Robert Curtis

Rory of the Hills

An Irish Tale

Robert Curtis

Rory of the Hills
An Irish Tale

ISBN/EAN: 9783741182266

Manufactured in Europe, USA, Canada, Australia, Japa

Cover: Foto ©Andreas Hilbeck / pixelio.de

Manufactured and distributed by brebook publishing software (www.brebook.com)

Robert Curtis

Rory of the Hills

RORY OF THE HILLS.

An Irish Tale.

BY ROBERT CURTIS, ESQ.,

AUTHOR OF

"THE IRISH POLICE-OFFICER," "CURIOSITIES OF DETECTION,"

ETC.

DUBLIN:
JAMES DUFFY, 15, WELLINGTON-QUAY,
AND
22, PATERNOSTER ROW, LONDON.
1870.

PREFACE.

The incidents upon which the following tale is founded have long since passed away; but there are doubtless some persons still living, who, should it fall into their hands, will recollect them as facts for which their memories can vouch.

I was myself a very young man, and had not long joined the Constabulary, at the time of their occurrence. But it was my connexion with that force which made me (as in all my other tales) personally acquainted with the facts which I have thus woven into a narrative. There are portions of this story which still dwell upon my memory with almost the same intense interest and *regret*, that I felt as I passed through what I may call the ordeal of the facts, for of course I was myself "The Chief" alluded to, where such a person has been necessarily brought forward.

Of *one* family mentioned in the tale, I have ascertained that there is not a single remnant, however far removed, whose feelings could be hurt by a reference to the transactions. And of *all* the rest, any relations who still survive may well be proud.

I have therefore no hesitation in committing the tale in its present form to a public, which has on former occasions given me so hearty and *sincere* a welcome, as to encourage me still to seek their favor.

October, 1870.

RORY OF THE HILLS.

CHAPTER I.

I COULD have wished that the incidents which I am about to describe in the following tale had taken place in some locality with a less Celtic, and to English tongues a more pronounceable name, than *Boher-na-Milthiogue*. I had at first commenced the tale with the word itself, thus: "Boher-na-Milthiogue, though in a wild and remote part of Ireland," &c. But I was afraid that, should an English reader take up and open the book, he would at the first word slap it together again between the palms of his hands, saying, "Oh, that is quite enough for me!" Now, as my English readers have done me vastly good service on former occasions, I should be sorry to frighten them at the outset of this new tale; and I have therefore endeavoured to lead them quietly into it. With my Irish friends no such circumlocution would have been necessary. Perhaps if I dissever and explain the word, it may enable even my English readers in some degree to approach a successful attempt at its pronunciation. I am aware, however, of the difficulty they experience in this respect, and that their attempts at some of our easiest names of Irish places are really laughable,—laughable, at least, to our Celtic familiarity with the correct sound.

Boher is the Irish for 'road,' and *milthiogue* for a 'midge;' Boher-na-Milthiogue, 'the midge's road.'

There now, if my English friends cannot yet pronounce the word properly, which I still doubt, they can at least understand what it means. It were idle, I fear, to hope that they can see any *beauty* in it; and yet that it is beautiful there can be no Celtic doubt whatever.

Perhaps it might have been well to have written thus far in the shape of a preface; but as nobody nowadays reads prefaces, the matter would have been as bad as ever. I shall therefore continue now as I had intended to have commenced at first.

Boher-na-Milthiogue, though in a wild and remote part of Ireland, is not without a certain degree of natural and romantic beauty, suiting well the features of the scene in which it lies.

Towering above a fertile and well-cultivated plain, frown and smile the brother and sister mountains of Slieve-dhu and Slieve-bawn, the solid masonry of whose massive and perpendicular precipices was built by no human architect. The ponderous and scowling rocks of Slieve-dhu, the brother, are dark and indistinct; while, separated from it by a narrow and abrupt ravine, those of Slieve-bawn, the sister, are of a whitish spotted gray, contrasting cheerfully with those of her gloomy brother.

There is generally a story in Ireland about mountains or rivers or old ruins which present any peculiarity of shape or feature. Now it is an undoubted fact, which any tourist can satisfy himself of, that although from sixty to a hundred yards asunder, there are huge bumps upon the side of Slieve-bawn, corresponding to which in every respect as to size and shape are cavities precisely opposite them in the side of Slieve-dhu. The story in this case is, that although formerly the mountains were, like a loving brother and sister, clasped in each other's arms, they quarrelled one dark night (I believe about the cause of thunder), when Slieve-dhu in a passion struck his sister a blow in the face, and staggered her back to where she now stands, too far for the possibility of reconciliation; and that she, knowing the superiority of her personal appearance, stands her ground, as a proud contrast to her savage and unfeeling relative.

Deep straight gullies, worn by the winter floods, mark the sides of both mountains into compartments, the proportion and regularity of which might almost be a matter of surprise, looking like huge stripes down the white dress of Slieve-bawn, while down that of Slieve-dhu they might be compared to black and purple plaid.

"Far to the north," in the bosom of the minor hills, lies a glittering lake,—glittering when the sun shines; dark, sombre, and almost imperceptible when the clouds prevail.

The origin of the beautiful name in which the spot itself rejoices, I believe to be this; but why do

I say 'believe?' it is a self-evident and well-known fact.

Along the base of Slieve-bawn there runs a narrow *roadeen*, turning almost at right angles through the ravine already mentioned, and leading to the flat and populous portion of the country on the other side of the mountains, and cutting the journey, for any person requiring to go there, into the sixteenth of the distance by the main road. In this instance the proverb would not be fulfilled, that "the longest way round was the shortest way home." Across one of the winter-torrent beds which runs down the mountain side, almost at the entrance of the ravine, is a rough-built rustic bridge, at a considerable elevation from the road below. To those approaching it from the lower level, it forms a conspicuous and exceedingly picturesque object, looking not unlike a sort of castellated defence to the mouth of the narrow pass between the mountains.

This bridge, towards sunset upon a summer's evening, presents a very curious and (except in that spot) an unusual sight. Whether it arises from any peculiarity of the herbage in the vicinity, or the fissures in the mountains, or the crevices in the bridge itself, as calculated to engender them, it would be hard to say; but it would be impossible for any arithmetician to compute at the roughest guess the millions, the billions of small midges which dance in the sunbeams immediately above and around the bridge, but in no other spot for miles within view. The singularity of their movements, and the peculiarity of their distribution in the air, cannot fail to attract the observation of the most careless beholder. In separate and distinct batches of some hundreds of millions each, they rise in almost solid masses until they are lost sight of, as they attain the level of the heathered brow of the mountain behind them, becoming visible again as they descend into the bright sunshine that lies upon the white rocks of Slieve-bawn. In no instance can you perceive individual or scattered midges; each batch is connected and distinct in itself, sometimes oval, sometimes almost square, but most frequently in a perfectly round ball. No two of these batches rise or fall at the same moment. I was fortunate enough to see them myself upon more than one occasion in high perfection. They reminded me of large balls thrown up and caught successively by some distinguished acrobat. During the performance, a tiny little sharp whir of music fills the atmosphere, which would almost set you to sleep as you sit on the battlement of the bridge watching and wondering.

By what law of creation, or what instinct of nature, or, if by neither, by what union of sympathy the movements of these *milthiogues* are governed—for I am certain there are millions of them at the same work in the same spot this fine summer's evening—would be a curious and proper study for an entomologist; but I have no time here to do more than describe the facts, were I even competent to enter into the inquiry. Fancy say fifty millions of midges in a round ball, so arranged that, under no suddenness or intricacy of movement any one touches another. There is no saying amongst them, "Keep out of my way, and don't be *pushin'* me," as Larry Doolan says.

So far the thing in itself appears miraculous; but when we come to consider that their motions, upwards to a certain point, and downwards to another, are simultaneous, that the slightest turn of their wings is collectively instantaneous, rendering them at one moment like a black target, and another turn rendering them almost invisible, all their movements being as if guided by a single will,—we are not only lost in wonder, but we are perfectly unable to account for or comprehend it. I have often been surprised, and so, no doubt, may many of my readers have been, at the regularity of the evolutions of a flock of stares in the air, where every twist and turn of a few thousand pairs of wings seemed as if moved by some connecting wire; but even this fact, surprising as it is, sinks into insignificance when compared with the movements of these *milthiogues*.

But putting all these inquiries and considerations aside, the simple facts recorded have been the origin of the name with which this tale commences.

CHAPTER II.

WINIFRED CAVANA was an only daughter, indeed an only child. Her father, old Ned Cavana of Rathcash, had been always a thrifty and industrious man. During the many years he had been able to attend to business—and he was an experienced farmer—he had realised a sum of money, which, in his rank of life and by his less prosperous neighbours, would be called "unbounded wealth," but which, divested of that envious exaggeration, was really a comfortable independence for his declining years, and would one of those days be a handsome inheritance for his handsome daughter. Not that Ned Cavana intended to huxter the whole of it up, so that she should not enjoy any of it until its possession might serve to lighten her grief for his death—no; should Winny marry some "likely boy," of whom her father could in every respect approve, she should have six hundred pounds, B.M.D.; and at his death—by which time Ned hoped some of his grandchildren would make the residue more necessary—she should have all that he was able to demise, which was no paltry matter. In the mean time they would live happily and comfortably, not niggardly.

With this view—a distant one, he still hoped—before him; and knowing that he had already sown a good crop, and reaped a sufficient harvest to live liberally, die peacefully, and be *berrid dacently*, he had set a great portion of his land upon a lease during his own life, at the termination of which it was to revert to his son-in-law, of whose existence, long before that time, he could have no doubt, and for whose name a blank had been left in his will, to be filled up in due time before he died, or, failing that event,—not his death, but a son-in-law,—it was left solely to his daughter, Winifred.

Winny Cavana was, beyond doubt or question, a very handsome girl—and she knew it. She knew, too, that she was "a catch;" the only one in that side of the country; and no person wondered at the many admirers she could boast of, though it was a thing she was never known to do; nor did she wonder at it herself. Without her six hundred pounds, Winny could have had scores of "bachelors;" and it was not very surprising if she was hard to be pleased. Indeed, had Winny Cavana been penniless, it is possible she would have had a greater number of open admirers, for her reputed wealth kept many a faint heart at a distance. It was not to be wondered at either, if a wealthy country beauty had the name of a coquette, whether she deserved it or not: nor was it to be expected that she could give unmixed satisfaction to each of her admirers; and we all know what censoriousness unsuccessful admiration is likely to cause in a disappointed heart.

Amongst all those who were said to have entered for the prize of Winny's heart, Thomas Murdock was the favourite—not with herself, but the neighbours. At all events he was the "likely boy" whom Winny's father had in his eye as a husband for his daughter; and in writing his will, he had lifted his pen from the paper at the blank already mentioned, and written the name Thomas Murdock in the air, so that, in case matters turned out as he wished and anticipated, it would fit-in to a nicety.

The townlands of Rathcash and Rathcashmore, upon which the Cavanas and Murdocks lived, was rather a thickly populated district, and they had some well-to-do neighbours, besides many who were not quite so well-to-do, but were yet decent and respectable. There were the Boyds, the Beattys, and the Brennans, with the Cahils, the Cartys, and the Clearys beyond them; the Doyles, the Dempseys, and the Dolans not far off; with the Mulveys, the Mooneys, and the Morans quite close. The people seemed to live in alphabetical batches in that district, as if for the convenience of the county cess-collector and his book. Many others lived still farther off, but not so far (in Ireland) as not to be called neighbours.

Kate Mulvey, one of the nearest neighbours, was a great friend and companion of Winny's. If Kate had six hundred pounds she could easily have rivalled Winny's good looks, but she had not six hundred pence; and notwithstanding her magnificent eyes, her white teeth, and her glossy brown hair, she could not look within miles as high into the clouds as Winny could. Still Kate had her admirers, some of whom even Winny's fondest glance, with all her money, could not betray into treachery. But it so happened that the person at whom she had thrown her cap had not (as yet, at least) picked it up.

CHAPTER III.

It was towards the end of October, 18—. There had been an early spring, and the crops had been got in favourably, and in good time. There had been "a wet and a windy May;" a warm bright summer had succeeded it; and the harvest had been now all gathered in, except the potatoes, which were in rapid progress of being dug and pitted. It was a great day for Ireland, let the advocates for "bread-stuffs" say what they will, before the blight and yellow meal had either of them become familiar with the poor. There were the *Cork reds*, and the *cups*, the *benefits*, and the *Brown's fancies*, for half nothing in every direction, besides many other sorts of potatoes, bulging up the surface of the ridges— there were no drills in those days; *mehils* in almost every field, with their coats off, at the digging-in.

"Bill, don't lane on that boy on the ridge wid you; he's not much more nor a *gossoon;* give him a start of you."

"*Gossoon aniow;* be gorra, he's as smart a chap on the face of a ridge as the best of us, Tom."

"Ay; but don't take it out of him too soon, Bill."

"Work away, boys," said the *gossoon* in question; "I'll engage I'll shoulder my loy at the end of the ridge as soon as some of ye that's spaking."

"It was wan word for the *gossoon* us he calls him, an' two for himself, Bill," chimed in the man on the next ridge. "Don't hurry Tom Nolan; his feet's sore afther all he danced with Nelly Gaffeny last night."

Here there was a loud and general laugh at poor Tom Nolan's expense, and the *pickers*—women and girls, with handkerchiefs tied over their heads— looked up with one accord, annoyed that they were too far off to hear the joke. It was well for one of them that they had not heard it, for Nelly Gaffeny was amongst them.

"It's many a day, Pat, since you seen the likes of them turned out of a ridge."

"They bate the world."

"They bang Banagher; and Banagher they say—"

"Whisht, Larry; don't be drawhing that chap down at all."

"I seen but wan betther the year;" said Tim Meaney.

"I say you didn't, nor the sorra take the betther, nor so good."

"Arra, didn't I? I say I did though."

"Where, *avic ma cree*?"

"Beyant at Tony Kilroy's."

"Ay, ay; Tony always had a pet acre on the side of the hill towards the sun. He has the best bit of land in the parish."

"You may say that, Micky, with your own purty mouth. I led his *mehil*, come this hollintide will be three years; an' there wasn't a man of forty of us but turned out eight stone of cups off every ten yards iv a four-split ridge. Devil a the like of them I ever seen afore or since."

"Lumpers you mane, Andy; wasn't I there?"

"Is it you, Darby? no, nor the sorra take the foot; we all know where you were that same year."

"Down in the lower part of Cavan, Phil. In throth, it wasn't cup potatoes was throublin' him that time; but cups and saucers. He dhrank a power of tay that harvest, boys."

Here there was another loud laugh, and the women with the handkerchiefs upon their heads looked up again.

"Well, I brought her home dacent, boys; an' what can ye say to her?"

"Be gor, nothing, Darby avic, but that she's an iligant purty crathur, and a credit to them that owns her, an' them that reared her."

"The sorrow word of lie in that," echoed every man in the *mehil*.

Thus the merry chat and laugh went on in every potato-field. The women, finding that they had too much to do to enable them to keep close to the men, and that they were losing the fun, of course got up a chat for themselves, and took good care to have some loud and hearty laughs, which made the men in their turn look up, and lean upon their loys.

Everything about Rathcash and Rathcashmore was prosperous and happy, and the farmers were cheerful and open-hearted.

"That's grand weather, glory be to God, Ned, for the time of year," said Mick Murdock to his neighbour Cavana, who was leaning with his arms folded, on a field-gate near the mearing of their two farms. The farms lay alongside of each other—one in the townland of Rathcash, and the other in Rathcashmore.

"Couldn't be bet, Mick. I'm upwards of forty years stannin' in this spot, an' I never seen the batin' of it."

"Be gorra, you have a right to be tired, Ned; that's a long stannin'."

"The sorra tired, Mick *a wochal*. You know very well what I mane, an' you needn't be so sharp. I'd never be tired of the same spot."

"Them's a good score of calves, Ned; God bless you an' them!" said Mick, making up for his sharpness.

"An' you too, Mick. They are a fine lot of calves, an' all reared since Candlemas."

"There's no denying, Ned, but you med the most of that bit of land of yours."

"'Tis about the same as your own, Mick; an' I think you med as good a fist of yours."

"Well, maybe so, indeed; but I doubt it is going into worse hands than what yours will, Ned."

"Why that, Mick?"

"Ah, that Tom of mine is a wild extravagant hero. He doesn't know much about the value of money, and never paid any attention to farming business, only what he was obliged to pick up from being with me. He thinks he'll be rich enough when I'm in my clay, without much work. An' so he will, Ned, so far as that goes; but it's only of book-larnin' an' horseracin' an' coorsin' he's thinkin', by way of being a sort of gentleman one of those days; but he'll find to his cost, in the latther end, that there's more wantin' to grow good crops than 'The Farmer's Calendar of Operations.'"

"He's young, Mick, an' no doubt he'll mend. I hope you don't discourage him."

"Not at all, Ned. The book-larnin's all well enough, as far as it goes, if he'd put the practice along with it, an' be studdy."

"So he will, Mick. His wild-oats will soon be all sown, an' then you'll see what a chap he'll be."

"Faix, I'd rather see him sowing a crop of

yallow Aberdeens, Ned, next June; an' maybe it's what it's at the Curragh of Kildare he'll be, as I can hear. My advice to him is to get marrid to some dacent nice girl, that id take the wildness out of him, and lay himself down to business. You know, Ned, he'll have every penny and stick I have in the world; and the lease of my houlding in Rathcashmore is as good as an estate at the rent I pay. If he'd give up his meandherin', and take a dacent liking to them that's fit for him, I'd set him up all at wanst, an' not be keeping him out of it until I was dead an' berrid."

The above was not a bad feeler, nor was it badly put by Old Mick Murdock to his neighbour. "Them that's fit for him" could hardly be mistaken; yet there was a certain degree of disparagement of his own son calculated to conceal his object. It elicited nothing, however, but a long thoughtful silence upon old Ned Cavana's part, which Mick was not slow to interpret, and did not wish to interrupt. At last Ned stood up from the gate, and smoothing down the sleeves of his coat, as if he supposed they had contracted some dust, he observed, "I'm afear'd, Mick, you are puttin' the cart before the horse; come until I show you a few ridges of red apples I'm diggin' out to-day. You'd think I actually got them carted in, an' threune them upon the ridges: the like of them I never seen."

And the two old men walked down the lane together.

But Mick Murdock's feeler was not forgotten by either of them. Mick was as well pleased—perhaps better—that no further discussion took place upon the subject at the time. He knew Ned Cavana was not a man to commit himself to a hasty opinion upon any matter, much less upon one of such importance as was so plainly suggested by his observations.

Ned Cavana, too, brooded over the conversation in silence, determined to throw out a feeler of his own to his daughter.

Ned had himself more than once contemplated the possibility as well as the prudence of a match between Tom Murdock and his daughter. The union, not of themselves alone, but of the two farms, would almost make a gentleman of the person holding them. Both farms were held upon unusually long leases, and at less than one-third of their value. If joined, there could be no doubt but, with the careful and industrious management of an experienced man, they would turn in a clear income of between five and six hundred a-year; quite sufficient in that part of the world to entitle a person of even tolerably good education to look up to the grand-jury list and a "justice of the pace."

The only question with Ned Cavana was: Did Tom Murdock possess the attributes required for success in all or any of the above respects? Ned, although he had taken his part with his father, *feared not.* Ay, there was another question: Was Winny inclined for him?—he feared not also.

The other old man had not forgotten the feeler he had thrown out either, nor the thoughtful silence with which it had been received; for Mick Murdock could not believe that a man of Ned Cavana's penetration had misunderstood him. Indeed, he was inclined to think that the same matter might have originated in Ned's own mind, from some words he had once or twice dropped, about poor Winny's prospects when he was gone, and the suspense it would be to him if she were not settled in life before that day; snaffled perhaps by some good-for-nothing extravagant fortune-hunter, with a handsome face, when she had no one to look after her."

There was but one word in the above which Mick thought could be justly applied to Tom; "extravagant" he undoubtedly was, but he was neither handsome,—at least not handsome enough to be called so as a matter of course,—nor was he good-for-nothing. He was a well-educated sharp fellow, if he would only lay himself down to business. He was not a fortune-hunter, for he did not require it; but idleness and extravagance might make him one in the end. Yet old Mick was by no means certain that the propriety of a match between these only and rich children had not suggested itself to his neighbour Ned as well as to himself. He hoped that if Tom had a dacent hankerrin' afther any one, it was for Winny Canava; but, like her father, he doubted if the girl herself was inclined for him. He knew that she was proud and self-willed. He was determined, however, to follow the matter up, and throw out another feeler upon the subject to his son.

CHAPTER IV.

It was now the 25th of October, just six days from All-Hallow Eve. Mick would ask a few of the neighbours to burn nuts and eat apples, and then, perhaps, he might find out how the wind blew.

"Tom," said he to his son, "I believe this is a good year for nuts."

"Well, father, I met a couple of chaps ere yesterday with their pockets full of fine brown shellers, coming from Clonard Wood."

"I daresay they are not all gone yet, Tom; an' I wish you would set them to get us a few pockets full, and we would ask a few of the neighbours here to burn them on All-Hallow Eve."

"That's easy done, father; I can get three or four quarts by to-morrow night. Those two very chaps would be glad to earn a few pence for them; they wanted me to buy what they had; and if I knew your intentions at the time, I should have done so; but it's not late. Who do you intend to ask, father?"

"Why, old Cavana and his daughter, of course, and the Mulveys; in short, you know, all the neighbours. I won't leave any of them out, Tom. The Cavanas, you know, are all as wan as ourselves, livin' at the doore with us; and they're much like us too, Tom, in many respects. Old Ned is rich, an' has but one child—a very fine girl. I am old, an' as rich as what Ned is, and I have but one child; I'll say,—though you're to the fore, Tom,—a very fine young man."

Old Mick paused. He wanted to see if his son's intelligence was on the alert. It must have been very dull indeed had it failed to perceive what his father was driving at; but he was silent.

"That Winny Cavana is a very fine girl, Tom," he continued; "and I often wonder that a handsome young fellow like you doesn't make more of her. She'll have six hundred pounds fortune, as round as a hoop; besides, whoever gets her will fall in for that farm at her father's death. There's ninety-nine years of it, Tom, just like our own."

"She's a conceited proud piece of goods, father; and I suspect she would rather give her six hundred pounds to some *skauhawn* than to a man of substance like me."

"Maybe not now. Did you ever thry?"

"No, father, I never did. People don't often hold their face up to the hail."

"*Na-bockleish*, Tom, she'd do a grate dale for her father, for you know she must owe everything to him; an' if she vexes him he can cut her out of her six hundred pounds, and lave the interest in his farm to any one he likes; and I know what he thinks about you, Tom."

"Ay, and he's so fond of that one that she can twist him round her finger. Wait now, father, until you see if I'm not up to every twist and turn of the pair of them."

"But you never seem to spake to her or mind her

at all, Tom; and I know, when I was your age, I always found that the girls liked the man best that looked afther them most. I'm purty sure too, Tom, that there's no one afore you there."

"I'm not so sure of that, father. But I'll tell you what it is: I have not been either blind or idle on what you are talking about; but up to this moment she seems to scorn me, father; there's the truth for you. And as for there being no one before me, all I can say is that she manages, somehow or other, to come out of the chapel-door every Sunday at the same moment with that whelp, Rory Lennon, from the mountain; *Rory of the Hills*, as they call him, and as I have heard her call him herself. Rathcash chapel is not in his parish at all, and I don't know what brings him there."

"Is it that poor penniless pauper, depending on his day's labour? Ah, Tom, she's too proud for that."

"Yes, that very fellow; and there is no getting a word with her where he is."

"Well, Tom, all I can say is this, an' it's to my own son I'm sayin' it,—that if you let that fellow pick up that fine girl with her six hundred pounds and fall into that rich farm, an' you livin' at the doore with her, you're not worth staggering-bob broth, with all your book-larnin' an' good looks, to say nothin' of your manners, Tom avic." And he left him, saying to himself, "He may put that in his pocket to balance his knife."

Thus ended what old Murdock commenced as a feeler, but which became very plain speaking in the end. But the All-Hallow Eve party was to come off all the same.

A word or two now of comparison, or perhaps, more properly speaking, of contrast, between these two aspirants to Winny Cavana's favour, though young Lennon was still more hopeless than the other, from his position.

Thomas Murdock was more conspicuous for the manliness of his person than for the beauties of his mind or the amiability of his disposition. Although manifestly well-looking in a group, take him singly, and he could not be called very handsome. There was a suspicious fidgetiness about his green-spotted eyes, as if he feared you could read his thoughts; and at times, if vexed or opposed, a dark scowl upon his heavy brow indicated that these thoughts were not always amiable. This unpleasing peculiarity of expression marred the good looks which the shape of his face and the fit of his curly black whiskers unquestionably gave him. In form he was fully six feet high, and beautifully made. At nineteen years of age he had mastered not only all the learning which could be attained at a neighbouring national school, but had actually mastered the master himself in more ways than one, and was considered by the eighty-four youngsters whom he had outstripped as a prodigy of valour as well as learning. But Tom turned his schooling to a bad account; it was too superficial, and served more to set his head astray than to correct his heart; and there were some respectable persons in the neighbourhood who were not free from doubts that he had already become a parish-patriot, and joined the Ribbon society. He was high and overbearing towards his equals, harsh and unkind to his inferiors, while he was cringing and sycophantic towards his superiors. There was nothing manly or straightforward, nothing ingenuous or affectionate about him. In fact, if ever a man's temper and disposition justified the opinion that he had "the two ways" in him, they were those of Thomas Murdock. His father was a rich farmer, whose land joined that of old Ned Cavana, of whom he was a contemporary in years, and with whom he had kept pace in industry and wealth.

Thomas Murdock was an only son, as Winny Cavana was an only daughter, and the two old men were of the same mind now as regarded the future lot of their children.

A few words now of Rory Lennon, and we can get on.

He was the eldest of five in family. They lived upon the mountain-side in the parish of Shanvilla, about two "*short* miles" from the Cavanas and Murdocks. His father and mother were both alive. They were respectable so far as character and conduct can make people respectable who are unquestionably poor. Their marriage was what has been sarcastically, but perhaps not inaptly, called by an English newspaper a "*potato marriage;*" that is—but no, it will not bear explanation. The result, however, after many years' struggling, may be stated. The Lennons had lived, and were still living, in a small thatched house upon the side of a mountain, with about four acres of reclaimed ground. It had been reclaimed gradually by the father and his two sons, —for Rory had a younger brother,—and they paid little or no rent for it. The second son and eldest daughter were now at service, "doin' for themselves;" and those at home consisted of the father, the mother, the eldest son, and two younger daughters, mere children. For the house and garden they paid a small rent, which "a slip of a pig" was always ready to realise in sufficient time; while a couple of goats, staggering through the furze, yoked together by the necks, gave milk to the family.

Rory, though not so well-looking as to the actual cut of his features, nor so tall by an inch and a half, as our friend Murdock, was far more agreeable to look upon. There was a confident good-nature in his countenance which assured you of its reality, and the honesty of his heart. His figure, from his well-shaped head, which was beautifully set upon his shoulders, to his small well-turned feet, was faultless. In disposition and character young Lennon was a full distance before the man to whom he was a secret rival, while in talent and learning he had nothing to fear by a comparison. He had commenced his education when a mere gossoon, at a poor-school with "his turf an' his read-a-ma-daisy," and as he progressed from A-b-e-l, bel, Abel, a man's name; A-b-l-e, ble, Able, powerful, strong; until finally he could spell Antitrinitarian pat; he then cut the concern, and was promoted by his parish-priest—"of whom more anon," as they say—to

Rathcash national school, where he soon stood in the class beside Tom Murdock, and ere a week had passed he "took him down a peg." This, added to his supposed presumptuous thoughts in the quarter which Tom had considered almost his exclusive right, sowed the seed of hatred in Murdock's heart against Lennon, which one day might bear a heavy crop.

That young Lennon was devotedly but secretly attached to Winny Cavana there was no doubt whatever in his own mind, and there were few who did not agree with him, although he had "never told his love;" and as we Irish have leave to say, there was still less that his love was more disinterested than that of his richer rival. There was another point upon which there was still less doubt than either, and that was that Winny Cavana's heart secretly leaned to *Rory of the Hills*, as young Lennon was familiarly called by all those who knew and loved him. One exception existed to this cordial recognition of Rory's good qualities, and that was, as may be anticipated, by Thomas Murdock, who always called him "*that* Lennon," and on one occasion, as we have seen, substituted the word "whelp."

Winny, however, kept her secret in this matter to herself. She knew her father would go "tanterin' tearin' mad, if he suspected such a thing." She conscientiously endeavoured to hide her preference from young Lennon himself, knowing that it would only get them both into trouble. Besides he had never (yet) shown a decided preference for her above

Kate Mulvey. Whether she succeeded in her endeavours is another question; women seldom fail when they are in earnest.

It is not considered amongst the class of Irish to which our *dramatis personæ* belong, as any undue familiarity, upon even a very short acquaintance, for the young persons of both the sexes to call each other by their Christian names. It is the admitted custom of the country, and Winny Cavana, rich and proud as she was, made no exception to the general rule. She even went further, and sometimes called young Lennon by his pet name. As regarded Tom Murdock, although she could have wished it otherwise, she would not make herself particular by acting differently. The first three letters of his name, coupled with the scowl she had more than once detected on his countenance, sounded unpleasantly upon her ear, Mur-dock. She always thought people were going to say, mur-*der* before the 'dock' was out. She never could think well of him; and although she called him Tom, it was more to be in keeping with the habit of the country, and as a refuge from the other name, than from a friendly feeling.

These were the materials upon which the two old men had to work, to bring about a union of their landed interests and their only children.

CHAPTER V.

The invitations for All-Hallow Eve were forthwith issued in person by old Murdock, who went from house to house in his Sunday clothes, and asked all the respectable neighbours in the politest manner. Rory Lennon, although he could scarcely be called a neighbour, and moreover was not considered as "belonging to their set," was nevertheless asked to be one of the party. Old Murdock had his reasons for asking him; although, to tell the truth, he and his son had a difference of opinion upon the subject. Tom thought to "put a spoke in his wheel" but was overruled by the old man, who said it would look as if they were afraid to bring him and Winny Cavana together; that it was much better to let the young fellow see at once that he had no chance, which would no doubt be an easy matter on that night: "it was betther to *humiliate* him at wanst."

Tom was ashamed not to acquiesce, but wished nevertheless that he might have had his own way. Rory Lennon lived too far from the Murdocks for the old man to go there specifically upon the mission of invitation; and the moment this difficulty was hinted by his father, Tom, who was not in the habit of making such offers, was ready at once to "go over to Shanvilla, and save his father the walk: he would deliver the message."

There was an anxiety in Tom's manner which

betrayed itself; and old Mick was not a man to *miss* a thing of the kind.

"No, Tom *a wochal*," he observed, "I won't put such a thramp upon you. Sure I'll see him a Sunda'; he always comes to our chapel."

"Fitter for him to stick to his own," said Tom.

"It answers well this turn, at all events," replied the old man.

Upon the following Sunday he was as good as his word. He watched young Lennon coming out of the chapel, and asked him, with more cordiality than Tom, who happened to be by, approved of.

Had nothing else been necessary to secure an acceptance, the fact of Tom Murdock being present would have been sufficient. The look which he caught from under the rim of Tom's hat roused Lennon's pride, and he accepted the old man's invitation with unhesitating civility. Lennon on this, as on all Sunday occasions, "was dressed in all his best;" and that look seemed to say, "I wonder where that fellow got them clothes, and if they're paid for:" he understood the look very well. But the clothes were paid for,—perhaps, too, more promptly than Tom's own; and a better fitting suit, from top to toe, was not to be met with in the whole parish. A "Caroline hat," smooth and new, set a wee taste jauntily upon his well-shaped head; a shirt like the drifted snow, loose at the throat, but buttoned down the breast with tiny blue buttons round as sweet-pea seeds; a bright plaid waistcoat, with ditto buttons to match, but a size larger; a pair of "spic au' span" knee-breeches of fine kerseymere, with unexceptionable steel-buttons and blue silk-ribbon strings, tied to perfection at the knee; while closely-fitting lamb's-wool long stockings showed off the shape of a pair of legs which, for symmetry, looked as if they had been turned in a lathe. Of his feet I have already spoken; and on this occasion they did not belie what I said.

Old Mick desired Rory Lennon "to bring Phil M'Dermott the smith's son with him. He was a fine young man, a good dancer, and had mended a couple of ploughs for him in first-rate style, an' very raisonable, for the winther ploughing."

Tom Murdock did not want for fine clothes, of course. Two or three suits were at his command; and as this was Sunday he had one of his best on. It was "given up to him" by most of the girls, that he was the handsomest and best-dressed man in the parish of Rathcash, and some would have added Shanvilla; yet he now felt, as he stole envious glances at young Lennon, that his case with Winny Cavana might not be altogether a "walk-over." All Tom's comparisons and metaphors had reference to horse-racing.

This little incident, however, cut young Lennon out of his usual few words with Winny; for, as a girl with a well-regulated mind, she could not venture to dawdle on the road until old Murdock had done speaking to Rory: she knew that would be remarked. She had never happened to see old Murdock speaking to Rory before, and her secret wonder now was,—"Could it be possible he was asking Rory Lennon for All-Hallow Eve?"

Quite possible, Winny; but you scarcely have time to find out before you meet him there, for another Sunday will not intervene before the party.

CHAPTER VI.

The last day of October came round apace, and about six o'clock in the evening the company began to arrive at old Mick Murdock's. Winny Cavana and her father took their time. They were near enough to make their *entrée* at any moment; and Winny had some idea, like her betters, that it was not genteel to be the first. She now delayed, however, to the other extreme, and kept her father waiting, under the pretence that she was finishing her toilet, until, on their arrival, they found all the guests assembled. Winny flaunted in, leaning upon her father's arm, "the admired of all admirers." Not being very learned in the mysteries of the toilet, I shall not attempt to describe the dresses of the girls upon this occasion, nor the elaborate manner in which their heads were set out, oiled and bedizened to an amazing extent, while the roses above their left ears seemed to have been all culled from the same tree.

Altogether there were about sixteen young persons, pretty equally divided as to boys and girls, besides some—and some only—of their fathers and mothers. Soon after the arrival of Ned Cavana and his daughter, who were *the* guests of the evening, supper was announced, and there was a general move into the "large parlour," where a long table was set out with a snow-white cloth, where plates (if not covers) were laid for at least twenty-four. In the middle of the table stood a smoking dish of *calcannon*, which appeared to defy them, and as many more; while at either end was a *raking* pot of tea, surrounded with cups and saucers innumerable, with pyramids of cut bread-and-butter nearly an inch thick.

The company having taken their seats, it was announced by the host that there were "two goold weddin'-rings in the *calcannon;*" but whereabouts, of course, no one could tell. He had borrowed them from two of the married women present, and was bound to restore them; so he begged of his young friends, for his sake as well as their own, to be careful not to swallow them. It was too well known what was to be the lot of the happy finders before that day twelvemonths, for him to say any thing upon that part of the subject. He would request of Mrs. Moran, who had seen more All-Hallow Eves than any woman there present—he meant no offence—to help the calcannon.

After this little introduction, Mrs. Moran, who by previous arrangement was sitting opposite the savoury volcano, distributed it with unquestionable impartiality. It was a well-known rule on all such occasions that no one commenced until all were helped, when a signal was given, and a simultaneous plunge of spoons took place.

Another rule was that all the married persons should content themselves with tea and bread-and-butter, in order that none of them might possibly rob the youngsters of their chance of the ring. Upon this occasion, however, this restriction had been neatly obviated by Mrs. Moran's experience in such matters; and there was a *knock-oge* of the same delicious food without any ring, which she called "the married dish." The tea was handed up and down from each end of the table until it met in the middle, and for some time there was a silent onslaught on the calcannon, washed down now and then by a copious draught of tea.

"I have it! I have it!" shouted Phil M'Dermott, taking it from between his teeth and holding it up, while his cheeks deepened three shades nearer to the colour of the rose in Kate Mulvey's hair, nearly opposite.

"A lucky man," observed Mrs. Moran, methodically, who seemed to be mistress of the mysteries. "Now for the lucky girl; and lucky every body will say she must be."

The words were scarcely finished when Kate Mulvey coughed as if she were choking; but pulling the other ring from her mouth, she soon recovered herself, declaring that she had nearly swallowed it.

Matters, as Mrs. Moran thought, had so far gone quite right, and a hearty quizzing the young couple got; but to tell the truth, one of them did not seem to be particularly satisfied with the result. The attack upon the calcannon from this point waxed very weak, for the charm was broken, and the tea and bread-and-butter came into play. Apples and nuts were now laid down in abundance, and the young girls might be seen picking a couple of pairs of nice nuts out of those on the plate, as nearly as fancy might suggest to match the figures of those whom they were intended to represent upon the bar of the grate. Almost as if by magic a regiment of nuts in pairs were seen smoking, and some of them stirring and purring on the flat bar at the bottom of the grate, which had been swept, and the fire brightened up for the purpose. Of course Mrs. Moran insisted upon openly putting down Phil M'Dermott and Kate Mulvey of the rings; for in general there is a secrecy observed as to *who* the *nuts* are, in order to save the constant girl from a laugh at the fickleness of her bachelor, should he go off in a shot from her side, and *vice versâ*. And here the mistress of the mysteries was not at fault. Kate Mulvey, without either smoking or getting red at one end (which was a good sign), went off like the report of a pistol, and was actually heard striking against the door as if to get out. There was a general laugh at Mrs. Moran's expense, who was told that it was a strong proof in favour of putting the pairs down secretly.

But Mrs. Moran was too experienced a mistress of her position to be taken aback, and quietly said, "Not at all, my dears. I have three times to burn them, if he does not follow her; but he has three minutes to do so."

As she spoke there was another shot. Phil M'Dermott could not stand the heat by himself, and was off to the door after Kate Mulvey.

This was a crowning triumph to Mrs. Moran, who quietly put back the second pair of nuts which she had just selected for another test of the same couple, and remarked that "it was all right now."

The couples, generally speaking, seemed to answer the expectations of their respective match-makers better than perhaps the results in real life might subsequently justify. It is not to be supposed that on this occasion Tom Murdock and Winny Cavana did not find a place upon the bar of the grate. But as Winny had given no encouragement to any one to put her down with him, and as the mistress of the mysteries alone could claim a right do so openly, as in the case of the rings, their place, with the result, could be known only to those who put them down, and perhaps a confidant.

There were a few pops occasionally, calling forth exclamations of "The good-for-nothing fellow!" or, "The fickle lass!" while some burned into bright balls—the admiration of all the true and constant lovers present.

The next portion of the mysteries were three plates, placed in a row upon the table; one contained earth, another water, and the third a gold ring. This was, by some, considered rather a nervous test of futurity, and some objections were whispered by the timid amongst them. The fearless and enthusiastic, however, clamoured that nothing should be left out, and a handkerchief to blind the adventurers was produced. The mystery was this: a young person was taken outside the door, and there blindfolded; he, or she, was then led in again, and placed opposite to the plates, sufficiently near to touch them; when told that "all was right," he with his forefinger pointed, placed it upon one of the plates. That with the earth symbolled forth sudden, or perhaps violent, death; that with the water, emigration or shipwreck; while that with the ring, of course a wedding and domestic happiness.

Young people were not generally averse to subject themselves to this ordeal, as, in nine cases out of ten, they managed either to be previously acquainted with the position of the plates, or, having been blindfolded by their own bachelor, to have a peep-hole down by the corner of their nose, which enabled them to secure the most gratifying result of the three.

With this usual course before his mind, Tom Murdock, as junior host, presented himself for the test, hoping that Winny Cavana, whom he had asked to do so, would blindfold him. But in this instance he had presumed too far; and while she hesitated to comply, the mistress of the mysteries came to her relief.

"No, no, Tom," she said, folding the handkerchief; "that is my business, and I'll transfer it to no one; come outside with me."

Tom was ashamed to draw back, and retired with Mrs. Moran to the hall. He soon returned, led in by her, with a handkerehief tied tightly over his eyes; there was no peephole by the side of his nose, let him hold back his head as he might, Mrs. Moran, took care of that. Having been placed near the table, he was told that he was exactly opposite the plates. He pointed out his forefinger, and threw back his head as much as possible, as if considering, but in fact to try if he could get a peep at the plates; but it was no use, Mrs. Moran had rendered his temporary blindness cruelly secure. At length his hand descended, and he placed his finger into the middle of the earth.

"Pshaw," said he, pulling the handkerchief off his eyes, "it is all humbug! Let Lennon try it."

"Certainly, certainly," ran from one to the other. It might have been remarked, however, if any one had been observing, that Winny Canava had not spoken.

Young Lennon then retired to the hall with Mrs. Moran, and was soon led in tightly blindfolded, for the young man was no more to her than the other; besides, she was strictly honourable. The plates had been re-arranged by Tom Murdock himself, which most people remarked, as it was some time before he was satisfied with their position. Lennon was then placed, as Tom had been, and told that "all was right." There was some nervousness in more hearts than one as he pointed his finger and brought down his hand. He also placed his finger in the centre of the plate with the earth, and pulled the handkerchief from his eyes.

"Now, you see," said Tom, "others can fail as well as me;" and he seemed greatly pleased that young Lennon had been as unsuccessful as himself.

A murmur of dissatisfaction now ran through the girls. The two favourites had been unfortunate in their attempts at divination, and there was one young girl there, who, when she saw Rory of the Hills' finger fall on the plate with the earth, felt as if a weight had been tied round her heart. It was unanimously agreed by the elderly women present, Mrs. Moran amongst the number, that these tests had turned out directly contrary to what the circumstances of the locality, and the characters of the individuals, would indicate as probable, and the whole process was ridiculed as false and unprophetic. "Time will tell, jewel," said one old croaking crone.

A loud burst of laughter from the kitchen at this moment told that the servant-boys and girls, who had also been invited, were not idle. The matches having been all either clenched or broken off in the parlour, and the test of the plates, as if by mutual consent, having been declared unsatisfactory, old Murdock thought it a good opportunity to move an adjournment of the whole party, to see the fun in the kitchen, which was seconded by Mrs. Moran, and carried *nem. con.*

CHAPTER VII.

HERE it was that the real fun was going on! From the centre of the ceiling hung a strong piece of cord, with cross sticks, about eighteen inches long, at the end. On each end of one of these sticks was stuck a short piece of lighted candle, while on the ends of the other were stuck small apples of a peculiarly good kind. The cross was then set turning, when some plucky hero snapped at the apples as they went round, but as often caught the lighted candle in his mouth, when a hearty laugh from the circle of spectators proclaimed his discomfiture. On the other hand, if fortunate enough to secure one of the apples, a clapping of hands, and shouts of "Well done!" proclaimed his victory.

A little to one side of this "merry-go-round" was a huge tub of spring-water, fresh from the pump, and as clear as crystal. It was intended that the performers at this portion of the fun should, stripped to the waist, dive for pence or whatever silver the bystanders chose to throw in. Up to this it had not come into play, for until their "betthers came down from the parlour" no silver was thrown in; and the youngsters were "loth to wet theirsel's for nothin'." Now, however, a *tenpenny-bit* from Tom Murdock soon glittered on the bottom of the tub, a full foot and a half under water. Forthwith two or three young fellows "peeled off," to prove their abilities as divers. The first, a blackhaired fellow, with a head as round as a cannon-ball, after struggling and bubbling until the people began to think he was smothering, came up without the prize. He was handed a kitchen towel to rub himself with; while one of the other young gladiators adjusted the tenpenny-bit in the middle of the tub, drew in a long breath and down he went like a duck. He was not nearly so long down as the other had been; he neither struggled nor bubbled, and came up with the money between his teeth.

"It wasn't your first time, Jamesy, anyhow," said one.

"How did you get a hoult of it, Jamesy avic?" said another.

But he kept drying his head and never minding them.

Another tenpenny was then thrown in by old Ned Cavana; it withstood repeated efforts, but was at last fairly brought up. Jamesy seemed to be the most expert, for having lifted this second tenpenny, his abilities were finally tested with a *fippenny-bit*, which after one or two failures he brought up triumphantly in his teeth; all the other divers having declined to try their powers upon it.

By this time the kitchen floor was very wet, and it was thought, particularly by the contributors to the tub, that there had been enough of that sort of fun. The girls, who were standing in whatever dry spots of the flags they could find, thought so too; they did not wish to wet their shoes before the dance; and there was another move back to the parlour.

Here the scene was completely changed, as if indeed by magic, as nobody had been missed for the performance. The long table was nowhere to be seen, while the chairs and forms were ranged along the walls, and old Murrin the piper greeted their entrance with an enlivening jig.

Partners were of course selected at once, and as young Lennon *happened* to be coming in from the kitchen with Winny Cavana at the moment, they were soon with arms akimbo footing it to admiration opposite each other. Not far from them another couple were exhibiting in like manner. They were

Tom Murdock and Kate Mulvey ; while several other pairs were "footing it" through the room. To judge from the self-satisfied smile upon Kate Mulvey's handsome lips, she was not a little proud or well pleased at having taken Tom Murdock from the belle of the party ; for she had too much self-esteem to think that it was the belle of the party had been taken from Tom Murdock.

I need not pursue the several sets which were danced, nor particularize the pairs who were partners on the occasion. Of course Tom Murdock took the first opportunity possible, to claim the hand of Winifred Cavana for a dance. Indeed he was ill-pleased, that in his own house he had permitted any chance circumstance to prevent his having opened the dance with her, and apologised for it—" but it happened in a manner over which he had no control." He had picked up that expression at a racecourse.

With all his bitterness he had the good sense not to make a scene by endeavouring to frustrate that which he had not the tact to obviate by pre-arrangement. Winny had made no reply to his apology, and he continued, " I did not ask Kate Mulvey to dance, until I saw you led out by young Lennon."

"That is a bad compliment to Kate," she observed.

" I can't help that," said he, gruffly ; "some people take time d-mn-bly by the forelock."

" That cannot apply to either him or me in this case ; there were two pairs dancing before he asked me."

Now although this was certainly not said by way of reproach to Tom for not himself being sooner, it was unanswerable, and he did not try to answer it. He was not however in such good humour as to forward himself much in Winny's good opinion, and Rory of the Hills, who watched him closely, was content that he should be her sole beau for the rest of the evening.

Refreshments were now brought in; cold punch for the boys, and "negus" for the girls; for old Murdock could afford to make a splash, and this he thought " was his time to do it."

After the liquor on the first tray was disposed of, and the glasses collected for a replenish, a solo jig was universally called for. The two best dancers in the province were present—Tom Murdock and Rory Lennon, so there could be no failure.

Old Murdock had never seen young Lennon dance until that night, and so far as he could judge, "he was not the man that Tom need be afraid of." He had often seen Tom's best dancing, and certainly nothing which young Lennon had exhibited there up to that time could at all touch it.

"Come, Tom," said he, "give the girls a specimen of what you can do, your lone," and he laid the poker and tongs across each other in the middle of the floor.

Paddy Murrin struck up a spirit-stirring jig, which no one could resist. The girls were all dancing it "to themselves," and young Lennon's feet were dying to be at it, but of course he must wait.

Indeed he was not anxious to exhibit in opposition to his host's son, but feared his reputation as a dancer would put him in for it.

Tom Murdock having been thus called on, was tightening the *fung* of one of his pumps, to begin. Turning then to Murrin, he called for "The Foxhunter's jig."

He now commenced, and like a knowing professor of his art, "took it easy" at the commencement, determined however to astonish them ere he had done. He felt that he was dancing well, but knew that he could dance much better, and would presently do so. He had often tried the "Poker and Tongs jig," but hitherto never quite to his satisfaction. He had sometimes come off perfectly victorious, without touching them, but as often managed to kick them about the floor. He was now on his mettle, not only on account of Winny Cavana, but also because "that whelp, Lennon, was looking on, which he had no right to be." For a while he succeeded admirably. He had tipped each division of the cross with both heel and toe, several times with rapid and successful precision; but becoming enthusiastic, as the plaudits passed round, he called to Murrin "to play faster," when after a few moments of increased speed, he tripped in the tongs, and came flat on his back upon the floor. He was soon up again, and a few touches of the clothes-brush set all to rights, except the irrepressible titter that ran round the room.

Of course there was an excuse—one of the *fungs* of his pump had again loosened and caught in the tongs. This was not merely an excuse, but a fact, upon which Tom Murdock built much consolation for his "partial failure," as he himself jocosely called it; but he was savage at heart.

There was a general call now from the girls for young Lennon, and "Rory of the Hills, Rory of the Hills," resounded on all sides. He would not rise, however; he was now more unwilling than ever to "dance a match," as he called it to himself, with his host's son.

The "partial failure" of his rival—and he was honest enough to admit that it was but partial, and could not have been avoided,—gave him well founded hopes of a triumph. He too had tried his powers of agility by the poker and tongs test, and oftener with success than otherwise. It was some time now since he had tried it, as latterly he had not much time to spare for such amusements. He was unwilling, but not from fear of failure, to get up; but no excuse would be taken; he was caught by the collar of his coat by two sturdy handsome girls, and dragged into the middle of the room. Thus placed before the spectators, he could not refuse the ordeal as it might be called.

He had his wits about him, however. He had seen Tom Murdock whisper something to the piper when he was first called on to stand up, and it proved that he was not astray as to its purport.

Recollecting the jig he was in the habit of dancing the poker and tongs to, he asked the piper to play it. Murrin hesitated, and at last came out with a stammer that "he had'nt it, but he'd give him one as good," striking up the most difficult jig in the Irish catalogue to dance to.

"No," said Lennon stoutly, "I heard you play the jig I called for a hundred times, and no later than last night, Pat, at Jemmy Mullarky's, as I passed home from work, and I'll have no other."

"I took whatever jig he happened to strike up," said Tom with a sneer.

"You might have had your choice, for that matter, and I daresay you had," replied Lennon, "and I'll have mine! It is my right."

"If a man can dance," continued Tom, " he ought to be able to dance to any jig that's given him; its like a man that can only say his prayers out of his own book." And there was a suppressed smile at Lennon's expense.

He saw it, and his blood was up in a moment.

"He may play any jig he chooses now," exclaimed Lennon, "except one, and that is the one *you* told him to play." Taking his chance that his suspicions were correct as to the purport of the whisper.

" I'll play the won I pled for the young masther himself; an' if that does'nt shoot you, you needn't dance at all," said Murrin, apparently prompted again by Tom Murdock.

This was a decision from which no impartial person could dissent, and Lennon seemed perfectly satisfied, but after all this jaw and interruption, he felt in no great humour to dance, and almost feared the result.

As he stood up he caught a glance from Winny's eye which banished every thought, save that of complying with that look. If ever a look planted an undying resolve in a man's heart it was that. It called him "Rory," as plain as if she had spoken it, and said, "don't let *that fellow* put you down," and quick as the glance was, it added "he's a nasty fellow."

To it now Rory went with his whole heart. He cared not what jig Pat Murrin played, "or any other piper," he was able for them.

At first the quiet tipping of his heel and toe upon the floor, with now and then a flat stamp which threw up the dust, was inimitable. As he got into the "merits of the thing," the music was obliged to vie with him in activity. It seemed as much as if he was dancing for the piper to play to, as that the piper was playing for him to dance. Those who were up to the merits of an Irish jig, could have told the one he was dancing to if there had been no music at all. There was a tip, a curl, or a stamp, for every note in the tune. In fact he played the jig upon the floor with his feet. He now closed the poker and tongs with confidence, while Tom Murdock looked on with a malicious hope that he too would bungle the business; and Winny Cavana looked on with a timid fear of the same result. But he danced through and amongst them as if by magic —a toe here, and a heel there, in each compartment of the crossed irons with the rapidity of lightning, but he never touched one of them.

"Quicker! quicker!" cried Murdock to the piper, seeing that Lennon was perfect master of his position.

"Aye, as quick as you like," stammered Lennon, almost out of breath; and the increased speed of the music brought forth more striking performance, testified to by the applause which greeted his finishing bow.

He caught a short glance again from Winny's eye, as he passed to a vacant seat. "Thank you, Rory, from my heart," it said, as plainly as the other had spoken when he stood up.

It was now well on in the small hours, and as old Murdock and his son had both ceased in a manner to do any more honours, their silence was accepted as a sort of "notice to quit," and there was a general move in search of bonnets and cloaks. Tom Murdock knew that he was in the dumps, and wisely left Winny to her father's escort. Lennon's way lay by the Mulveys, and he was "that far" with Kate and some others. Indeed, all the branch roads and pathways were echoing to the noisy chat and opinions of the scattered party on their several ways home.

CHAPTER VIII.

THE after-reflections of those most interested in the above gathering were various, and it must be admitted to some extent unsatisfactory. First of all old Murdock was keen enough to perceive that he had not furthered his object in the least by having given the party at all. From what Tom had told him he had kept a close watch upon young Lennon, of whose aspirations towards Winny Cavana he had now no doubt, and if he was not sure of a preference upon her part towards him, he was quite certain that she had none towards Tom. This was the natural result of old Murdock's observations of Winny's conduct during the evening,—who, while she could and did hide the one, could not, and did not, hide the other.

Tom Murdock was the least satisfied of them all with the whole business, and sullenly told his father, who had done it all to serve him, that "he had done more harm than good, and that he knew he would by asking that whelp Lennon; and he hoped he might never die till he broke every bone in his body. By hook or by crook, by fair means or foul, he must put a stop to his hopes in that quarter."

His father was silent. He felt that he had not advanced matters by his party. Old Cavana was not the sharp old man in these matters, either to mind or divine from how many points the wind blew, and quietly supposed all had gone on smoothly, as he and old Murdock wished.

Winifred had been more than confirmed in her dislike to Tom Murdock, while her secret preference for Rory of the Hills had been in no respect diminished. She had depth enough also to perceive that Kate Mulvey was anxious enough to propitiate the good opinion, to which she had taken no pains to hide her indifference. She was aware that Kate Mulvey's name had been associated with young Lennon's by the village gossips, but she had seen nothing on that night to justify any apprehension, if *she* chose to set herself to work. She would take an opportunity of sounding her friend upon this momentous subject, and finding out how the land really lay. If that was the side of her head Kate's cap was inclined to lean to, might they not strike a quiet and confidential little bargain between them, as regarded these two young men?

Kate Mulvey's thoughts were not very much at variance with those of her friend Winny. She, not having the same penetration into the probable results of sinister looks, and scowling brows; or not, perhaps, having ever perceived them, had thrown one of the nicest caps that ever came from a smoothing-iron at Tom Murdock, but she feared he had not yet picked it up. She was afraid, until the night of the party, that her friend and rival—yes, it is only in the higher ranks of society that the two cannot be united—had thrown a still more richly trimmed one at him; but on that night, and she had watched closely, she had formed a reasonable belief that her fear was totally unfounded. She was not quite sure that it had not been let drop in Rory of the Hill's way, if not actually thrown at him. These girls, in such cases, are so sharp!

The very same thought had struck her. She also had determined upon sounding her friend Winny, and would take the first favourable opportunity of having a confidential chat with her upon the subject. The girls were very intimate, and were not rivals, only they did not know it. We shall see by-and-by how they "sounded" each other.

Young Lennon's after-thoughts, upon the whole, were more satisfactory than perhaps those of any of the other principal persons concerned. If Winny Cavana had not shown him a decided preference over the general set of young men there, she had certainly being still less particular in her conduct and manner towards Tom Murdock. These matters, no doubt, are managed pretty much the same in all ranks of society, though, of course not with the same refinement; and to young Lennon, whose heart was on the watch, as well as his eyes, one or two little incidents during the night gave him some faint hopes that, as yet at least, his rich rival had not made much way against him. Hitherto, young Lennon had looked upon the rich heiress of Rathcash as a fruit too high for him to reach from the low ground upon which he stood, and had given more of his attention to her poorer neighbour Kate Mulvey. He, however, met with decided reluctance in that quarter, and being neither cowardly, ignorant, nor shy, he had improved one or two favourable occasions with Winny Cavana at the party, whom he now had some, perhaps delusive, notion was not so far above his reach after all.

These are the only persons with whose after-thoughts we are concerned. There may have been some other by-play on the part of two or three fine young men and handsome girls, who burned themselves upon the bar, and danced together after they became cinders, but as they are in no respect mixed up with our story, we may pass them by without investigating their thoughts, further than to declare that they were all well pleased, and that the praises of old Murdock's munificence rang from one end of the parish to the other.

CHAPTER IX.

I MUST now describe a portion of the garden which stretched out from the back of old Ned Cavana's premises. A large well-enclosed farm-yard almost immediately at the rear of the house, gave evidence of the comfort and plenty belonging not only to the old man himself, but to everything living and dead about the place; and as we shall be obliged to pass through this farm-yard to get into the garden, we may as well describe it first. Stacks of corn, wheat, oats, and barley, in great variety of size, pointed the pinnacles of their finishing touch to the sky. Sticking up from some of these were sham weather-cocks, made of straw, in the shape of fish, fowl, dogs, and cats, the handiwork of Jamesy Doyle, the servant boy,—the same black-headed urchin who lifted the tenpenny-bit out of the tub at old Murdock's party. They were fastened upon sticks, which did not turn round, and were therefore put up more to frighten away the sparrows than for the purpose of indicating which way the wind blew, or, more likely still, as mere specimens of Jamesy Doyle's ingenuity. The whole yard was covered a foot deep with loose straw, for the double purpose of giving comfort to two or three litters of young pigs, and that of being used up, by the constant tramping, into manure for

the farm; for cows, heifers, and calves strayed about
it without interruption. A grand flock of geese, as
white as snow and as large nearly as swans, marched
in from the fields, headed by their gander, every
evening about the same hour, to spend their night
gaggling, and watching, and sleeping by turns under
the stacks of corn, which were raised upon stone
pillars with mushroom metal-caps, to keep out the
rats and mice. A big black cock, with a hanging
red comb and white jowels, and innumerable hens
belonging to him, something on the Brigham Young
system, marched triumphantly about, culling his
favourites every now and then with a quick melancholy little chuckle as often as he found a tit-bit
amongst the straw. Ducks, half as large as the
geese, coming home without a feather ruffled, in a
mottled string of all colours, from the stream below
the hill, diving, for variety, into the clean straw,
emerging now and then, and smattering with their
flat bills in any little puddle of water that lay between the pavement in the bare part of the yard.
"Bullydhu," the watch-dog, as evening closed,
taking possession of a small wooden house upon
wheels,—Jamesy Doyle's handiwork too,—that it
might be turned to the shelter, whichever way the
wind blew. It was a miracle to see Bully getting
into it, the door was so low; another piece of consideration of Jamesy's for the dog's comfort. You
could only know when he was in it, by seeing his
large soft paws under the arch of the low door.

Beyond this farmyard—farm in all its appearance
and realities—was the garden. A thick, high, furze-

hedge, about sixty yards long, ran down one side of it, from the corner of the farmyard wall; and at the further end of this hedge, which was the square of the garden, and facing the sun, was certainly the most complete and beautiful summer-house in the parish of Rathcash, or Jamesy Doyle was very much mistaken. It also was his handiwork. In fact there was nothing Jamesy could not turn his hands to, and his heart was as ready as his hands, so that he was always successful, but here he had outstripped all his former ingenuity. The bower was now of four years standing, and every summer Jamesy was proud to see that nature had approved of his plan by endorsing it with a hundred different signatures. With the other portions of the garden or its several crops, we have nothing to do; we will therefore linger for a while about the furze hedge and in "Jamesy's bower" to see what may turn up. But I must describe another item in the locality.

Immediately outside the hedge there was a lane, common to a certain extent to both farms. It might be said to divide them. It lay quite close to the furze hedge, which ran in a straight line a long distance beyond where "Jamesy's bower" formed one of the angles of the garden. There was a gate across the lane precisely outside the corner where the bower had been made, and this was the extent of Murdock's right or title to the commonality of the lane. Passing through this gate, Murdock branched off to the left with the produce of his farm. It is a long lane, they say, that has no turning, and although the portion of this one with which we are concerned was only sixty yards long, I have not, perhaps, brought the reader to the spot so quickly as I might. I certainly could have brought him to it through the yard without putting even the word 'farm' before it, or without saying a word about the stacks of corn and the weather-cocks, the pigs, cows, heifers and calves, the geese, ducks, cock and hens, "Bullydhu" and his house, &c.; and with a hop, step, and a leap, I might have placed him in "Jamesy's bower," if he had been the person to occupy it—but he was not. With every twig, however, of the hedge and the bower it is necessary that my readers should be well acquainted; and I hope I have succeeded in making them so.

Winny Cavana was a thoughtful thrifty girl, an experienced housekeeper, never allowing one job to overtake another where it could be avoided. Of course incidental difficulties would sometimes arise; but in general she managed every thing so nicely and systematically that matters fell into their own time and place as regularly as possible.

When Winny got the invitation for Mick Murdock's party, which was only in the forenoon of the day before it came off, her first thought was, that she would be very tired and ill-fitted for business the day after it was over. She therefore called Jamesy Doyle to her assistance, and on that day and the next, she got through whatever household jobs would bear performance in advance, and instructed Jamesy as to some little matters which she used to oversee herself, but which on this occasion she would entrust solely to his own intelligence and judgment for the day after the party. She could not have committed them to a more competent or conscientious lad. Any thing Jamesy undertook to do, he did it well, as we have already seen both in the haggard, the garden, and the tub—for it was he who brought up the fippenny-bit at Murdock's, and he would lay down his life to serve, or even to oblige Winny Cavana.

Having thus purchased an idle day after the party, Winny was determined to enjoy it, and after a very late breakfast—for her father, poor soul, was dead tired—she called Jamesy, and examined him as to what he had done or left undone. Finding that, notwithstanding he had been up as late as she had been herself the night before, he had been faithful to the trust reposed in him, and that everything was in trim order, she then complimented him upon his snapping and diving abilities.

"How much did you take up out of the tub, Jamesy?" she asked.

"Be gorra, Miss Winny, I took up two tenpenny bits an' a fippenny."

"And what will you do with all that money, Jamesy? it is nearly a month's wages."

"Be gorra, my mother has it afore this, Miss Winny."

"That is a good boy, Jamesy, but you shouldn't curse."

"Be gorra, I won't, miss; but I didn't think that was cursing, at all at all."

"Well, it is swearing, Jamesy, and that is just as bad."

"Well, Miss Winny, you'll never hear me say it agen."

"That's right, James. Is the garden open?"

"It is, miss; I'm after bringing out an armful of leaves to bile for the pigs."

Winny passed on through the yard into the garden. It was a fine mild day for the time of year, and she was soon sitting in the bower with an unopened story-book in her lap. It was a piece of idle folly, her bringing the book there at all. In the first place she had it by heart—for books were scarce in that locality, and were often read—and in the next she was more in a humour to think than to read. It was no strange thing, under the circumstances, if, like some heroines of a higher stamp "she fell into a reverie."

"How long she remained thus," to use the patent phrase in such a case, must be a mere matter of surmise; but a step at the gate outside the hedge, and her own name distinctly pronounced, caused her to start. Eaves-dropping has been usually condemned, and "listeners" they say, "never hear good of themselves." But where is the young girl, or indeed any person, hearing their own name pronounced, and being in a position to listen unobserved, who would not do so. Our heroine, at all events, was not "above that sort of thing," and instead of hemming, or coughing, or shuffling her feet in the gravel, she cocked her ears and held her breath. We would be a little indulgent to a person so sorely tempted, whatever our readers may think.

"If Winny Cavana," she heard, "was twice as

proud, an' twice as great a lady, you may believe me, Tom, she wouldn't refuse you. She'll have six hundred pounds as round as the crown of your hat; an' that fine farm we're after walkin' over; like her, or not like her, take my advice an' don't lose the fortune an' the farm."

"Not if I can help it, father. There's more reason than you know of why I should secure the ready money of her fortune at any rate; as to herself, if it wasn't for that, she might marry Tom Naddy *th' aumaudhawn* if she had a mind."

"Had you any chat with her last night, Tom? Oh! then wasn't she lookin' elegant!"

"As elegant as you please, father, but as proud as a peacock. No, I had no chat with her, except what the whole room could hear; she was determined on that, and I'm still of opinion that you did more harm than good."

"Not if you were worth a *thrawneen*, Tom. Arrah avic machree, you don't understand her; that was all put on, man alive. I'm afeerd she'll think you hav'nt the pluck in you; she's a sperited girl herself, and depend upon it she expects you to spake, an' its what she's vexed at, your dilly-dallyin. Why did you let that fellow take her out for the first dance? I heerd Mrs. Moran remark it to Kitty Mulvey's mother."

"That was a mistake, father; he had her out before I got in from the kitchen."

"They don't like them mistakes, Tom, an' that's the very thing I blame you for; you should have stuck to her like a leech the whole night, they like

a man that's in earnest. Take my advice, Tom
avic, an' put the question plump to her at wanst for
Shraftide. Tell her I'll lay down a pound for you
for every pound her father gives her, and I'll make
over this place to you out an' out. Old Ned an' I
will live together while we last, an' that can't be
long, Tom avic. I know he'll settle Rathcash upon
Winny, and she'll have the interest of her fortune
besides—

"Interest be d—d!" interrupted Tom; "won't
he pay the money down?"

"He might do that same, but I think not; he's
afeared it might be dribbled away, but with Rathcash, an' Rathcashmore joined, the devil's in it if
she can't live like a lady; at all events, Tom, you
can live like a gentleman; ould Ned's for you
entirely, Tom, I can tell you that."

"That is all very well, father, and I wish you
could make me think that your words would come
true, but I'm not come to four-and-twenty years of
age without knowing something of the way girls
get on; and if that one is not set on young Lennon,
my name is not Tom Murdock; and I'll tell you
what's more, that if it wasn't for her fortune and
that farm, he might have her and welcome. There
are many girls in the parish as handsome, and
handsomer for that matter, than what she is, that
would just jump at me."

"I know that, Tom agra, but maybe it's what
you'll only fix her on that whelp, as you call him,
the stronger, if you bo houldin' back the way you
do. They like pluck, Tom; they like pluck I tell

you, an' in my opinion she's only makin blief, to dhraw you out. Try her, Tom, try her."

"I will, father, and if I fail, and that I find that spalpeen Lennon is at the bottom of it, let them both look out, that's all. For his part I have a way of dealing with him that he knows nothing about, and as for her—"

Here Jamesy Doyle came out into the lane from the farmyard, and father and son immediately branched off in the direction of their own house, leaving Tom Murdock's second part of the threat unfinished.

But Winny had heard enough. Her heart, which had been beating with indignation the whole time, had nearly betrayed itself when she heard Rory of the Hills called a spalpeen.

One thing she was now certain of, and the certainty gave her whole soul relief,—that if ever Tom Murdock could have had any chance of success through her father's influence, and her love for him, it was now entirely at an end for ever. Should her father urge the match upon her, she had, as a last remedy, but to reveal this conversation, to gain him over indignantly to her side.

Winny was seldom very wrong in her likings or dislikings, although perhaps both were formed in some instances rather hastily, and she often knew not why. In Tom Murdock's case, she was glad, and now rather "proud out of herself," that she had never liked him.

"I knew the dirt was in him," she said to herself as she returned to the house. "I wish he did not live so near us, for I foresee nothing but trouble and vexation before me on his account. I'm sorry Jamesy Doyle came out so soon. I'd like to have heard what he was going to say of myself, but sure he said enough. Rory of the Hills may despise himself and his threat." And she went into the house to prepare the dinner.

Tom Murdock, notwithstanding his shortcomings, and they were neither few nor far between, was a shrewd clever fellow in most matters. It was owing to this shrewdness that he resolved to watch for some favourable opportunity, rather than seek a formal meeting with Winny Cavana '*at wanst,*' as had been advised by his father.

CHAPTER X.

It is not to be wondered at that two persons, equally clever in all respects, and having a similar though not identical object in view, should have pretty much the same thoughts respecting the manner of carrying it out, and finally pursue the same course to effect their purpose. But the matter involves some nicety, if not difficulty, when it so happens that those two persons have to work upon each other in a double case. It is then a matter of diamond cut diamond; and if, as I have suggested, both are equally clever, the discussion of the subject between them would make no bad scene in a play. Winny wanted to find out something from Kate Mulvey, and at the same time to hide something from her.

Kate Mulvey was on precisely the same intent with Winny Cavana in both ways; so that some such tournament must come off between them the first time they met, with sufficient opportunity to "have it out" without interruption.

You have seen that Winny had determined to sound her friend Kate, as to how her land lay between these two young men. If Kate had not made a like determination as to sounding Winny, she was, at all events, ready for the encounter at any moment, and had discussed the matter over and over in her own mind. Their mutual object, then, was to find out which of the young men was the real object of the other's affections; and up to the present moment each believed the other to be a formidable rival to her own hopes.

Winny was not one who hesitated about any matter which she felt to require immediate performance; and as she knew that some indefinite time might elapse before an opportunity could occur to have her chat out with Kate Mulvey, she was resolved to make one.

Her father's house, as the reader has seen in the commencement, was not on the roadside. There was no general pass that way; and except persons had business to old Cavana's or Mick Murdock's, they never went up the lane, which was common to both the houses of these rich farmers. It was not so with the house where Kate Mulvey resided. Its full front was to the high-road, with a space not more than three perches between. This space had been originally what is termed in that rank of life.

"a bawn," but was now wisely converted into a cabbage-garden, with a broad clean gravel-walk running through the centre of the plot, from the road to the door. It was about half a mile from Cavana's, and there was a full view of the road, for a long stretch, from the door or window of the house—that is, of Mulvey's.

It was now a fine mild day towards the end of November. Old Mick Murdock's party had ceased to be spoken of, and perhaps forgotten, except by the few with whom we have to do. Winny Cavana put on her every-day bonnet and her every-day cloak, and started for a walk. Bully-dhu capered round her in an awkward playful manner, with a deep-toned howl of joy when he saw these preparations, and trotted down the lane before her. As may be anticipated, she bent her steps along the road towards Mulvey's house. She knew she could be seen coming for some distance, and hoped that Kate might greet her from the door as she passed. She was not mistaken; Kate had seen her from the first turn in the road towards the house, and was all alive on her own account. She had tact and vanity enough, however,—for she had plenty of time before Winny came alongside of the house,—to slip in and put on a decent gown, and brush her beautiful and abundant hair; and she came to the door, as if by mere accident, but looking at her very best, as Winny approached. Kate knew that she was looking very handsome, and Winny Cavana, at the first glance, felt the very same fact.

"Good-morrow, Kate," said Winny; that's a fine day."

"Good-morrow kindly, Winny; won't you come in and sit down awhile?"

"No, thank you; the day is so fine, I'm out for a walk. You may as well put on your bonnet, and come along with me; it will do you good, Kitty."

"With all my heart; step up to the house, and I'll be ready in two twos." But she was not so sure that it would do her good.

The girls then turned up to the house, for Kate had run down in her hair to shake hands with her friend. Winny would not go in, but stood at the door, ordering Bully-dhu not to growl at Captain, and begging of Captain not to growl at Bully-dhu. Kate was scarcely the "two twos" she gave herself, until she came out ready for the road; and the two friends, and the two dogs, having at once entered into most amicable relations with each other, went off together.

Winny was resolved that no "awkward pause" on her part should give Kate reason to suppose there was anything unusual upon her mind, and went on at once, as if from where she had left off.

"The day was so fine, Kate," she continued, "that I was anxious to get some fresh air. I have been churning, and packing butter, every day since Monday, and could not get out. Biddy Murtagh is very clean and honest, but she is very slow, and I could not leave her."

"It is well for you, Winny, that has the butter to pack."

"Yes, Kate, I suppose it will be well for me some day or other; but as long as my poor father lives—God between him and harm!—I don't feel the want of any thing."

"God spare him to you, Winny mavourneen! He's a fine hale old man, and I hope he'll live to be at the christening of many a grandchild. If report speaks thrue, Winny dear, that same is not unlikely to come round."

"Report does not always speak the truth, Kate; don't you know that?"

"I do; but I also know that there's seldom smoke without fire, and that it sometimes makes a good hit. And sure, nothin's more rasonable than that it's right this time. Tom's a fine young fellow: an' like yourself, sure, he's an only child. There wasn't such a weddin' this hundred years—no, nor never—in the parish of Rathcash, as it will be—come now!"

"Tom is a fine young man, Kate; I don't deny it—"

"You couldn't—you couldn't, Winny Cavana! you'd belie yoursel' if you did," said Kate, with a little more warmth of manner than was quite politic under the circumstances.

"But I don't, Kate; and I can't see why *you* need fly at me in that way."

"I beg your pardon, Winny dear; but sure every body sees an' knows that you're on for one another; an' why not?—wasn't he as cross as a bag of cats at his father's party because he let 'that whelp' (as he called him) Rory Lennon take you out for the first dance?"

E

"Rory of the Hills is no whelp; he could'nt call him a whelp. Did he call him one?"

"Didn't you hear him? for if you didn't, you might; it wasn't but he spoke loud enough."

"It is well for him, Kate, that Rory didn't hear him. He's as good a man as Tom Murdock at any rate. He didn't fall over the poker and tongs as Tom did."

"That was a mere accident, Winny. I seen the *fung* of his pump loose myself; didn't I help to shut it for him, afther he fell?"

"You were well employed indeed, Kate," said Winny sneeringly.

"You would have done it yourself if he axed you as he did me," replied Kate.

"Certainly not," said Winny.

So far they seemed both to have the worst of it, in spite of all their caution. What they wanted was to find out how the other's heart stood between these two young men, without betraying their own— which latter they had both nearly done.

There was a pause, and Kate was the next to speak.

"Not but I must admit that Rory of the Hills is a milder, better boy in some respects than Tom. He has a nicer way with him, Winny, and I think it is easier somehow to like him than to like Tom.

"Report says you do, Kate dear."

"But you know, Winny, report does not always spake thrue, as you say yourself."

"Ay, but as you said just now, Kate, it sometimes makes a good hit."

"Well, Winny, I wish *you* joy at all events, with all my heart. Both your fathers is anxious for your match; an' sure when the two farms is joined in one, with you an' Tom, you can live like a lady. I suppose you'll hould your head too high for poor Kate an' Rory of the Hills then."

There was a sadness in Kate's tone as she said this, which, from ignorance of how matters really stood, was partly genuine, and, from anxiety to find it out, was partly assumed.

But she had turned the key, and the door flew open. Winny could fence with her feelings no longer.

"Kate Mulvey," she exclaimed, "do not believe the reports you hear about me and Tom Murdock. I'm aware of what you say about his father and mine been anxious to unite the farms by our marriage. I don't want to say any thing against Tom Murdock; but he'll never call me wife. There now, Kate jewel, you have the truth. I'll be well enough off, Kitty, without Tom Murdock's money or land; and when I really don't care for him, don't you think it would be much better and handsomer of him, to bestow himself and it upon some nice girl without a penny" (and she glanced slyly at Kate, whose cheeks got rosy red), "than to be striving to force it upon one that doesn't want it—nor wish for it? And don't you think it would be much better and handsomer for me, who has a nice little fodeen, and must come in for my father's land,—God between him and harm!—to do the same, if I could meet with a nice boy that really cared for myself, and not for my money? Answer me them questions, Kate?"

Kate was silent; but her eyes had assumed quite a different expression, if they had not altogether turned almost a different colour. The weight of Winny's rich rivalry had been lifted from her heart, and so far as that obstacle had been dreaded, the coast was now clear. Of course she secretly agreed in the propriety of Winny's views, and it was only necessary that she should now do so openly.

"You didn't answer me them questions yet, Kate."

"Well I could, Winny, if I liked it; but I don't wish to have act, hand, or part in setting you against your father's wishes."

"You need not fear that, Kitty; my father won't force me to do what I really do not wish to do. He never put the matter to me plainly yet, but I expect it every day. He's always praising Tom Murdock, and hinting at the business, by saying he wishes he could see me comfortably settled; that he is growing old and is not the man he used to be; and all that. I know very well, Kate, what he means, both ways; and, 'God between him and harm!' I say again; but he'll never see me Tom Murdock's wife. I have my answer ready for them both."

"Well, Winny, as you seem determined, I suppose I may spake; and, to tell you the truth, I always thought it would be a pity to put them two farms into one, and so spoil two good establishments; for sure any one of them is lashings, Winny, for any decent boy and girl in the parish; an' what's more, if they were joined together to-morrow, there is not a gentleman in the county would think a bit the better of them that had them."

"Never, Kitty, except it was some poor broken-down fellow that wanted to borrow a couple of hundred pounds, and rob them in the end. And now, Kitty, let us be plain and free with one another. My opinion is that Tom could raise you— I won't say out of poverty, Kate; for, thanks be to God, it is not come to that with you, and that it never may—but into comfort and plenty; and that I could, some day, do the same, if I could meet with a nice boy that, as I said, would care for myself and not for my money. If Tom took a liking to you, Kitty, you might know he was in earnest for yourself; I *know* he's only put up to his make-belief liking for me by his own father and mine. But, Kitty dear, I'm afraid, like myself, you have no fancy for him."

"Well, Winny, to tell you the truth, I always believed what the neighbours said about you an' him; and I tried not to think of him for that same reason. There's no doubt, Winny dear, but it would be a fine match for me; but I know he's out an' out for you: only for that, Winny, I could love every bone in his body—there now! you have it out."

"He'll soon find his mistake, Kate dear, about me. I'm sure the thing will be brought to a point before long between us, and between my father and me too. When Tom finds I'm positive, he can't be blind to your merits and beauty, Kitty,—yes, I will say it out, your beauty!—you needn't be putting your hand to my mouth that way; there's no mistake about it."

"Ah, Winny, Winny dear, you are too lenient to me entirely; sure I couldn't sit or stand beside you in that respect at all, an' with your money; sure they'll settle it all between themselves."

"They may settle what they like, Kitty; but they can't make me do what I am determined not to do; so as far as that goes you have nothing to fear."

"Well, Winny dear, I'm glad I know the truth; for now I won't be afeared of crossing you, at any rate; and I know another that would'nt be sorry to know as much as I do."

"Who, Kitty? tell us."

"Ah, then now, Winny, can't you guess? or maybe it's what you know better than I do myself."

"Well I suppose you mean Rory of the Hills; for indeed, Kitty, he's always on the top of your tongue, and the parish has it that you and he are promised. Come now, Kitty, tell us the truth. I told you how there was no truth in the report about me and Tom Murdock, and how there never could be."

If this was not leading Kate Mulvey to the answer most devoutly wished for, I do not know what the meaning of the latter part of the sentence could be. It was what the lawyers would call a "leading question." The excitement too of Winny, during the pause which ensued, showed very plainly the object with which she spoke, and the anxiety she felt for the result.

Kate did not in the least misunderstand her. Perhaps she knew more of her thoughts than Winny was aware of, and that it was not then she found them out for the first time; for Kate was a shrewd observer. She had gained her own object, and it was only fair she should now permit Winny to gain hers.

"Ah, Winny dear," she said, after a contemplative pause, "there never was a word of the kind between us. You know, Winny, in the first place, it wouldn't do at all—two empty sacks could never stand; and in the next place, neither his heart was on me, nor mine on him. It was all idle talk of the neighbours. Not but Rory is as nice a boy as there is to be found in this or any other parish, and you know that, Winny; don't you now?"

"Kitty dear, there's nobody can deny what you say, and for that self-same reason I believed what the neighbours said regarding you and him."

"Tell me this now, Winny,—you know we were reared, I may say, at the door with one another, and have been fast friends since we were that height" (and she held her hand within about two feet of the ground, at the same time looking fully and very kindly into her friend's face)—"tell me now, Winny dear, did it fret you to believe what you heard? Come now."

"For your sake, and for his, Kitty, it could not fret me; but for my own sake—there now, don't ask me."

"No, avourneen, I wont; what need have I, Winny, when I see them cheeks of yours,—or is it the sun that cum suddenly out upon you, Winny ashtore?"

"Kate Mulvey, I'll tell you the truth, as I believe you have told it to me. For many a long day I'm striving to keep myself from liking that boy on your account. I think, Kate, if I hadn't a penny-piece in the world no more than yourself, I would have done my very best to take him from you; it would have been a fair fight then, Kitty; but I didn't like to use any odds against you, Kitty dear; and I never gave him so much as one word to go upon."

"I'm very thankful to you, Winny dear; an' signs on the boy, he thought you were for a high match with rich Tom Murdock; an' any private chat Rory an' I ever had was about that same thing."

"Then he has spoken to you about me! O Kitty, dear Kitty, what used he to be saying of me? do tell me!"

"The never a word I'll tell you, Winny dear. Let him spake to yourself; which maybe he'll do when he finds you give Tom the go-by; but I'm book sworn; so don't ask me."

"Well, Kitty, I'm glad I happened to come across you this morning; for now we understand each other, and there's no fear of our interrupting one another in our thoughts any more."

"None, thank God," said Kitty.

By this time the girls had wandered along the road to nearly a mile from home. They had both gained their object, though not in the roundabout *sounding* manner which we had anticipated, and they were now both happy. They were no longer even the imaginary rivals, which it appears was all they had ever been; and as this light broke upon them the endearing epithets of "dear" and "jewel" became more frequent and emphatic than was usual in a conversation of the same length.

Their mutual confidences, as they retraced their steps, were imparted to the fullest extent. They now perfectly "understood each other," as Winny had said; and to their cordial shake-hands at the turn up to Kate Mulvey's house, was added an affectionate kiss as good as if they swore never to interfere with each other in love-affairs.

CHAPTER XI.

WINNY CAVANA, as far as her own feelings and belief were concerned, had not made a bad morning's work of it. Hitherto she had supposed that Kate Mulvey had forestalled her in the affections of Rory of the Hills. The neighbours had given them to each other, and she feared that Rory was not free from the power of her charms. With these doubts, or almost with this belief, upon her mind, she could not have met her father's importunities about Tom Murdock with the same careless and happy determination which matters, as they now stood, would enable her to do. Being assured, from her conversation with Kate, that there was nothing between her and Rory, she could "riddle" more easily some circumstances

and expressions which, to say the least of it, were
puzzling, with a belief that these two persons were
mutually attached. Winny knew now how to reconcile them, and the view she took of them was any
thing but favourable to her father's wishes or Tom
Murdock's hopes.

She could not hope, however,—perhaps she did
not wish,—for any interview with Rory just then,
when her change of manner, emanating from her
knowledge of facts, might draw him out, for her
heart now told her that this would surely come.
She had some fears that her father might sound her
about Rory, and she wished to be able to say with a
clear conscience that he had never spoken, or even
hinted at the subject, to her; but she was determined
nevertheless to act towards her father, and subsequently towards Tom Murdock, as if her troth and
Rory's had been already irrevocably plighted. She
was in hopes that if she had an interview with her
father upon the subject of Tom Murdock in the first
instance, the unalterable dislike which she would
exhibit to the match might save her the horrible
necessity of going through the business with the
man himself. But poor Winny had settled matters
in her own mind in an order in which they did not
occur; and it so happened that, although she thought
her heart had gone through enough of excitement
for one day, and that she would, for the rest of that
evening, hide beneath the happiness which was
creeping over, she was mistaken.

Tom Murdock had seen her pass down the road;
and hastily putting on one of his best coats and his

very best hat, he followed her, determined to have good news in return for his father's advice; but he was disappointed. Before he could overtake her, he perceived that she had been joined by Kate Mulvey, and that they went coshering away together. Of course he saw that it was "no go," as he said, for that time; but he would watch her returning, when he could not fail to meet her alone.

"Hang me," said he, as he saw them walking away, "if I don't think Kate Mulvey is the finest girl of the two, and very nearly as handsome as ever she was—some people say handsomer. If it was not for her money, and that grand farm she'll have, I'd let her see how soon I could get a girl in every other respect as good, if not better, than she is. Look at the two of them: upon my faith, I think Kate is the highest stepper of the two."

Tom paused for a few moments, if not in his thoughts, at least in the expression of them; for all the above had been uttered aloud. Then, as if they had received a sudden spur which made him start, he muttered with his usual scowl, "No, no; I'll follow it up to the death if necessary. That whelp shall never have it to say that Tom Murdock failed, and perhaps add, where he did not. I'll have her, by fair means if I can; but if not, by them five crosses," and he clasped his hands together, "she shall be mine by foul. Sure it is not possible they are goin to meet that whelp this blessed moment!" And he dogged them at so long a distance behind, that, even if their conversation had been less interesting, they would not have been aware of his stealthy espionage.

When they turned to return, he turned also, and was then so far before them, that, with the bushes and the bends in the road, he could not be perceived. Thus he watched and watched, until, to his great satisfaction, he saw them part company at Kate's house. Winny Cavana, as we have seen, had still some distance to walk ere she reached the lane turning up to her father's; and Kate having gone in and shut the door, Tom strolled on, as if by mere accident, until he met Winny on the road.

Tom was determined to be as mild and as bland, as cordial and good-natured as possible. He felt there had always been a sort of undefined snappish battle between him and Winny; and he had the honesty of mind, as well as the vanity, to blame his own harsh and abrupt manner for this. Perhaps it arose no less from a consciousness of his personal advantages than from a belief that in his position as an only son and heir to his father's interest in a rich and profitable farm, he had no great need of those blandishments of expression so generally requisite in making way to a young and unhackneyed heart. He resolved, therefore, upon this occasion to give Winny no cause to accuse him of uncouthness of manner; neither was he inclined to be uncouth when he beheld the glowing beauty of her face, heightened, as he thought, solely by the exercise of her walk; but not a little increased, without his knowledge of the fact, by the new light which had just dawned upon the horizon of her hopes.

Her heart bounced in her bosom as she saw him approach.

"Good morning, Winny," he said, holding out his hand.

"Good morrow, kindly, Tom," she replied, wishing to be civil, and taking it. She knew she was "in for it" as she expressed it to herself; but encouraged "by the hope within her springing," and softened by the anticipation of its fulfilment, she was determined to be kind but firm.

"Have you been walking far, Winny? Upon my life, it seems to agree with you. It has improved your beauty, Winny, if that were possible."

"Tom, don't flatter me; you're always paying me compliments, and I often told you that I did not like it. Besides, you did not let me answer your question until you begin at your old work. I walked about a mile of the road with Kate Mulvey."

"Kate Mulvey is a complete nice girl. You are not tired, Winny, are you?"

"Ah! then, what would tire me? is it a mile of a walk, and the road under my feet? I could walk to *Boher-na-Milthiogue* and back this minute."

By this time they had come to the end of the lane turning up to Rathcash House.

"I'm glad to find you are not tired, Winny. You may as well come on towards the cross; I have something to say to you."

"And welcome, Tom; what is it?"

Winny felt that the thing was coming, and she wished to appear as careless and unconscious as possible. When she recollected all Kate Mulvey

F

had said to her, she was just in the humour to have it over. Upon reflection, too, she was not sorry that it should so happen before the grand passage between her and her father upon the same subject. She could the more easily dispose of the case with him, having already disposed of it with Tom himself. She therefore went on, past the end of her own lane; and Tom, taking this for an unequivocal token in his favour, was beginning to get really fond of her,—at least he thought so.

"Well, Winny, I'm very glad I happened to meet you, and that you seem inclined to take a walk with me; for to tell you the truth, Winny, I can't help thinking of you."

"Perhaps you don't try, Tom."

"True for you, Winny dear; I wouldn't help thinking of you if I could, and I couldn't if I would."

"Is that the way with you, Tom?"

But Winny did not smile or look at him, as he had hoped she would have done.

"You know it is, Winny dear; but I can keep the truth, in plain English, from you no longer."

"See that, now! Ah then, Tom, I pity you."

And Tom could not tell from her manner, or from the tone of her voice, whether she was in earnest or only joking. He preferred the former.

"Well, Winny Cavana, if you knew how much I loved you, you would surely take pity on me, my own *colleen dhass.*"

"Faith, Tom, I believe it's in earnest you are, sure enough."

"In earnest! Yes, Winny, by the bright sky over me—and it is not brighter than your own eyes—I am in earnest! It is a long day now since I first took to loving you, though it was only of late you might have picked it out of my looks. Ah! Winny dear, if you hadn't a penny-piece but yourself, I would have spoken to you long ago. But there was a great deal of talk among the neighbours about the joining of them two farms together, and I was afraid you might think—"

"I understand. You were afraid I might think it was my money and the farm you were after, and not myself. Was not that it, Tom?"

"Just so, Winny, but I am indeed in earnest, and for yourself alone, Winny dear; and I'm willing to prove my words by making you my wife, and mistress of all I have coming Shraftide, God willing." And he took her by the hand.

She withdrew it at once, after a slight struggle, and replied, "Tom Murdock, put such a thing totally out of your head, for it can never be,—never, by the same oath you swore just now, and that is the blue heaven above me!" And she turned back towards the lane.

"I cross, Winny." Don't say that. I know that your father and mine would both be willing for the match. As to what your father would do for you, Winny mavourneen, I don't care a *boughalawn bui;* for I'm rich enough without a cross of his money or his land. My own father will make over to me by lawful deed, the day you become my wife, his house and furniture, together with the whole of his land and cattle. Your father, I know, Winny, would do the same for you, for he has but yourself belonging to him; and although your fortune or your land has nothing to say to my love, yet, Winny dear, between us, if you will consent to my prayer, for it is nothing less, there's few grandees in the country could compare to you,—I'll say nothing for myself. Winny dear, only say the word."

"No, Tom, I'll say no word but what I'm after saying; and you are only making matters worse, talking of grandeur and riches that way. You would only be striving at what you would not be able for, nor allowed to keep up, Tom; and as for myself, I'd look well—wouldn't I?—stuck up on a new side-car, and a drawn bonnet and feathers, coming down the lane of a Sunday, and the neighbours thronging to Mass,—aping my betters, and getting myself and yourself laughed at. Devil a one, Tom, but they'd call you Lord *Boher-na-Milthiogue*. No, Tom; put it out of your head; that is my first and last word to you." And she hastened her step.

"No, Winny, you won't leave me that way, will you? By all the books that were ever shut and opened, you may make what you please of me. I'll never ask to put yourself or myself a pin's-point beyond what we always were, either in grandeur or any thing else. But wouldn't it be a fine thing, Winny dear, to have our children able to hold up their heads with the best in the county, in a manner?"

"Ay, in a manner, indeed. No, Tom; they would never be any thing but the Murdocks of Rathcashmore—grandchildren of ould Mick Murdock and ould Ned Cavana, the common farmers."

"And what have you to say against old Mick Murdock?" exclaimed Tom, beginning to feel that his suit was hopeless, and flaming up inwardly in the spirit which was most natural to him.

"Nothing, indeed, Tom; you need not be so angry, I meant no offence; I said as much against my own father as against yours, if there was any thing against either. But we must soon part now, Tom, and let us part friends at all events, living as we do within a stone's-throw of each other." She held out her hand, but he took it coldly and loosely. He felt that his game was up.

"Take my advice, Tom Murdock"—this was the second time she had found it necessary to overcome her antipathy to pronounce the name—"take my advice, and never speak to me again upon the subject. Sure, there's many a fine handsome girl would be glad to listen to you; and I'll now ask you one question before we part. Wouldn't it be better and fitter for you to bestow yourself and your land upon some handsome young girl who has nothing of her own, and was, maybe, well inclined for you, and to rise her up to be independent, than to be striving to force yourself and it upon them that doesn't want your land, and cannot care for yourself? Why don't you look about you? there's many a girl in the parish as handsome, and handsomer, than I am, that would just jump at you."

Winny had no sooner uttered these latter words than she regretted them. She did not wish Tom Murdock to know that she had overheard him. She was glad however to perceive that, in his anger, he had not recognised them as a quotation from his conversation with his father at the gate.

There was a silence now for a minute or so. Tom's blood was up; his hopes of success were over, and he was determined to speak his mind in an opposite direction.

"Have I set you thinking, Tom?" said Winny, half timidly.

"I'm d—d but you have, Winny Cavana; and I'll answer your question with one much like it. And would not it be better and fitter for *you*—of course it would—to bestow yourself and your fortune and your land upon some handsome young fellow that has nothing but his day's wages, and was well inclined for you, and to rise him up out of poverty, than to spoil a good chance for a friend by joining yours to them that has enough without it? Why didn't you follow up your first question with *that*, Winny Cavanagh?" And he stopped short, enjoying the evident confusion he had caused.

Winny thought too for a few moments in silence. She was considering the probability of Tom Murdock's having overheard her conversation with Kate Mulvey from behind some hedge. But the result of her calculation was that it was impossible.

She was right. It was a mere paraphrase of her own question to him, and only shows how two clever people may hit upon the same idea, and express it in nearly the same language. And the question was prompted by his suspicions in the quarter already intimated.

"Yes, I see how it is," he exclaimed, breaking the silence, and giving way to his ungovernable temper. "But, by the hatred I bear to that whelp, *that* shall never be, at all events. I'll go to your father this moment, and let him know what's going on."—

"And who do you dare to call 'a whelp,' Tom Murdock? If it be Rory of the Hills, let me tell you that his little finger is worth your whole head and heart—body and bones together."

"There, there—she acknowledges it. But I'll put a spoke in that whelp's wheel,—for it was him I called a whelp, since you must know,—see if I don't; so let him look out, that's all."

"I have acknowledged nothing, Tom Murdock. A word beyond common civility never passed between Rory of the Hills and myself; and take care how you venture to interfere between my father and me. You have got your answer, and I have sworn to it. You have no right to interfere further."

By this time they had reached the end of the lane again; and Winny with her heart on fire, and her face in a flame, hurried to the house. Fortunately, her father had not returned from the fields, and rushing to her own room, she locked the door, took off her bonnet and cloak, and "threw herself" (I believe that is the proper expression) upon the bed. Perhaps a sensation novelist would add that she "burst into an agony of tears."

CHAPTER XII.

Winny lay for nearly an hour meditating upon the past, the present, and the future. Upon the whole she did not regret what had occurred, either before or after she had met Tom Murdock, and she cooled down into her accustomed self-possession sooner than she had supposed possible.

One grand object had been attained. Tom Murdock had come to the point, and she had given him his final and irrevocable answer, if she had twenty fathers thundering parental authority in her ears. A spot of blue sky had appeared too in the east, above the outline of Shanvilla mountain, in which the morning star of her young life might soon arise, and shine brightly through the flimsy clouds—for she could call them nothing but flimsy now—which had hitherto darkened her hopes. What if Tom Murdock was a villain!—and she believed he was: what dared he—what could he do? pshaw, nothing! But, oh! that the passage of arms between herself and her father was over. "Then," thought she, "all might be plain sailing before me."

But, Winny, supposing all these matters fairly over,—and the battle with your father is likely to be as cranky and tough upon his part, as it is certain to be straightforward and determined upon yours,— there will still be a doubtful blank upon your mind and in your heart, and one the solution of which you cannot, even with Katey Mulvey's assistance, seek an occasion to fill up. Ah! no, you must trust to chance for time and opportunity for that most important of all your interviews. And what if you be mistaken after all, and, if mistaken, crushed for ever by the result!

Let Winny alone for that. Women seldom make a bad guess in such a case.

Winny's mental and nervous systems having both regained their ordinary degree of composure, she left her room and proceeded through the house upon her usual occupations. She was not, however, quite free from a certain degree of anxiety at the anticipated interview with her father. He had not in any way intimated his intention to ask certain questions touching any communication she might have received from Tom Murdock, together with her answers thereto; and yet she felt certain that on the first favourable occasion he would ask the questions, without any notice whatever. She had subsided for the day, after a very exciting morning upon two very different subjects. Yes; she called them different, though they were pretty much akin; and she would now prefer a cessation of her anxiety for the remainder of that afternoon at least.

So far she was fortunate. Her father did not come in until it was very late; and being much fatigued by his stewardship of the day, he did not appear inclined to enter upon any important subject, but fell asleep in his arm-chair, after a hasty and (Winny observed) scarcely-touched dinner.

Winny was an affectionate good child. She was

devotedly fond of her father, with whose image were associated all her thoughts of happiness and love, since she was able to clasp his knees and clamber to his lap. Even yet no absolute allegiance of a decided nature claimed the disloyalty of her heart; but she felt that the time was not far distant when either he must abdicate his royalty, or she must rebel.

"It is clearly my duty now," she said to herself, "not to delay this business about Tom, upon the chance of his being the first to speak of it: tomorrow, before the cares and labours of the day occupy his mind, and perhaps make him ever so little a bit cross, I will tell him what has happened. I am afraid he will be very angry with me for refusing that man; but it cannot be helped: not for all the gold they both possess would I marry Tom Murdock. I shall not betray his sordid villany, however, until all other resources fail; but I know my father will scorn the fellow as I do, when he knows the whole truth—but, ah! I have no witness," thought she, "and they will make a liar of me."

If the old man could have ever perceived any difference in the kind and affectionate attention so uniformly bestowed upon him by his fond daughter, perhaps it might have been upon that night after he awoke from a rather lengthened nap in his easy-chair.

Winny had sat during the whole time gazing upon the loved features of the sleeping old man. She could not call to mind, from the day upon which her memory first became conscious, a single unkind, or even a harsh word which he had uttered to her. That he could be more than harsh to others she knew, and she was now in her nineteenth year; fifteen clear years, she might say, of unbroken memory. She could remember her fifth birth-day quite well, and so much as a snappish word or a commanding look she had never received from him; not, God knows, but he had good reason, many's the time, for more than either. And there he lay now, calm, and fast asleep, the only one belonging to her on the wide earth, and she meditating an opposition in her heart to his plans respecting her,—all, she knew, arising from the great love he had for her, and the frustration of which, she was aware, would vex him sore. "O Tom Murdock, Tom Murdock, why are you Tom Murdock? or Rory of the Hills, why did I ever see you?" was the conclusion to this train of thought, as she sat still, gazing on her sleeping father.

Then a happier train succeeded, and a fond smile lit up her handsome face. "Ah! no, no! I am the only being belonging to him, the only one he loves. The father who for nearly twenty years never spoke an unkind word—and if he had reason to reprove me did so by example and request, and not the rod—has only to know that a marriage with Tom Murdock would ensure my misery to make him spurn him, as I did myself. As to the other boy, I know nothing for certain myself about him, and I can fairly deny any accusation he may make; and I am certain he has been put up to it by old Murdock through his son. Yet even on this score I'll deny as little as I can."

Here it was her father awakened; and Winny had only time to conclude her thoughts by wondering how that fellow dare call Rory "a whelp."

"Well, father dear," she said, "you have had a nice nap; you must have been very tired. I wish I was a man, that I might help you on the farm."

"Winny darlin', I wouldn't have you anything but what you are for the world. I have not much to do at all on the farm but to poke about, and see that the men I have at work don't rob me by idling; and I must say I never saw honester work than what they leave after them. But, Winny, I came across old Murdock shortly after I went out, and he came over my land with me, and I went over his with him, so that we had rather a long walk. I'll engage he's as tired as what I am. I did not think his farm was so extensive as it is, or that the land was so good, or in such to-au-op caun-di-shon." And poor old Ned yawned and stretched himself.

Winny saw through the whole thing at once. The matter of a marriage between herself and Tom Murdock, and a union of the farms, had doubtless been discussed between her father and old Mick Murdock, and a final arrangement, so far as *they* were concerned, had been arrived at. A hitch upon her part she was certain neither of them had ever dreamt of; and yet "hitch" was a slight word to express the opposition she was determined to give to their wishes.

She knew that if her father had got so far as where he had been interrupted by the yawn, when he was fresh after breakfast the whole thing would have come out. She was, however, a considerate girl; and although she knew there was at that moment a good opening, where a word would have brought the matter on, she knew that the result would have completely driven rest and sleep from the poor old man's pillow for the night, tired and fatigued as he was. She therefore adroitly changed the conversation to his own comforts in a cup of tea before he went to bed.

"Yes, mavourneen," he said, "I fell asleep before I mixed a tumbler of punch, and I'll take the tea now instead; for, Winny, my love, you can join me at that. Do you know, Winny, I'm very thirsty?"

"Well, father dear, I'll soon give you what will refresh you."

While Winny was busying herself for the tea, putting down a huge kettle of water in the kitchen, and rattling the cups and saucers until you'd think she was trying to break them, the old man wakened up into a train of thought not altogether dissimilar to that which Winny herself had indulged in over his sleeping form.

Winny was quite right. The whole matter had been discussed on that day between the old men during their perambulations round the two farms; the respective value and condition of the land forming a minute calculation not unconnected with the other portion of their discourse,—settlements, deeds of conveyance, &c., &c., had all been touched upon.

Winny was right in another of her surmises, although at the time she scarcely believed so herself.

Old Murdock, taking his cue from Tom, told old Ned that if he found Winny at all averse to marrying Tom, he was certain young Rory of the Hills would be at the bottom of it—at least Tom had more than hinted such to him.

Old Ned was furious at this, declaring that if Tom Murdock was never to the fore, his daughter should never bestow his long and hard earnings upon a pauper like that, looking for a day's wages here and there, and as often without it as with it; how dare the likes of him lift his eyes to his little girl! But he'd soon put a stop to that, if there was anything in it, let what would turn up. Every penny-piece he was worth in the world was in his own power, and there was a very easy way of bringing Miss Winny to her senses, if she had that wild notion in her head.

Poor old Ned, in his indignation for what he thought Winny's welfare, forgot that she was the only being belonging to him in the world, and that when it came to the point he would find it impossible to put his threat of "cutting her off" into execution.

Old Murdock was delighted with this tirade against young Rory of the Hills, whom he looked upon as the only real obstacle to Tom's acquisition of land and money, to say nothing of a handsome wife.

"Be studdy with her, Ned," said he, "she has a very floostherin' way wid her where you're concerned; I often remarked it. Don't let her come round you, Ned, wid her pilaverin' about 'that whelp,' as Tom calls him."

"An' he calls him quite right. If he daars to look up to my little girl, he'll soon find out his mistake, I can tell him."

"Nothin' would show him his mistake so much as to have Tom's business an' hers settled at Shraft, Ned."

"I know that, Mick; an' with the blessing I'll spake to her in the mornin' upon the subjict. I dunna did Tom ever spake to herself, Mick?"

"If he didn't, he will afore to-morrow night; he's on the watch to meet with her by accident; he says it's betther nor to go straight up to her, an' maybe frighten her."

"Very well, Mick; I'll have an eye to them; maybe it would be betther let Tom himself spake first. These girls are so dam' proud; an' I can tell you it is better not vex Winny."

Of course these two old men said a great deal more; but the above is the pith of what set old Ned Cavana thinking the greater part of the night; for the tea Winny made was very strong, and, as he said, he was thirsty, having missed his tumbler of punch after dinner. He fell asleep, however, much sooner than he would have done had the sequel to his plans become known to him before he went to bed.

CHAPTER XIII.

THE next morning Winny presented herself at the breakfast table looking more attractive and more tidily dressed, her rich glossy hair better brushed and smoothed down more carefully than was usual at that hour of the day. Her daily custom, like all other country girls who had household concerns to look after, was not to "tidy herself up" until they had been completed. She was not ignorant, however, of the great advantage which personal neatness added to beauty gave a young girl who had a cause to plead. And although the man upon whom she might have to throw herself for mercy was her father, she was not slow on this occasion to claim their advocacy for what they might be worth. But she had also prayed to God to guide her in all her replies to the parent whom she was bound to honour and obey, as well as to love. She had not contented herself with having set out her own appearance to the best advantage, but she had also set out the breakfast-table in the same way. The old blue-and-white teapot had been left on the dresser, and a dark-brown one, with a figured plated lid, taken out of the cupboard of Sunday china. Two cups and saucers, and plates "to match," with two real ivory-hafted knives laid beside them. There was also some white *broken* sugar in a glass bowl, which Winny had won in a lottery at Carrick-on-Shannon from a "bazaar man." There was nothing extraordinary in all this for persons of their means, though, to tell the truth, it was not the everyday paraphernalia of their breakfast-table. Winny had not been idle either, in furnishing the plates with a piping-hot potato-cake, a thing of which her father was particularly fond, and which she often gave him; but this one had a few carraway-seeds through it, and was supposed to be better than usual. Then she had a couple of slices of nice thin bacon fried with an egg, which she knew he liked too. All this was prepared, and waiting for her father, whose fatigue of the day before had caused him to sleep overlong.

While waiting for him, it struck Winny that he must think such preparations out of the common, and perhaps done for a purpose. Upon reflection she was almost sorry she had not confined her embellishments to her own personal appearance, and even that, she began to feel, might have been as well let alone also. But she had little time now for reflection, for she heard her father's step, as he came down stairs.

She met him at the door, opening it for him.

"Good morrow, father," she said; "how do you find yourself to-day? I hope you rested well after your long walk yesterday."

"After a while I did, Winny; but the tea you made was very strong, an' I didn't sleep for a long time after I went to bed."

"Well, 'a hair of the hound,' you know, father dear. I have a good cup for you now too; it will not do you any harm in the morning when you have the whole day before you. And I have a nice potato-cake for you, for I know you like it."

"Troth I b'lieve you have, Winny; an' I smell the carraways that I like. But, Winny, sure the ould blue teapot's not broken, is it?"

"No, father; but I was busy with the potato-cake

this morning, and had not time to wash it out last night, so I took out number one to give it an airing; and I put down the other things to match."

The portion of this excuse which was true was far greater than that which was not; and Winny, who as a general rule was truthful, was satisfied with it—and, reader, so must you be.

"Never mind, Winny, you are mistress here, an' I don't want any explanation; it wasn't that made me spake; but I'd be sorry th' ould blue teapot was bruck, for we have it since afore you were woll in your teens. You're lookin' very well this mornin,' Winny agra."

"Hush, father; eat your cake, and don't talk nonsense. There's an egg that black Poll laid this morning, and here's some butter I finished not five minutes before you came in yesterday evening. Shall I give you some tea?"

"If you plase, Winny dear." And the old man looked at his daughter with undeniable admiration.

They then enjoyed a neat and comfortable breakfast, which indeed neither of them seemed in a hurry to bring to an end. The old man was constrained and silent, and left all the talk to Winny, who, it must be admitted, never felt it more difficult to furnish conversation. Old Ned looked at her once or twice intently, as if wondering at her being much finer than usual; and then he looked at the breakfast gear; and the expression of his face was as if he suspected something. These looks, both at herself and the table, did not escape Winny's notice, but she never met them, always interrupting any exclamation which was likely to follow them, with some question or remark of her own, such as, "Do you like that cake, father?" "That is the muil cow's butter; I always keep her milk by itself, and churn it in the small churn for you, father; you said you liked it. Here, Bully-dhu, is a piece of cake for you."

With some such heterogeneous questions or remarks as this, she managed to parry his looks, or at all events the observations which were likely to follow them, and direct for the moment—ah! Winny, it was only for the moment!—his thoughts from whatever was upon them, and which Winny believed she knew right well.

But this suspense on both sides must come to an end. Old Ned, from his conversation with Mick Murdock, had determined not to speak to his daughter until he knew Tom had done so. But Winny did not know this, and dreaded every moment a thunder-clap would come which she was herself preparing for her father, and she was anxious, if it was only for the sake of propriety, to tell her story unprovoked.

The old man now stood up from the table, saying he would be likely to be out all day, as he was preparing to get down some wheat. But Winny, when it came to the point, could only stammer out in a feeble voice, that she wanted to speak to him before he went.

"Now's your time, Winny dear, for I have a great dale to do before dinner-time; an' I must be off to the men."

"Father dear, I may as well tell you at once—I'm in trouble—about—about—about—Tom—Murdock." And she threw her arms round his neck, and laid her cheek upon his shoulder.

"An' is that all, mavourneen? Ah! Winny, Winny, I knew it would come to this!—mavourneen macree, I knew it would. But there, Winny jewel, don't be crying—don't be crying; sure you know I'm not the man to cross your wishes; no—no, my own girl, I'd neither oppose you nor force you for the world; aren't you the only one I have on airth? an' sure isn't your happiness mine, Winny dear? There, Winny, don't cry; sure you may do as you like, mavourneen macree, you may."

Winny knew that all this was uttered under a misconception, and it gave her but little comfort. There was *one* part of it, however, she would not forget.

"Oh, father," she sobbed out upon his breast, "Tom Murdock has asked me to marry him." And the tears rolled down her cheeks.

"Why, then, Winny dear, dhry up them tears; sure I know they're on my account, at the thoughts of partin' me; but won't you be livin' at the doore with me while I last? Isn't it what I always hoped an' prayed for?—och! Winny, Winny, but you're the lucky girl this day, an' I'm the lucky man, for it will add ten years to my life."

And he kissed her yielding lips over and over again. But she did not speak; while the big tears continued to course themselves down her pale but beautiful cheeks.

"Don't—don't, Winny asthore; don't be crying on my account; sure I may say we'll not have to part at all. Mick an' I have it all settled, mavourneen; he's to build you a grand new house where th' ould one stan's, an' I'm to furnish it from top to toe; and Mick an' I will live here, not three hundred yards from the pair of you. O Winny, Winny, but it's I is the happy man this day! There, don't be cryin', I tell you; sure I would not gainsay you for the world;" and he kissed her again. But still she did not speak.

"There, Winny, there; don't be sobbin' an' cryin' I tell you. Why, what's the matter with you, Winny mavrone?"

"O father, father, it never can be!" she exclaimed in broken sobs, and clinging to his neck closer than ever.

"Nonsense, Winny! what's the matther, I say? why can't it be? Of course you did not refuse Tom's offer?"

"I did, father—indeed I did. I never can care for Tom Murdock; father, I could never be happy with that man. Don't ask me to marry him."

"Is the girl mad? To be sure I will, Winny. There's but the two of you in it, an' with Mick's farm an' mine joined,—the leases are all as one as 'free simple,'—you'd be as grand as many ladies an' gentlemen in the country;" and he disengaged himself from her arms and strode towards the door.

Winny thought he was going; but he had no notion of it at so unsettled a point. She rushed between him and the door.

"Father, don't go!" she cried; "for God's sake don't leave me that way!"

"Winny, it's what I'm greatly surprised at you, so I am. My whole life has been spent in puttin' together a dacent little fortun' for you; I never had one on airth I loved but yourself an' your poor mother—God rest her sowl! I never spoke a cross word to you, Winny jewel, since I followed her to the grave, four days after you were born; an' now, in my old days, when I haven't long to last, you're goin' to brake my heart, an' shorten them same. O Winny, Winny, say its only jokin' you are, an' I'll forgive you, cruel as it was."

"No, father, I'm telling you the real truth; people seldom joke with the tears running down their cheeks; look at them, father. I know all you say is true; and indeed it will break my own heart to oppose you, if you do not yield. But listen here, father dear: sure after all your love and kindness to me for the last eighteen or twenty years, I may say, you won't go now and spoil it all by crossing my happiness without any necessity for it. Tom put all the grandeur and wealth before me himself, that the joining of the two farms and marrying him would bring to me. But it is no use, father; I never liked that man, and I never can. Oh! don't ask me, father asthore; I'm contented and happy as I am."

"Winny, I never found you out in a lie since you could first spake, an' I'm sure you won't tell me one now. Listen to me, Winny. Tom Murdock is a fine handsome young fellow, an' well to do in the world, with a grand education, an' fit to hould his own any where; and I say he's any young girl's fancy, or ought to be, at any rate. You an' he have been reared at the doore with each other. What you are yourself, Winny asthore, I need not say, for every one that sees you knows it; and well they may, for sure you spake for yourself. It seldom happens—indeed, Winny, I never knew it—that a boy an' girl like you an' Tom, reared at the doore that way, fail but what they take a likin' to each other. It seems Tom done his part, both as to the likin' an' spakin', as he ought to do in both; but you, Winny, have done neither. Now, Winny, I can't but think that's very strange, an' I have but the one way to riddle it. Tell me now, honestly and plainly, is there any one that cum afore Tom in his request? Answer me that, Winny!"

"I will, father, honestly and truly. It is not that any one has come between me and Tom that made me refuse him. The very thing that you say, of our being reared at the door with one another, has made me dislike him. I have seen too much of his ways, and heard too many of his words, ever to like him, father; there is no use in trying to make me, for I never can."

"But, Winny jewel, you have hardly answered my question yet. Are you secretly promised, Winny, to any other young man that you're afeard I wouldn't like? that's the plain question. The truth now, Winny,—the truth, Winny!"

"No! father, certainly not. Tom Murdock is the only man that ever asked me."

"Was there ever anything betune you an' young Lennon, Rory of the Hills, as I have heard you call him myself?"

"Never, father; Rory never spoke to me upon such a subject, and further than that, he has paid me less compliments and spoken less to me upon any subject than fifty young men in the parish."

It so happened, however, that the name had heightened Winny's colour, and her father, looking at her with an admiring and affectionate smile said:

"Fifty, Winny! well, in throth, I don't wonder at it, or a hundred an' fifty, if they were in the parish."

Winny took advantage of his smile.

"There, father dear, don't be angry with your poor colleen; she'll do better than to marry riches with misery. Thank God, and you, father, she will have more than enough without coveting Tom Murdock's share." And she held up her beautiful lips, and looked in the old man's face with eyes swimming in tears.

Old Ned had fought the battle badly, and lost it. He bent down his head to meet his daughter's caress, and pressed her to his heart.

"There, Winny mavourneen," he exclaimed; "I have not loved you as the apple of my eye, since your poor mother died, for me to thwart you now. You shall never marry Tom Murdock except with your own free will and consent, asthore. As you say, Winny dear, we neither want nor covet his share. But sure, Winny dear, I thought you were for him all along."

"Oh! thank you, thank you a thousand times, father dear; that is so like you. I knew you would not break your Winny's heart."

But Winny Cavana was too honourable, even towards the man she hated, to tell her father of the conversation she had overheard between old Murdock and his son at the gate. She had gained her cause without that.

CHAPTER XIV.

Tom Murdock had no fixed purpose in any where he went after Winny Cavana left him discomfited upon the road. He wandered on past Kate Mulvey's, on towards Shanvilla, but not with any hope or wish to come across Rory of the Hills. His intentions of "dealing with him" were yet distant and undefined. What naturally occupied his thoughts was the humiliation he felt at Winny Cavana having refused him. Although he had complained to his father that "he did not think she was for him," yet upon a due consideration of his personal appearance, and his position in the country, he felt persuaded in his own mind that his father was right, and that nothing was required to secure success but to go boldly and straightforward to work. Tom had hinted to his father, although the old man had not observed it, or if so, had taken no notice of it, that there were more reasons than he was aware of for his wishing to secure Winny Cavana's ready money at all events; and his exclamation when his father spoke of only the interest, might have awakened him to the dread, at least, that there really was some cause with which he was unacquainted, why he dwelt so much more upon the subject of her fortune than the land. The fact was so. Tom Murdock was a worse young man than anyone—except his immediate associates—was aware of. In addition to his other accomplishments, perhaps I should rather say his attributes, he possessed a degree of worldly cunning which would have sufficed to keep any four ordinary young men out of trouble. But he required it all, for he had four times more villany —not to answer for, for it was unknown, but on his conscience—than any young man of like age in the parish.

One great keeper of a secret—for the time being, at least—is plenty of money. With plenty of money you can keep people in the dark, or blind them with the brightness of the glare. You can keep them in the country, or you can send them out of it, as circumstances require. You can bribe people to be silent, or to tell lies, as you like. But a villain who has not plenty of money cannot thrive long in his villany. When his money fails, his character oozes out, until he becomes finally exposed.

Tom Murdock had practically learned some of the above truths by his experience in life, short as it was, better than any thing he had learned at Rathcash National school. The latter part of it was what he now feared, but did not wish to learn.

Tom could not have been in the habit of going to

Dublin, to Armagh and Sligo (no one knew in what capacity,) three or four times a-year, where he played cards, and bet high, without money of his own; supposing even that his expenses on the road (which was shrewdly suspected) had been paid. He could not have sent half-a-dozen young *friends* to America, and compromised scores of actions ere they came before a court of law, without money. He could not have kept a brace of greyhounds, and a race mare, at Church's hotel in Carrick-on-Shannon, as "Mr. Marsden's," without money; and more money in all these cases, from the secrecy which was required, than almost the actual cost might involve. There were other smaller matters, too, which increased the necessity for Tom Murdock to be always in possession of some ready cash. This, from his position as heir to Rathcashmore, and heir presumptive, if not apparent, to Rathcash along side of it, he had as yet found no difficulty in procuring upon his own personal security; and to do him justice, he had hitherto avoided mixing up his father's name or responsibility in any of his borrowing transactions. Then there was the usurious interest which these money-lenders, be they private or public, charge upon loans, to be added to Tom's liabilities. If he was pressed by Paul, he robbed Peter to pay him; and when (after long forbearance) he was pressed by Peter, he robbed Paul back again. Upon all these and such-like occasions, Winny Cavana's fortune, which he said would be paid down, was the promptest guarantee he could hold out for payment; for ultimately, he said, they could not lose, as he must some day or other "pop into the old chap's shoes," and in the mean time he was paying the interest regularly.

Winny Cavana's instinct had not deceived her; but had she known one-half so much as some of Tom Murdock's bosom friends could tell her, she would have openly spurned him, and not have treated his advances with even the forced consideration she had done.

He wandered on now towards Shanvilla, without, as we have seen, any fixed purpose. Personally humiliated as he had been by Winny's refusal of him, his thoughts dwelt more upon the fact that he could no longer reckon upon her fortune to pay off the tormenting debts, which were every day pressing more heavily upon him; for he could not but believe that her refusal of him would get abroad. The Peters had been robbed often enough, and they would now let the Pauls fight their battle the best way they could with Tom Murdock himself: they were safe now, and they would keep themselves so. They had told Tom this,—"not that they doubted him, but their money was now otherwise employed;" Tom began to fear, therefore, that an exposure must soon break out.

How could he face his father, too. He would undoubtedly lay his failure to the score of his own impetuous and uncouth manner of seeking her favour; for he had often charged him with both, particularly towards Winny Cavana. One or two of his creditors had given up even the pretence of being civil, and had sworn "they would go to his father for payment, if not promptly settled with."

It was no great wonder if Tom wandered through the country with no fixed purpose, and finally arrived, tired and ill-humoured, at his father's house.

The old man had missed him "from about the place" all the forenoon, and had naturally set down his absence to the right cause. He had been candid in his advice to his son, "to spake up bowldly, and at wanst, to Winny;" and he was sincere in his belief that she would "take him hoppin'." This day, suspecting that he was on the mission, he had "kep' himself starvin'," and delayed the dinner for his return. He had ordered Nancy Feehily to have "a young roast goose, an' a square of bacon, an' greens for dinner agen misther Tom cem home." He anticipated "grand chuckling" over Tom's success, of which he made no more doubt than he did of his own existence.

"At last, Tom a wochal, you're cum," he said, as his son entered the door. "But where the sorra have you been? I think Winny's at home this betther nor two hours, for I seen her going in. Well, Tom, you devil! didn't I tell you how it id be?—*dhitidtch!*" he added, making an extraordinary noise with his tongue against the roof of his mouth, and giving his son a poke in the ribs with his forefinger.

"No! but did not I tell you how it would be? There, father! that bubble's burst, and I'm sorry I ever made an *onshiough* of myself."

"Faix, an', Tom, you must be an *onshiough* if that bubble burst, unless it's what you blew it out yourself. Di ye mane to say you spoke to her plain, as I tould you to do, Tom avic?"

"As plain as the palm of my hand, father, I put the whole thing before her in the kindest and fondest manner ever a man spoke. I told her how my whole heart and soul was waiting for her this three or four years past—God forgive me for the lie."

"Amen, Tom, if it was one; but maybe it wasn't, man. You're vexed now, Tom agra; but it won't be so. I tell you she only wants to see if you'll follow her up afther she giving you one refusal. What did she say, agra?"

Here Nancy Feehily brought in the roast goose and square of bacon, with a dish of smoking "Brown's fancies" in their jackets, and a check was given to the conversation. The old man, as he had said, had "kep' himself starvin'," and Tom could not keep himself from a like infirmity in his ramble through the country. He was not one of those who permitted a mental annoyance to produce a physical *spite* in return; he did not, as they say, cut his nose to vex his face, nor quarrel with his bread and butter; so, between them, they did ample justice to Nancy Feehily's abilities as a cook.

"You don't mane to say she refused you, Tom?" said the old man, after the girl had left, and while he was waiting for his son to cut him another slice of bacon.

"She did, father; but let me alone about her now: I'll tell you no more until I make myself a rousing tumbler of punch after dinner. She shall not take away my appetite, at all events."

Nor did she. Tom never ate a better dinner in his life, and his father followed his example. Old Mick had taken the hint, and said no more upon the subject. There was nothing but helping of goose, and slices of bacon, and cutting large smiling potatoes through the middle, with a dangerous sound of the knife upon the cloth, until the meal was ended.

Then, when the things had been removed, and Tom had made his rouser to his satisfaction, and his father had done the same, Tom told him precisely what had taken place between him and Winny Cavana.

Old Murdock listened with an attentive stare until his son had told him all. He then put out his tongue and made another extraordinary sound, but very different from the one already alluded to; and exclaimed, "Bad luck to her impudence, say I!"

"And I say amen, father."

"Tell me, Tom, do you think that fellow Lennon is at the bottom of all this? Did you put that to her?"

"I did, father, and she was not a bit puzzled or flustrificated about him. She spoke of him free and easy; but she denied that there was ever a word between them but common civility."

"An' maybe it's the thruth, Tom avic. You'll find anyhow that she'll change her tune afther her father gets spakin' to her on the subject. He'll be as stout as a bull, Tom; I know he will. He tould me he'd never give in, and that he'd threaten to cut her fortun' off, and make over his interest in the land to the Church for charitable purposes, if she tuck up the smallest notion of that pauper, that scullion, he called him. Don't be down about it, Tom. They say that wan swallow makes no summer; an' I say, wan wild goose makes no winter. My advice to you now, Tom, is, to wait a while; don't be goin' out at all, neither here nor there for some time. I'll let on I don't know what can be the matther with you; an' you'll see she'll came an' be hoppin' round you like a pet robin."

"I hope you are right, father, but I don't think so; I never saw a woman more determined in my life—she took her oath."

"Pshaw, Tom, that's nothin'. Don't torment yourself about it now; mark my words, her father will soon bring her to her senses."

"I do not much care whether he does or not as to herself; only for that six hundred pounds, the most of which I want badly. I would not envy any man that was tied to the like of her."

"Arra, Tom jewel, what would you want wid the most of six hundred pounds? sure, if you got it itself, you oughtn't to touch a penny of it."

Tom had not intended to say what he had said; it slipt out in his vexation. But here his worldly cunning and self-possession came to his aid, and he replied,

"Perhaps not, indeed, father; but there is a spot of land not far off which will soon be in the market, I hear, and it would be no bad speculation to buy it. I think it would pay six or seven per cent. interest."

Tom knew his father's weakness for a bit of land, and was ready enough.

"Oh, that's a horse of another colour, Tom. Arra, where is it? I didn't hear of it."

"No matter now, father. I cannot get the money, so let me alone about it. I wish the d—l had the pair of them."

"Whist, whist, Tom avic; don't be talking in that way. Sure af it's a safe purchase for six per cent, the money might be to be had. Thanks be to God, we're not beholdin' to the hussy's dirty drib for money."

Here a new light dawned upon Tom. Might he not work a few hundreds out of his father in some way or other for this pretended purchase, and then say that it would not be sold after all; and that he had relodged the money, or lost it, or was robbed—or—or something? The thought was too vague as yet to take any satisfactory shape; but the result upon his mind at the moment was, that his father was too wide awake to be dealt with in that way.

"Well, father," he said, "I shall be guided by your advice in this business still, although I have done no good by taking it to-day; but listen to me now, father."

"An' welcome, Tom. I like a young man to have a mind of his own, an' to be able to strike out a good plan; an' then, if my experience isn't able to back it up, why I spake plainly, an' tell him what I think."

"My opinion is, father, that I ought to go away out of this place altogether for a while. You know

I am not one that moping about the house and garden would answer at all. I must be out and going about, father, or I'd lose my senses."

This was well put, both in matter and manner, and the closing words told with crowning effect. Tom had said nothing but the fact; such were his disposition and habits, that he had scarcely exaggerated the effects of a close confinement to the premises, while of sound bodily health.

"Begorra, Tom, what you say is the rale thruth. What would you think of going down to your aunt in Armagh for a start?"

"No use, father,—no use; I could be no better there than where I am. Dublin, father, or the Continent, for a month or six weeks might do me some good."

"Bedads, Tom, that id take a power of money, wouldn't it?"

"Whether you might think so or not, father, would depend upon what you thought my health and happiness would be worth; here I cannot and will not stay, that is one sure thing."

"Well, Tom, af she doesn't come round in short, afther her father opens out upon her, we'll talk it over, and see what you would want; but my opinion is, you won't have to make yourself scarce at all—mind my words."

Here Tom fell into such a silent train of thought, that all further conversation was brought to an end. Old Mick believed his son to be really unhappy "about that impident hussey;" and having made one or two ineffectual efforts "to rouse him," he left him to his meditations.

At the moment they were fixed upon a few of his father's closing words, "see what you'll want." "Want—want!" he repeated to himself. "A dam' sight more than you'll fork out, old cock."

Old Mick busied himself about the house, fidgeting in and out of the room—upstairs and downstairs; while Tom was silently arranging more than one programme of matters which must come off, if he would save himself from ruin and disgrace.

His father had ceased to come into the room, indeed his step had not been heard through the house or on the stairs for some time, and it was evident he had gone to bed. But Tom sat for a full hour longer, with scarcely a change of position of even hand or foot. At length, with a sudden sort of snorting sigh, he stood up, stretched himself, with a loud and weary moan, and went to his room.

CHAPTER XV.

ANY help which old Murdock was in the habit of getting from his son upon the farm, and it was at no time of much value, either in labour or advice, had latterly dwindled down to a mere careless questioning as to how matters were going on, and his father began to fear that he was "beginning to go to the bad." Poor old man! how little of the truth he knew!

There was now always something cranky and unpleasant in Tom's manner. He was often from home for days together, and when at home, often out at night until very late; and if questioned in the kindest manner by his father upon the subject, his answers were snappish and unsatisfactory. Poor old Mick—deluded Mick—laid down both his wanderings and his crankiness to the score of his love for Winny Cavana, and the uncertainty of his suit.

From one or two encouraging and cheery expressions his father had addressed to him, Tom knew this to be the view he had taken of his case, and he was quite willing to indulge the delusion. Now that matters had come to an open rupture between him and Winny—for notwithstanding his father's hopes, he had none—it was convenient for him that his father should continue of the same mind,—nay more, his father himself had suggested a step, which, if he could manage with his usual ability, might turn to his profit, and relieve to a certain extent some of the perplexities by which he was beset.

Old Mick had spent a long and fatiguing day, not merely in his peregrinations through the farm, but from anxiety and watching, having observed Winny go out earlier than usual, and seeing that Tom soon after had followed her down the road. He was rather surprised in about an hour afterwards to see Winny return alone, and at not having seen Tom for nearly two hours later in the day, when he returned cross and disappointed, as we have seen. The "untoward circumstances" detailed in the conversation after dinner with his son, had not the same depressing effects upon the old man as upon Tom; for he really believed that they were not only not past cure, but according to his notions of how such matters generally went on, that they were on a fair road to success. He, therefore, enjoyed a night's sound asleep, while Tom lay tossing and tumbling, and planning and scheming,—and occasionally cursing Rory Lennon, whom he could not persuade himself was not, as his father said, at the bottom of all this. It was near morning, therefore, before he had fretted himself to sleep.

Early the next day old Mick determined to ascertain the actual state of facts. He was up betimes, and having seen what was necessary to be done for the day upon the farm, he set the operations going, and returned to breakfast. Tom had not yet stirred; and as Nancy had told the old masther that she heered him struggling with the bed-clothes, an' talkin' to himself until near morning, he would not allow her to call him, but went to breakfast by himself, telling her to have a fresh pot of tay, an' a dacent breakfast for him when he got up. "Poor fellow," he said to himself, "I did not think that girl had so firm a hoult of him."

Old Mick's anticipations of how matters really stood, and his confidence in Ned Cavana's firmness, were doomed to be shaken, if not altogether disappointed. Old Ned saw him hanging "about the borders" with a watchful look directed towards his house. He took it for granted that Tom had mentioned something of what had occurred to him, and he knew at once what he was lingering about for.

Ned had undoubtedly led old Murdock to suppose that he would be "as stout as a bull" with Winny about marrying his son; but when Ned had spoken thus sternly upon the subject, he had not anticipated any opposition upon Winny's part to the match. He did not see how she could object, nor did he see why. Mick had imbibed some slight idea of the kind from what Tom had told him; but Ned had combated this idea with great decision, and some sternness; more by way of showing his neighbour how he could exercise his parental authority, than from any great dread that he would be ever called on to assert it.

But Ned Cavana knew not the nature of his own heart. He had miscalculated the extent of his love for Winny, or the influence her affectionate and devoted life could exercise over that love, in a case where such a dispute might come between them. Thus we have seen him yield to that influence almost without argument, and certainly without a harsh or angry word. When it came to the point that he had to confront her tears, where was the fury with which he met old Murdock's insinuations and suggestions?—where the threats of cutting her off, not *with* but *without* a shilling, and leaving it all to the Church? Where the steady determination with which he had resolved to "bring her to her senses?"—all, all lost in the affectionate smile which beamed upon her pleading love.

Ned Cavana knew now that old Murdock was on the watch for him. He believed that Tom had told him what had taken place between him and Winny; and although he did not dread any alteration in his promise to his daughter, he felt that he could deal more stoutly with old Murdock, with the recollection of Winny's tears fresh on her cheeks, than if the matter were to lie over for any time. He therefore strolled through the farmyard, and out on the lane we have already spoken of, and turned down towards the fields at the back of his garden. This movement was not of course unnoticed by the man who was on the watch for some such, and accordingly he sloped down towards the gate, at which he and his son had held the conversation—a conversation which had confirmed Winny in her preconceived opinion of Tom Murdock's character and motives.

The two old men thus met once again at the same spot at which the reader first saw them together.

"I'm glad you cum out, Ned," said Murdock, "for I was wating to see you, to tell you about Tom. He done his part yesterda' illegant, an' you may spake to the little girl now as soon as you plaise."

"I have spoken to her, Mick. She tould me all about it herself last night."

"Well, she didn't resave Tom at all the way he thought she would, nor the way she led him to think she would, aidher. I hope she tould the thruth to you, Ned, and didn't make b'lief to be shy an' resarved, as she did to Tom. Poor boy, he's greatly down about it."

"She did; she tould me the whole thruth, Mick avic, and it's all no use; she won't marry Tom—that's the long an' the short of it."

"Why, then, she mightn't be cosherin wid him the way she was, Ned, and ladin the poor young boy asthray as to her intintions when she brought him to the point."

"My little girl never done anything of the kind, Mick; she'd scorn to do it."

"Well, no matther; she done it now, Ned; and as for Tom, he's the very boy that i'd nather humbug a little girl, nor allow her to humbug him. Did you spake stout to her, Ned?"

"I said all that was necessary, Mick awochal; but I seen it was no use, an' I wouldn't disthress the crathur."

"Disthress the crathur, *aniow!* Athen, may be it's what you don't much care how that poor boy 'ithin there is disthressed through her mains."

"As for that, Mick, it needn't, nor it won't disthress Tom a bit. There's many a fine girl in the parish that i'd answer Tom betther nor my little girl; and when I find that she's not for him, Mick awochal, I tell you, I won't disthress the colleen by harsh mains, so say no more about it."

"Athen, Ned, I think you tuck it aisy enugh afther all you tould me d'other day; you'd do this, an' you'd do that, an' you'd cut her off wid a shillin', an' you'd bring her to her senses, an' what wouldn't you do, Ned? I tould you to be studdy, or she'd cum over you wid her pillaver; and I tell you now what I tould you then, that it is all through the mains of that pauper Lennon she has done this—a purty *scauhawn* for her to be wastin' your mains an' your hard earnin's upon. Arrah Ned, I wondher you haven't more sense than to be dcludhered by that beggarman out of your little girl an' your money."

"No, Mick, young Lennon has nothing to say to it; if he never was born, Winny wouldn't marry Tom. I would not misbelieve Winny on her word, let alone her oath; an' she tould me she tuck her oath to Tom that she'd never marry him. He taxed her wid young Lennon, an' so did I; an' she declared, an' I believe her there too, Mick, that there never was a word between them upon such a subject, an' let there be no more now between us. It can't be helped. But I will not disthress my little girl by spakin' to her any more about Tom."

"Oh! very well, Ned; that'll do. But, be the book, Tom's not the boy that'll let himself be med a fool of by any one; an' I'm the very fellow that is able an' willin' to back him up in it."

"Athen what do you mane, Mick?—for the devil a wan of me can undherstan' that threat, af it beant the law you mane, an' sure the gandher in the yard beyant id have more sense than to think iv that. My little girl never held out the smallest cumhither upon Tom; but, instead iv that, she tells me that she always med scarse iv herself wheen he was to the fore. So af it be law you mane, Mick, you may do your worst."

"No, it isn't the law I mane, Ned. Law is dear at best, an' twiste as dear at worst; but I mane to say that I'll back up poor Tom 'ithin there, that's brakin' his heart about Winny; an' if you have any regard for her, you'll do the same thing; an' you'll see we'll bring the thing round, as we ought: that's what I mane. The girl can't deny but what she med much iv Tom, until that other spalpeen cum across her. Tom's no fool, an' knows what a girl mains very well."

"She does deny it, Mick, an' so she can. But there's no use, I tell you, in sayin' any more about it. I can see plane an' aisy enough that Winny isn't for him. I tould her I wouldn't strive to force her likin' or dislikin', an' I wont; so just tell Tom that the girl is in earnest. She tould him so herself, an' you may tell him the same thing. He can't think so much about her, Mick, as you let on, for there never was any courting betune them from first to last. I'll spake to you no more about it, Mick, an' you needn't spake to me."

With this final resolve, Ned turned his back completely round upon his neighbour, and walked with a hasty but firm step into the house.

Old Mick stood for some moments looking after him in a state of perplexed surprise. He had some fears, though they were not very great, that Winny's influence over her father was sufficiently strong to determine him according to her wishes, if she was really averse to a match with his son; but this latter was a point upon which he had scarcely any fears at all; except such as were suggested by the hints his son himself had thrown out about young Lennon. Upon this part of the case he had spoken to Ned in such a way as to make him determined to be very strict and decided in his opposition to any leaning on his daughter's part in that quarter.

Old Mick, as he stood and looked, was perplexed on both these parts of the case. If he believed that Winny Cavana had really and decidedly refused to marry his son, he could only do so upon the suspicion that young Lennon was the mainspring of the whole movement. And, again, to suppose she had preferred a "secret colloguing with that pauper," behind her father's back, to an open and straightforward match with a rich young man, and what he called a handsomer man than ever Lennon was, or ever would be, and with her father's full consent, was what he could not bring himself to believe of any sensible girl. But this he did believe, that if "that young whelp" was really not at the bottom of Winny's refusal, a marriage with his son, be it brought about *by what means it could*, would end in a reconciliation, not only of Winny to so great a match, but of old Ned, as a necessary consequence, to his daughter's acquiescence.

With these thoughts, and counter-thoughts, he too turned towards his house, where he found Tom just going to his breakfast, in no very good humour with the past, the present, or the future.

His father "bid him the time of day," and said, "he had to look after a cow that was on for cavin'," and that he'd be back by the time he had done his breakfast. This was a mere piece of consideration upon old Mick's part.

Loss of appetite and uneasiness of manner in a handsome young man of two-and-twenty is unhesitatingly set down by the old crones of a parish to his being "in love," and they are seldom at a loss to supply the *colleen dhass* to whom these symptoms are attributable. In Tom's case, however, there were other matters than love which were accountable for the miserable attempt at breakfast he had made, notwithstanding the elaborate preparations Nancy Feehily had made to tempt him. His father was surprised to find him so soon following him to the fields. But Tom, knowing his father's energy of action when a matter was on his mind, suspected he had not been to that hour of the day without managing an interview with old Cavana, and was on the fidgets to know what passed. But love—as love— had nothing whatever to say to his want of relish for so good a breakfast as had been set before him.

He met his father returning towards the house, not far from the celebrated gate already so often mentioned in this story. The spot where they now met was a little more favourable for a conference than the gate in question, for, unlike it, there was no private bower for eavesdroppers to secrete themselves in.

"Well, father," said Tom, breaking into the subject at once, "have you seen the old fogie about Winny?"

"I have, Tom, an' matthers is worse nor I thought. She has cum round him most complately; for the present anyhow."

"I told you how it would be, father, and be d—d!"

"Whist, Tom, don't be talkin' that way; there's one thing I'm afther being purty sure of, an' that is, that that spalpeen has nothin' to say to it. It's all perverseness just for a while, an' she'll cum round afther a bit."

"Well, father, I'll cut my stick for that bit, be it long or short; so tell me what can you do for me about money. You know if she was never in the place, it's nothing to keep me here stravaging about the road."

"Thrue for you, Tom avic. It isn't easy, however, layin' a man's hand upon what you'd want wid you for a start; but sure my credit is good in the bank, an' sure I'll put my name upon a bill-stamp for you for twenty or thirty pounds. Take my advice an' don't go past your aunt's in Armagh. Tom, she's an illigant fine women, an' will resave you wid a *ceade mille a faltha*, an' revive you out an' out afore you put a month over you. There's not a man in Armagh has a better thrade than her husband, Bill Wilson the carpenter,—cabinet-maker, I believe they call him,—an' b'lieve my words, she'll make the most of her brother's son. Who knows, Tom avic? Arrah, maybe you'd do betther down there nor at home. Any way, Winny won't be gone afore you come back, an' if we can't manage wan thing, maybe we would another—*thig um thu?*"

"Well, I hope so; but, father, I'll be off before Sunday, and this is Wednesday."

"You'll have lashins of time, Tom; but the sorra wan but I'll be very lonely; for although, Tom, you do be wandherin' from home by day, and stoppin' out late sometimes by night, sure I know you're not far off, an' I always hear you lettin' yourself in betune night an' mornin'. Though Cæsar does'nt bark at you, I hear him whinin' an' shufflin' when you're coming to the back doore."

"No matter about that now, father; I suppose I can get the money to-morrow or after, and start for my aunt's?"

"Any minute, Tom. I'm never without a bill-stamp in the house in regard of the fairs. Come in, an' I'll dhraw it out at wan'st, an' I'll engage they'll give you the money on it at the bank; don't be the laste taste afeared of that, Tom."

Whether Tom then intended to be guided by his father's advice, and not go past his aunt's in Armagh, it is not easy to say; but at all events he "let on" that he would not do so. When he got his heels loose, with a trifle of cash in his pocket, he could turn his steps in any direction he wished.

They then returned to the house, and old Mick, putting on his spectacles, opened a table-drawer in the parlour, where he kept his writing-materials, accounts, receipts, &c. After some discussion, which had well-nigh ended in an argument, as to whether the amount should be twenty or thirty pounds, a bill was ultimately drawn by the son upon the father for the former sum, at three months. Tom had other reasons than the mere increase of ten pounds in the amount, for wishing to have the word thirty instead of twenty written in the bill; however, he could not screw more than the latter sum out of the old man, which he said was ample to take him to his aunt's in Armagh, where he'd get lashins an' lavins of the best of everything. Tom knew that for this purpose it would be ample, and therefore failed to bring forward any arguments to sustain his view as to the necessity of making it thirty; but as it was he himself who wrote it out, he patted the blotting-paper over it in great haste—a matter which was not of course observed by the old man, nor, if it had been, would he have supposed there was anything unusual, much less for a purpose, in the act. The father having read it carefully over, and seeing that it was all correct, wrote his name with some dignity of manner across the bill. This portion of the writing Tom took care to let dry without any blotting at all, for he held it to the fire instead. Neither did the old man observe this unusual course, the manifest mode being to have used the blotting-paper, as in the first instance.

The latter being now thus far perfected, Tom asked his father if he could have Blackberry—one of the farm horses—to go into C. O. S. early next morning.

"An' welcome, Tom, if he was worth a hundred pounds," said the old man locking the drawer.

CHAPTER XVI.

Tom spent the remainder of that day very quietly, most of it in his own room. His first employment, whatever it may have been, was over an old portfolio, where he kept his own writing materials. What were the chief subjects of his calligraphy is not known. Perhaps love-letters to such of his numerous *enamoratas* as could read may have formed a portion, nor is it impossible but the police might have given a trifle to have laid their hands upon some others. Neither were likely to see the light, however, as Tom Murdock kept that old portfolio carefully locked up in his box.

The next morning, at an unusually early hour for him, Tom proceeded upon Blackberry, fully caparisoned with the best saddle and bridle in the place, to C. O. S.; where, after ten o'clock, he found no difficulty in procuring cash upon his father's acceptance.

Now, although in the first instance Tom had no notion of stopping at his aunt's in Armagh, or perhaps of going there at all, upon reflection he changed his mind altogether upon the subject. He had some congenial spirits there besides his aunt— spirits with whom he occasionally had had personal communication, as well as more frequent epistolary correspondence. Beyond Armagh, therefore, upon second thoughts he resolved not to go upon this occasion. As to any depression of spirits on account of Winny Cavana, he had none, except the loss of her fortune, which would have stood to him so well in his present circumstances. And here he remembered that his father had told him the interest of "that same" was all he would have touched, and even that at only three per cent; so that for the mere present he had done as well, if not better. What he had drawn out of the bank upon his father's credit, would settle the two harassing and intricate cases, which two different attorneys, on the part of those whom he had most grievously wronged, had threatened to expose in a court of law. He would have some over—he took care of that—to take him to Armagh and back, where he could not manage *this time* to go at the expense of "the fund." He did not purpose, however, to stop very long at his aunt's. He would tell Winny when he came back that her refusal of him had driven him away—he knew nor cared not whither; but that he found it impossible to live without sometimes seeing her, if it was only from his own door to hers: yes, he would follow that business up the moment he returned. In the mean time it might not be without some good effect his being absent for a short time.

Such were the thoughts and plans with which Tom, after he had settled with the attorneys, left his poor old father, we may say completely alone; for after the rather sharp words which had taken place between the two old men, he could hardly continue his customary visits, or half-casual, half-projected meetings with Ned Cavana, by their respective mearings. Hitherto in this respect, more than in actual visits, the intercourse between these two old men had been habitual, indeed it may be said of daily occurrence, mutually watched for. If one saw the other overlooking his men, either sowing or reaping, or planting or digging, according to the time of the year, the habit almost amounted to a rule, that, whichever saw the other first quitted his own men, and sloped over towards his neighbour to have a look at what was going on, and having there exhausted the pros and cons of whatever the work might be, a general chat was kept up, and the visit returned on the spot.

Now, however, matters were to a great extent changed. This "untoward circumstance" between Tom Murdock and Winny Cavana, together with the subsequent conversation upon the subject between the fathers, rendered this friendly intercourse impossible. From all his son had told him, old Mick thought Winny Cavana had treated him badly, and he considered that old Ned had "gone back of his word" to himself. He was a plucky, proud old cock, and his advice to Tom would be "to see it out with the pair of them, without any *pillaver*."

What he meant by "seeing it out," he hardly knew himself, for he had repudiated the law in a most decided manner when taxed with it by Ned. What, then, could he mean by "seeing it out." Perhaps Tom would not require his advice upon the subject.

From this day forth, however, old Mick was not the man he used to be. A man at his age, however well he may have worn,—ay, even to have obtained the name of an evergreen,—generally does so, having his mind at ease, as well as his body in health—the one begets the other; and so an old man thrives, and often looks as well at seventy, as he did at sixty. But these old evergreens sometimes begin to fail suddenly if the cold wind of disappointment blows roughly upon their hitherto happy hearts; and Tom Murdock was not three weeks away, when the remarks of the people returning from the chapel, respecting old Mick, were that "they never saw a man so gone in the time." And the fact was so.

Old Mick Murdock had been all his life a cheerful, chatty man, one with whom it was a comfort to "be a piece of the road home." Moreover, he had always been erect in person, with a pair of cheeks like a scarlet Crofton apple—not the occasional smooth flush of delicacy, but the constant hard rough tint of perfect health. There were many young men in the parish whom a walk alongside of old Mick Murdock for a couple of miles would put out of breath, while you would not see a heave, however slight, out of old Mick's chest.

Look at him now: "he has not a word to throw to a dog," as the saying has it; he is beginning to stoop in his gait, and more than once already he has struck his heel against the ground in walking. As yet it is not a drag, and those indications of a break-up in his constitution are comparatively slight. Ere long, however, you will see him with a stick, and you will be hardly able to recognise him as the Mick Murdock of a few months before.

Tom, as we have seen, having settled with the attorneys, started for his aunt's; where, as his father had predicted, he was received with open arms, and a joyful clapping of hands, and a *ceade mille a'faltha*. "Oh! then, Tom, avic macree, but it's you that's welcome, an' shure I needn't ax you how you are. Oh! but it's you that's grown the fine young man since I seen you last. An' let me see—how long ago is that now, Tom agra? It'll be four years coming Easthre Sunda' next, since I was down in

Rathcashmore. An' how is Mick, a wochal? an' how's *herself*, Tom, the 'colleen dhass,' you know?" And she gave him a poke with her finger between the ribs. "Ah, Tom avic, you needn't look so shy; shure I know all about it, an' why wouldn't I? It'll be an illigant match for the pair iv ye; as good for the wan as for the other—coming Shraft, Tom, eh? In troth Winny will be a comfort to you, as well as a credit; that's what she will, won't she, Tom?"

"Let me alone now, aunt; I'm tired after the journey; and it's not of her I'm thinking."

"See that now—arra *na bocklish*, Tom, don't be afther telling me that; shure didn't Mick himself write to me two or three times to let me know how matters was going on, and the grand party he gev on Hallow-Eve, and the fun ye all had, and how you danced wid her a'most the whole night."

"Nonsense, aunt! Did he tell you how any body else danced?"

"No, the sorra word he said about any wan that was there, barrin' yourself an' herself."

"Well, never heed her now. I'll tell you more about her to-morrow or next day, and maybe ask your advice upon the subject at the same time."

Their conversation was here interrupted, as Tom thought very opportunely, by the entrance of Bill Wilson, whose welcome for his wife's nephew, was as hearty, in a manner, as that which he had received from herself. The conversation, of course, now "became general;" and Bill Wilson, although he had never been out of Armagh, seemed to have every body down about Tom's country pat by heart, for he asked for them all by name, not forgetting, although he had left her to the last, to ask for Winny Cavana. It was evident to Tom, from his manner, that he was up to the project in that quarter; and as evident, that like his aunt, he knew nothing of how matters up to this had turned out, or how they were likely to end. He answered his uncle's questions, however, with reasonable self-possession; and his aunt, having perceived from his last observation to herself that there was "a screw loose," turned the conversation very naturally to the subject of Tom's physical probabilities, saying,

"Athen, Tom jewel, maybe it's what you're hungry, an' would like to take something to eat afore dinner; sure an' sure it's the first question I ought to have axed you."

"No, aunt, I thank you kindly, I'll take nothing until your dinner; there's a friend of mine lives in the skirts of the town, I want to see him, and I'll be back in less than an hour."

"A friend of yours, Tom? athen sure if he is, he ought to be a friend of ours: who is he, Tom awochal?"

"Oh! no, aunt, you never heard of him. He's a boy I have a message to from a friend in the country."

"Why, then, Tom, you'll be wanting to know the way, in this strange place, an' shure I'll send the girl wid you to show you. Shure, how could you know, an' you never in Armagh afore?"

"No, aunt, I say. I have a tongue in my head,

and I'm not an *onshiough*. I'll find him out without taking your girl from her business."

"Athen, Tom jewel, whoever bought you for an *onshiough*, would lay out his money badly, I'm thinking; an' although you were never in this big city afore, the devil a bit afeared I am but you'll find your way, an' we'll have lashins iv everything that's good for you, and a *cead mille a faltha*, when you come back."

Tom then left them, bidding them a temporary good-by. He did not think it at all necessary to enlighten his aunt to the fact that he had paid periodical visits to Armagh from time to time, and had on these occasions passed her very door. But these visits were of short duration, and have been only hinted at. They were sufficient, however, to familiarise him with the portions of the city to which he now directed his steps. But as we are not aware of the precise spot to which he went, nor acquainted with those whose society he sought, we shall not follow him.

His aunt, after he had left, was in no degree sparing in her praises of him to her husband, who had never seen him before, but who indorsed every word she said with the greatest promptitude and good-humour, "as far as he could see."

Bill Wilson was no fool. He gave his wife's nephew a hearty and sincere welcome, and he knew it would be an ungracious thing not to acquiesce in all that she said to his advantage; but it was an indiscreet slip to add the words "as far as he could see." It implied a caution on his part, which did not say much for the confidence he ought to have felt in his wife's opinion, and went merely to corroborate her praises of his personal appearance.

" 'As far as you can see,' Bill! Well indeed that far you can find no fault at all, at all; that's shure an' sartin. Where would you find the likes iv him, as far as that same goes, William Wilson?—not in Armagh, let me tell you. I ax you did you ever see a finer head iv hair, or a finer pair iv eyes in a man's head, or a handsomer nose, or a purtier mouth? an' the whiskers, Bill—ah! them's the dark whiskers from Slieve-dhu; none of your moss-coloured whiskers that you see about here, Bill. Look at the hoith iv him! He's no leprehaun, Bill Wilson; an' I say if you go out an' walk the town for three hours, you'll not meet the likes iv him till you come back again to where he is himsel'."

"Faix, an' I won't try that, Mary, for I believe every word you're afther sayin'. But, shure, I didn't mane to make little of the young man at all."

"You said 'as far as you could see,' Bill; an' shure we all know how far that is. But amn't I tellin' you what is beyant your sight,—what he is to the backbone, for larnin', an' every thin' that's good, manly, an' honest? There now, Bill, I hope you don't misdoubt me,—'as far as you can see,' indeed!"

"Well, Máry, I meant nothing against him by that; indeed I believe, and I'm shure, he's as good as he's handsome. But I must go out now to the workshop to look after the men. Let me know when he comes back."

Tom was not so long away as he had intended. The person whom he went to look for was not at home, and he returned to his aunt at once. He had not many acquaintances in Armagh, and they were such as might be better pleased with a visit *after dark* than so early in the day.

Before "the dinner", was prepared, Tom had another chat with his aunt, and, as a matter of course, she could not altogether avoid the subject of Winny Cavana. She had been given to understand by her brother, that a successful courtship was carrying on between Tom and her. But the humour in which Tom had received her first quizzing upon the subject at once told that intelligent lady of the "loose screw" on some side of the question. Upon so important a matter, a married woman, and own aunt to such a fine young man, one of the parties concerned, Mrs. Wilson could not permit herself to remain ignorant. Her direct questions in the first instance, and her dexterous cross-examination afterwards, showed Tom the folly of hoping to evade a full confession of his having been refused; and it may be believed that he set forth in no small degree how ill-treated he had been by the said Winny Cavana and her father.

His aunt consoled him, so far as she could, with hopes that matters might not be so bad as he apprehended; reminding him at the same time of the extent of the sea, and the number of good fishes which must still be in it uncaught. That shrewd woman could also perceive, from Tom's manner, under his confession, as well as his first ill-humour, that the loss of Winny Cavana's fortune, and the reversion of her fat farm, were more matters of regret to him than the loss of herself.

"And why not," she thought, under the impression of Winny's ill-treatment of "such a fine han'-som' young fellow as her nephew. Shure, couldn't he have his pick an' choice of any girl in that, or any other parish ; ay, or among her acquaintances in Armagh, for that matter. But as for young Lennon! she was sartin shure Winny couldn't be such a born idgiot as to make much of the likes of him, where Tom was to the fore."

She thus encouraged her nephew, taking much the same view of his case as old Mick had done, and giving him pretty much the same advice—"not to dhraw back at all, but to persavare an' get a hoult in her by hook or by crook, an' thrust to a reconciliation afthewards. He might take her word for it, it was more make b'lief than anything else. Don't give it up, Tom ; them sort of girls like persavarince ; I know I did, awochal, in my time. What's on her mind is, that it's afther her money you are, an' not hersel'."

"The devil a much she's out there, aunt; but I wish I could make her think otherwise."

"Lissen here, Tom ; 'a council's no command,' they say, an' my advice is this :—Let on, when you go back, that you could get an illigant fine girl in Armagh wid twiste her fortune ; but that nothing would tempt you to forsake your own little girl at home, that was a piece iv your heart since ye were both the hoith of a creepeen; do you see? an' I'll back you up in it. Tell her she may bestow her fortune upon Kate Mulvey or any one she likes; that herself is all you want. You know she won't do that when it comes to the point."

"Not a bad plan, aunt. But sure I should let on to my father, and to everyone in the neighbourhood; and they'll be asking me who she is, and about her father and her mother, and all about her; and I should have answers ready, if I mean the thing to look like the truth."

"An' won't I give you all that as pat as A B C? Don't I know the very girl that'll answer to a T, Tom?"

"Why then, aunt dear, mightn't you bring me across her in earnest?"

"Faix, an! I could not, Tom, for a very good reason—that I'm not acquainted wid her, except to see her sometimes; an' I know her name, an' who she is, an' her father's name, and how he med his money. They're as proud as paycocks, I can tell you; and nather the one nor the other would look the same side iv the street wid the likes iv us, Tom; but they don't know that at Rathcash; an' shure, if Winny thries to find out about them, she'll find that you're tellin' the truth as far as the names an' money goes, an' I'll let on to be as thick as two pickpockets wid them."

Tom was silent. The closing words of his aunt's speech made him wish that he could pick some of their pockets of about a hundred pounds.

The plan, however, seemed a good one, and had the effect of putting Tom Murdock into good humour; and when Bill Wilson joined them at dinner, Tom was so agreeable and chatty, that Bill thought his wife, although she was Tom's aunt, had not said a word too much for him; and he regretted more than ever that he had used the words "so far as he could see." He anticipated—nay, he dreaded—that they would be brought up to him again that night with greater force than ever.

CHAPTER XVII.

THE most part of ready cash, whatever the sum may have been, which Tom had received at the bank, having been, as he called it, "swallowed up by them cormorants, the attorneys," he had, after all, but a trifling balance in his pocket. He was determined, therefore, to live quietly for some time at his aunt's upon "the lashins and lavins," taking her advice, and arranging with her his plans of operations upon his return to Rathcashmore. And his aunt's advice, in a prudent and worldly point of view, was not to be controverted, if anything could tend towards the attainment; of his object; that was the question.

It was impossible, however, that Tom could rest altogether satisfied with the company of his aunt and her husband, and three or four children between ten and seventeen years of age; particularly as the eldest of his cousins was a long-necked boy with big stuck-out ears, who worked in his father's shop, instead of a graceful girl with dark hair and fine eyes, whose domestic duties must keep her in the house as her mother's assistant, or perhaps enable her, when she could be spared, to guide him through the principal parts of the town, of which he would have feigned the most profound ignorance. But the eldest child, just past seventeen, as we have seen, happened to be a boy, not a girl, and Tom did not consider this the best arrangement that could be wished. In consequence, he sometimes spent an evening from home, with one or other, or perhaps with *all* the congenial spirits with whom, as a *delegate*—for the truth may be confessed—from another county, he could claim brotherhood. On this occasion, however, he was not on official business in Armagh; and whatever intercourse took place between them was of a purely social nature.

Tom was not altogether such a *mauvais sujet* as perhaps the reader has set him down in his own mind to be, from the inuendos which have been thrown out respecting him, as well as the actual portions of his character which have made themselves manifest. It must be confessed—nay, I believe it has been admitted not many lines above—that he was a Ribbonman; and although that includes all that is murderous and wicked, when a necessity arises, yet in the absence of such necessity, a Ribbonman may not be altogether void of certain good points in his character. It is the frightful *obligation* which he *labours* under that makes a villain of him, should circumstances require the aid of his iniquity. Apart from this, and from what is termed an agrarian grievance, a Ribbonman may not be a bad family-man, although the training he undergoes in "The Lodge," is ill-calculated to nourish his domestic sympathies.

Tom had now been upwards of a month enjoying the hospitality of his aunt; and notwithstanding that she had done all in her power to entertain him, and "make much" of him, he was beginning to tire of the eternal smoke and flags, and stacks of chimneys, which were always the same to the eye: no bright "blast of sun," no sudden dark cloud, made any difference in them; there they were, always the same dull colour, no matter what light shone upon them. No wonder, then, Tom Murdock began once more to long for the fresh breeze that blew about the wild hills of Rathcashmore, the green fields of his father's farm, and the purple heather of Slievedhu, with the white rocks of Slieve-bawn by her side.

Absence too had done more really to touch Tom's heart with respect to Winny Cavana than to wean him from the "saucy slut," as he had called her in pique on his departure. He had "come across,"—this is the Irish mode of expressing "had been introduced to,"—through his aunt's assistance, several of what she called illigant fine girls, nieces of her husband and others, and his heart confessed that none of them "were a patch" upon Winny Cavana, after all. He thus became fidgety, and began to speak of returning home. Of course the aunt opposed her hospitality to such a step, for the present at least: "Just as we were beginning to enjoy you,

Tom avic," said she; and of course her husband made a show of joining her, although he knew there had been more beer drunk in the house in the last month than in the six preceding ones; neither did the cold meat turn out to half the account. He knew this by his pocket, not by his knowledge of the cookery. Tom, however, made no promise of further sojourn than "to put the following Sunday over him," and it was now Thursday. But the next morning's post hurried matters. It brought him a letter from his father, which prevented his aunt from pressing his stay beyond the following day, when it was finally settled by Tom that he would start for home. "It ran thus," as is the common mode of introducing a letter in a novel or story :—

"Dear Tom,—This comes to you hoppin' to find you in good health, which I am sorry to say, it does not leave me at present; but thank God for all his mercies. I was very lonesum entirely after you left me; and the more, dear Tom, as I had not my ould neighbour Ned Cavana to spake to, as used to be the case afore that young chisel of a daughter of his cum round him to brake wid us. She's there still, seemingly as proud as ever; but she'll be taken down a peg wan of these days, mark my words. I have wan piece of good news for you, Tom avic; an' that is, that young Lennon never darkened their doore since you went; and more be token, she never spoke a word to him on Sunda's afther Mass, but went straight home with her father from the chapel. This I seen myself; for although I have been very

daunny since you left me, I med bowld wid myself
not to lose prayers any Sunda' wet or dhry, for no
other purpose but to watch herself an' that chap.
So, dear Tom, you needn't be afeard of him. I
think, indeed, I seen him going down the road the
three Sunda's with Kate Mulvey; so I think Winny
tould the truth to her father about him. Dear Tom,
I have not been well at all at all for the last three
weeks, an' I am not able to be out all day as I used
to be, an' I hardly know how matters are goin' on
upon the farm. I see old Ned a'most every day
from the doore or the garden, where I sometimes go
out when it's fine; I see him wandherin' about his
farm as brisk an' as hard as ever. I think nothin'
would give that man a brash. Dear Tom, I did not
like writin' to you to say I was lonesum or unwell
until you had taken a turn out of yourself at your
aunt's; but I am not gettin' betther, an' I think
the sight iv you would do me good. Tell your aunt
to let you cum home to me now. Indeed, dear
Tom, I'm too long alone; an' havin' no one to spake
to makes me fret, though I wouldn't interfere with
you for a while afther you went. If ould Ned
Cavana was the man I took him to be, he wouldn't
let the few words that cum betune us keep him
away from me all this time, an' I not well; but he
never put to me, nor from me, since you left, nor I
to him. Dear Tom, cum back to me as soon as you
can, an' maybe we'll get the betther of him an'
Winny, afther all. Hopin' your aunt, an' the chil-
der, an' Bill himself, is all in good health, I remain
your father till death— Michael Murdock."

Tom, as I have hinted, was not without his good points, and, as he read over the above letter from his poor lonely father, his heart smote him for having been so long away, and where, to tell the truth to himself, he had no great fun or pleasure. His conscience, moreover, accused him of one glaring act of ingratitude, and villany, he might call it, towards the poor old man. There was something tender and self-sacrificing in the letter, yet it was not without a complaining tone all through, that brought all Tom's better feelings uppermost in his heart; and he resolved to start for home early the next morning. He now felt that he had business at home, which at one time he had never contemplated taking the smallest trouble about, besides keeping his poor old father better company than he had hitherto done. Yet, with all this softening of his disposition, he was never more determined to carry out his object with respect to Winny Cavana, by fair means—or by *foul!*

What his father had said about young Lennon gave him hopes that, in the end, a scheme which he had planned for the latter might not be *necessary*.

Tom knew there could be no use in writing to his father to say he would soon be home with him. The nearest post-town was seven miles from Rathcashmore; and although any person "going in had orders" to call at the post-office, and bring out all letters for the neighbours of both the Rathcashes, yet were he to write now, his letter was sure to lie there for some days, and he would undoubtedly be home before its receipt. Thus he argued, and therefore endeavoured to content himself with the resolution he had formed to make no delay; and whatever "his traps" may have been, they were got together and locked in his box at once.

He had engaged to meet a *particular friend* on the following evening, Friday, partly on *business*, previous to returning to *his own part* of the country. But he would now anticipate this visit by going there at once, so as to enable him to leave for home early next morning. He hoped to find his father better than his letter might lead him to suppose; and he had no doubt his presence and society, which he was determined should be more constant and sympathising than heretofore, would serve to cheer him.

Nothing, then, which his aunt could say, and certainly nothing which her husband had added to what she did say, had any effect towards altering Tom's resolution to start for home on the following morning. By this means he hoped to reach his father on the evening of the second day,—railways had not been then established in any part of Ireland, not even the Dublin and Kingstown line,—and he would save the poor old man from the lonesome necessity of going to church on Sunday, "be it wet or dry."

He carried out his determination without check or hindrance, and arrived at the end of the lane leading up to Rathcashmore house soon after dusk in the evening of Saturday. He travelled by car from C—k; and the horse being neither too spirited, nor too *fresh* after his journey, stood quietly on the road, with his head down, and his off fore-leg in the "first position," until the driver returned, having left Tom Murdock's box above at the house.

The meeting between old Mick and his son was as tender and affectionate on the old man's part as could well be, and as much so on Tom's as could well be expected. Old Mick had some secret anticipations,—presentiment, perhaps I should have called it,—that they would never part again in this world, until they parted for the last time. Daily he felt an increasing weakness of limb, weariness of mind, which whispered to his heart that that parting was not far distant. His son's arrival, however, had the effect which he promised to himself. He seemed to improve both in spirits and in health. If he had not thrown away the stick,—which the reader was forewarned he would adopt,—he made more use of it cutting at the *kippeens*, and whatever else came in his way, than as a help to his progress.

———•———

CHAPTER XVIII.

NEW-YEAR's day is always a holiday. And well it is for the girls and boys of a parish, of a district, of a county, aye, of all Ireland, if it should rise upon them in the glowing beauty of a cloudless sun. Then indeed the girls "are drest in all their best." Many a new bright ribbon has been purchased on the previous market-day, and many a twist and turn the congregation side of their bonnets has had. A bow of new ribbon, blue or red, according to their complexion,—for these country girls are no more fools in such a matter than their betters,—has been held first to this side of their bonnet, then to that; then the long ends have been brought across the top this way, then that way, temporarily fastened with pins in the first instance, until it is held at arm's-length, with the head a little to one side, to test the final position. Their petticoats have been swelled out by numbers, not by crinoline, which as yet was unknown, even to the higher orders. But "be this as it may," the girls of the townlands of Rathcash, Rathcashmore, and Shanvilla made no contemptible turn-out upon the new-year's day after Tom Murdock had returned from Armagh. The boys, too, were equally grand, according to their style of dress. Some lanky, thin-shanked fellows in loose trousers and high-low boots; while the well-formed fellows, with plump calves and fine ankles, turned out in their new *corderoy* breeches, woollen stockings, and *pumps*. I have confined myself to their lower proportions, as in most cases the coats and vests were much of the same make, though perhaps different in colour and material, while the well-brushed "*Caroline*" hat was common to all.

Conspicuous amongst the girls in the district in which our story sojourns were, as a matter of course, Winny Cavana and Kate Mulvey, with some others of their neighbours who have not being mentioned, and who need not be.

Winny, since the little episode respecting her refusal of Tom Murdock, and his subsequent departure, had led a very quiet meditative life. She could not help remarking to herself, however, that she had somehow or other become still more intimate with Kate Mulvey than she had used to be ; but for this she could not account—though perhaps the reader can. She had always been upon terms of intimacy with Kate ; had frequently called there, when time would permit, and sat for half an hour, or sometimes an hour, chatting, which was always reciprocated by Kate, whose time was more on her own hands. In what then consisted the increase of intimacy can hardly be said. Perhaps it merely existed in Winny's own wish that it should be so, and the fact that one and the other, on such occasions, now always threw a cloak around her shoulders and accompanied her friend a piece of the way home. Sometimes, when the day was tempting, a decided walk would be proposed, and then the bonnet was added to the cloak. What formed the burden of their conversation in these chats, which to a close observer might be said latterly to have assumed a confidential appearance, must be so evident to the reader's capacity that no mystery need be observed on the subject. To say the least, Rory of the Hills came in for a share of it, and, as a matter of almost necessity, Tom Murdock was not altogether left out.

Kate Mulvey, after the *éclaircissement* with Winny, believed she could do her friend some good without doing herself any harm, a principle upon which alone most people will act. With this view she took an early opportunity to hint something to Rory of the result of the interview between herself and Winny ; and although she did it in a very casual,

and at the same time a clever, manner, she began to
fear that so far as her friend's case was concerned,
she had done more harm than good. The fact of
Tom Murdock's proposal and rejection subsequent
to the interview adverted to, had not become public
amongst the neighbours; and before Winny had an
opportunity of telling it to Kate, Rory had left his
father's house to seek employment in the North.
It is not unlikely that he was tempted to this step
by something which had fallen from Kate Mulvey
respecting Winny and Tom Murdock, although the
whole cat had not yet got out of the bag.

Hitherto poor Rory's heart had been kept pretty
whole, through what he considered a well-founded
belief that Winny Cavana, almost as a matter of
course, must prefer her handsome rich neighbour to
a struggling labouring man like him. Tom, he
knew, she saw almost every day, while at best she
only saw him for a few minutes on Sundays after
chapel. Rory knew the meaning of the word pro-
pinquity very well, and he knew as well the danger
of it. He knew, too, that if there were no such
odds against him, he could scarcely dare aspire to
the hand of the rich heiress of Rathcash. He knew
the disposition of old Ned Cavana too well to believe
that he would ever consent to a "poor devil" like
him "coming to coort his daughter." He believed
so thoroughly that all these things were against him,
that he had hitherto successfully crushed every
rising hope within his breast. He had schooled
himself to look upon a match between Tom Murdock
and Winny Cavana as a matter so natural, that it

would be nothing less than an act of madness to endeavour to counteract it. What Kate Mulvey, however, had "let slip" had roused a slumbering angel in his soul. He was not wrong then, after all, in a secret belief that this girl did not like Tom Murdock overmuch. Upon what he had founded that belief he could no more have explained—even to himself—than he could have dragged the moon down from heaven; but he did believe it: he even combated it as a fatal delusion, and yet it was true. But how did this mend the matter as regarded himself? Not in the slightest degree, except so far as that the man he most dreaded, and had most reason to dread, was no longer an acknowledged rival to his heart. Hopes he still had none.

But Rory of the Hills was now in commotion. The angel was awake, and his heart trembled at a possibility which despair had hitherto hidden from his thoughts.

For some time past he had not only not avoided a casual meeting with Winny, but delighted in them with a safe, if not altogether a happy, indifference. He looked upon her as almost betrothed to Tom Murdock; circumstances and reports were so dovetailed into one another, and so like the truth.

Although there was really no difference in rank between him and Winny, except what her father's well-earned wealth justified the assumption of, his position as a daily labourer kept him aloof from an intimacy of which those in circumstances more like her own could boast; and poor Rory felt that it was a matter for boast. Thus had he hitherto refrained from attempting to "woo that bright particular star," and his heart was comparatively safe. But now—ay, *now*—what was he to do? "Fly, fly!" said he: "I'll go seek for employment in the North. To America, India, Australia—anywhere. Kate Mulvey may have meant it as kindness; but it would have been more kind to have let me alone. This horrible knowledge of that one fact will break my heart."

And Rory of the Hills did fly. But it was no use. But there were many reasons quite unconnected with Winny Canava which rendered a more speedy return than he had intended unavoidable. A stranger beyond the precints of his own parish, he found it impossible to procure permanent employment amongst those who were better known, and who "belonged to the place:" a great consideration in the minds of the Irish, high and low. The bare necessaries of life, too, were more expensive in the North than about his own home; and for the few days' employment which he got, he could scarcely support himself, while his father and family would feel the loss of his share of the earnings at home. No; these two separate establishments would never do. He could gain nothing by it but the gnawing certainty of never seeing, even at a distance, her in whom he now began to feel that his heart delighted. Besides, he could manage to avoid her altogether by going to his own chapel; yes, he felt it a duty he owed to his father not to let him fight life's battle alone, and—he returned. We question whether this *duty* to his *father* was his sole motive; and we shall see whether he did not subsequently consider it a *duty* to prefer the good preaching of Father Roche of Rathcash, to the somewhat indifferent discourses of good Father Farrell in *his own* chapel.

Rory had not been more than ten days or a fortnight away, and he was now following the usual routine, of a day idle and a day working, which had marked his life before he went.

But we were talking of a new-year's day, and it will be far spent if we do not return to it at once, and so we shall lose the thread of our story.

The day, as we had wished a few pages back, had risen in all the beauty of a cloudless sun. There had been a slight frost the night before, but as these slight frosts seldom bring rain until the third morning, the country people were quite satisfied that the promise of a fine day on this occasion would not be broken. The chapel-bells of Rathcash and Shanvilla might be heard sounding their clear and cheerful call to their respective parishioners that the hour of worship had drawn near, and the well-dressed happy congregation might be seen in strings along the road and across the pathways through the fields, in their gayest costume, laughing and chatting with an unbounded confidence in the faithfulness of the sky.

Tom Murdock, the reader knows, had returned, but he had not as yet seen Winny Cavana. One Sunday had intervened; but upon his father's advice he had refrained from going "for that wan Sunda' to chapel." Neither, on the same advice, had he gone near old Ned's house. The old man—that is, old Murdock—had endeavoured to spread a report that his son Tom was engaged to be married to a very rich girl in Armagh. He took his own views of all matters, whether critical or simple, and had his own way of what he called managing them. He was not very wrong in some of his ideas, but he sometimes endeavoured to carry them out too persistently, after anybody else would have seen their inutility.

On this New-year's day, too, he had hinted something about his son's not going to Mass, but Tom would not be controlled, and quickly "shut up"—that is the *fashionable* phrase now-a-days—the old man upon the subject. His opinion, and he did not care to hide it, was, "that he did not see why he should be made a mope of by Winny Cavana, or any other conceited piece of goods like her." His father's pride came to his aid in this instance, and he gave way.

Rathcash chapel was a crowded place of worship that day. Amongst the congregation, as a matter of course, were Winny Cavana and Kate Mulvey, both conspicuous by their beauty and solemnity. Tom Murdock too was there;—doubtless he was handsome, and he was solemn also, but his solemnity was of a different description. It was that generated by disappointment, with a dream of villany in perspective.

Tom was not a coward, even under the nervous influence of rejected love. Physically, he was not one in the matters of everyday life; and morally, he wanted rectitude to be one when he ought. He therefore resolved to meet Winny Cavana, as she came out of chapel, as much as possible as if nothing had happened, and to endeavour to improve the acquaintance as opportunity might permit. He purposed to himself to walk home with her, and determined, if possible, that at least a friendly intercourse should not be interrupted between them.

Rory of the Hills had steadily kept his resolution, notwithstanding our doubts, and had not gone to Rathcash chapel for the last four or five Sundays: he was even beginning to think that Father Farrell, after all, was not quite so much below Father Roche as a preacher.

At length there was a rustling of dresses and a shuffling of feet upon the floor, which proclaimed that divine worship had ended; and the congregation began to pour out of Rathcash chapel,—men in their dark coats and Caroline hats, and women in their best bonnets and cloaks. Tom Murdock was out almost one of the first, and sauntered about, greeting some of the more distant neighbours, whom he had not seen since his return. At length Winny and Kate made their appearance. Winny would have hurried on, but Kate "stepped short," until Tom had time to observe their approach. He came forward with more cowardice in his heart than he had ever felt before, and Winny's reception of him was not calculated to reassure him. Kate was next him, and held out her hand promptly and warmly. Winny could scarcely refuse to hold out hers: but there was neither promptness nor warmth in her manner. An awkward silence ensued on both sides; until Kate, with more anxiety on her own behalf, than tact or consideration on her friend's, broke in with half a score of inquiries, very kindly put, as to his health—the *very long* time he was away—how the neighbours *all* missed him so much—what he had been doing—how he left his aunt—how he liked Armagh, &c.—ending with a *hope* that he had come home to *remain*.

Winny was glad she had so good a spokeswoman with her, and did not offer a single observation in her aid. To say the truth, there was neither need nor opportunity; for Kate seemed perfectly able, and not unwilling, to monopolise the conversation. Tom endeavoured to be sprightly and at his ease, but made some observations far from applicable to the subjects upon which his loquacious companion had addressed him. He had hoped that when they came to the end of the lane, turning up to their houses, that Kate Mulvey would have gone towards her own home, and that he must then have had a word with Winny alone; but the manner in which she hastened her step past the turn, saying, "Kate, you know we are engaged to have a walk 'our lone' to-day," showed him that no amelioration of her feelings had taken place towards him; and without saying more than "Well, this is my way," he turned and left them.

Bully-dhu was standing near the end of Winny's house, looking from him; and as he recognised his mistress on the road, commenced to wag his huge tail, as if asking permission to accompany them. "Call him, Winny," said Kate; "he may be of use

to us; and at all events, he will be *company;* and
she laid a strong emphasis upon the last word.
Winny complied, and called the dog as loud as she
could. Poor Bully wanted but the wind of the
word, and tore down the lane with his mouth wide
open, and his tail describing large circles in the air.
He had well-nigh knocked down Tom Murdock as
he passed, but he did not mind that; and bounding
out upon the road, cut such capers round Winny as
were seldom seen, keeping up at the same time a
sort of growling bark, until the enthusiasm of his
joy at the permission had subsided.

CHAPTER XIX.

WINNY and Kate had agreed to take a long walk
after mass on the day in question. This was not a
mere trick of Winny's to get rid of Tom Murdock.
Certainly they had not agreed that it should be
"their lone;" this was as chance might have it;
and it was a gratuitous addition of Winny's, as
calculated to attain her object; and we have seen
how promptly she succeeded.

The day was fine; and they now wandered along
the road, so engaged in chat that they scarcely knew
how far they were from home. They had turned
down a cross-road before they came to Shanvilla, the
little village where Rory of the Hills lived. Kate
would have gone on straight; but Winny could not
be induced to do so. Kate had her own reasons for
wishing to go on, while Winny had hers for being

determined not; so they turned down the road to their left, intending, as they had Bully-dhu with them, to come home through the mountain-pass by Boher-na-milthiogue. They had chat enough for the whole road. Prayers had been over early, although it was second Mass; and the country people generally dine later on a holiday than usual. It gives the boys and girls more time to meet and chat and part, and in some instances to make new acquaintances. But whether it had been agreed upon or not, Winny and Kate appeared likely to have their walk alone upon this occasion; and as neither of them could choose their company, they were not sorry to find the road they had chosen less frequented than the one they had left. Bully-dhu scampered through the fields at each side of them, and sometimes on a long distance in front, occasionally running back to a turn to see if they were coming.

They were now beyond two miles from home, and two-and-a-half more would have completed the circle they had intended to take; but they were destined to return by the same way they came, and in no comfortable or happy plight.

They were descending a gentle hill, when at some distance below them they perceived a number of young men engaged playing at what they call "long bullets." They would instinctively have turned back, not wishing, unattended as they were except by Bully-dhu, to run the gauntlet of so many young men upon the roadside, most of whom must be strangers; but the said Bully-dhu had been enjoying himself considerably in advance, and they called and called to no purpose. They could not whistle; and if Bully heard them call, he did not heed them. He had seen a large brindled mastiff coming towards him from the crowd with his back up, and a growl of defiance which he could not mistake. Bully was no coward at any time; but on this occasion his courage was more than manifest, being, as he considered, in sole charge of his mistress and her friend. He was not certain but his antagonist's attack might be directed as much against them as against himself; and he stood upon the defensive, with his back up also, the hairs of which, from behind his ears to the butt of his tail, bristled "like quills upon the fretful porcupine." An encounter was now inevitable. The mastiff had shown a determination that nothing but a death-struggle should be the result, and rushed with open mouth and a roar of confident superiority upon his weaker rival. It was no even match; nothing but poor Bully-dhu's indomitable courage and activity could enable him to stand a single combat with his antagonist for five minutes. The first snarling and growling on both sides had now subsided, and they were "locked in each other's arms" in a silent rolling struggle for life or death. A dog-fight of even the most minor description has charms for a crowd of youngsters; and of course the "long bullets" were left to take care of themselves, and all the players, as well as the spectators, now ran up the road to witness this contest, which was, indeed, far from a minor concern. Poor Winny had screamed when she saw her dog first rolled by so furious and, as she saw at once, so superior a foe. She would have rushed forward but that Kate restrained her, as both dangerous and useless. She therefore threw herself against the bank of the ditch by the roadside, continuing to call out "for God's sake for somebody to save her poor dog! Was there no person there who knew her, and would save him?"

The crowd had by this time formed a ring round the infuriated animals. Some there were who would have been obedient to Winny's call for help; but the case at present admitted of no relief. Notwithstanding poor Bully-dhu's pluck and courage he had still the worst of it; in fact, his was altogether a battle of defence, while that of the mastiff was one of ferocious attack. He had seized Bully in the first instance at an advantage by the side of the neck under the ear, meeting his teeth through the skin, while the blood flowed freely from the wound, colouring the mud of the road a dark crimson round where they fought, and nearly choking the mastiff himself, as he was occasionally rolled under in the strife. Now they were upon their hind-legs again, wrestling like two stout boys for a fall; now Bully was down, and the mastiff rolled his head from side to side, tightening his grip, while the bloody froth besmeared himself and his victim, as he might now almost be called.

Some men at this point, more humane than the rest, took hold of the mastiff by the tail, while others struck him on the nose with a stick. They might as well have struck the rocks of Slieve-dhu or Slieve-bawn. The mastiff was determined on death, and death he seemed likely to have. His master was there, and seemed anxious to separate them. He even permitted him to be struck on the nose, claiming the privilege only of choosing the thickness of the stick.

"He's loosening, boys!" said one fellow; "he's tired of that hoult, an' can do no more with it; stan' back, boys, an' give the black dog fair play, he's not bet yet; he never got a grip iv th'other dog yet; give him fair play, boys, an' he'll do good business yet. There! Tiger's out iv him now, and the black dog has him; be gorra he's a game dog any way, boys! I dunna who owns him." This man seemed to be an "expert" in dog-fighting. Tiger had got tired of the hold he had had, and considering a fresh grip would be better, not by any means influenced by the blows he had received on the nose, he had given way; believing, I do suppose, that he had already so mastered his antagonist, that he could seize him again at pleasure. But he had reckoned without his host, Bully-dhu took advantage of the relief to turn on him, and seized him pretty much in the same way he had been seized himself, and with quite as much ferocity and determination. The fight did not now seem so unequal; they had grip for grip, and there was a general cry amongst the crowd to let them see it out. Indeed there appeared to be no alternative, for they had both resisted every exertion to separate them.

"It's no use, boys," said the expert; "you might cut them in pieces, an' they wouldn't quit, except to get a better hoult; if you want to part them, hould them by the tails, an' watch for the loosening of wan or th'other, and then drag them away."

"Stan' back, boys," said another. "The black dog's not bet yet; stan' back, I say!"

Bully-dhu had made a great rally of it. It was now evident that he would have made a much better fight from the first, if he had not been seized at an advantage which prevented him from turning his head to seize his foe in return. They had been by this time nearly twenty minutes in deadly conflict; and the mastiff's superior strength and size began now to tell fearfully against poor Bully-dhu. He had shaken himself completely out of Bully, and made a fresh grip, not far from the first, but still nearer the throat. The matter seemed now coming to a close, and the result no longer doubtful. Every one saw that if something could not be done to disengage Tiger from that last grip, the black dog must speedily be killed.

Here Winny, who heard the verdict from the crowd, could be restrained no longer, and rushed forward praying for some one, for them all, to try and save her dog. They all declared it was a pity; that he was a grand dog, but no match for the mastiff. Some recommended one thing, some another. Tiger was squeezed, and struck on the nose; a stick was forced into his mouth with a hope of opening his teeth and loosening his hold; but it was all useless, and poor Winny gave up all for lost, in a fit of sobbing and despair.

At this moment a man, who had not originally been of the party, was seen running at full speed down the hill. It was Rory of the Hills, who at this juncture had come accidently upon the top of the hill immediately above them, and at once recognising *some* of the party on the road, rushed forward to the rescue. He cast but a glance at the dogs. He knew them *both*, and how utterly hopeless a contest it must be for Bully-dhu. Like an arrow from a bow, he flew to a cabin hard by, and seizing a half-lighted sod of turf from the fire, he returned to the scene. "Now, boys," he cried, "hold them fast by the tails and hind-legs, and I'll soon separate them." Two men seized them—Tiger's own master was one. Although there were many young men there who would have looked on with savage pleasure at an even fight between two well-matched dogs, even to the death, there was not one who could wish to stand by and see a noble dog killed without a chance by a superior foe, and they all hailed Rory of the Hills, from his confident and decisive manner, as a timely deliverer. The dogs having been drawn by two strong men to their full length, but still fastened by the deadly grip of the mastiff on Bully-dhu's throat, Rory blew the coal, and applied it to Tiger's jaw. This was too much for him. He could understand squeezes, and even blows on the nose and head, or perhaps in the excitement he never felt them; but the lighted coal he could not stand, and yielding at once to the pain, he let go his hold. The dogs were then dragged away to a distance; Rory of the Hills carrying poor

Bully-dhu in his arms, more dead than alive, to where Winny sat distracted on the road-side.

"O Rory! he's dead or dying!" she cried, as the exhausted animal lay gasping by her side.

"He's neither!" almost roared Rory; "have you a fippenny-bit, Winny, or Kate? if I had one myself, I wouldn't ask you."

"Yes, yes," exclaimed Winny, taking an old bead-purse from her pocket, and giving him one. She knew not what it was for, but her confidence in Rory's judgment was unbounded, and her heart felt some relief when it was not a needle and thread he asked for.

"Here," said Rory to a gossoon, who stood looking at the dog, "be off like a hare to Biddy Molldoon's for a naggin of whiskey, and you may have the change for yourself, if you're back in less than no time; make her put it in a bottle, not a cup, that you may run the whole way without spilling it."

The boy started off, not very unlike—either in pace or appearance—to the animal he was desired to resemble, for he had a cap made of one of their skins.

Rory of the Hills, although a very steady, temperate young man, was not altogether so much above his compeers in the district as not to know "where a dhrop was kept," which to the uninitiated (English of course,) means a sheebeen house. Perhaps, *to them*, I am only explaining one thing by another which equally requires explanation.

During the interval of the boy's absence, Rory of the Hills was examining the wounds in poor Bullydhu's neck and throat. The dog still lay gasping, and occasionally scrubbling with his fore-legs, and kicking with his hind, while Winny reiterated her belief that he was dying. Rory now contradicted her rather flatly. He knew she would excuse the rudeness from the hope which it held forth.

"There will be nothing on him to signify indeed, Winny, after a little," he said kindly, feeling that he had been harsh but a moment before; "see, he is not even torn; only cut in four places."

"In four places! O Rory, in four!"

"Yes; but they are only where the other dog's teeth entered, and came through; see, they are only holes; the dog is quite exhausted, but will soon come round. Come here, Winny, and feel him yourself."

Winny stretched over, and Rory took her hand to guide it to the spots where her poor dog had been wounded. Poor Bully looked up at her, and feebly endeavoured to wag his tail, and Winny smiled and wept together. Rory was a very long time explaining to her precisely where the wounds were, and how they must have been inflicted; and he found it necessary to hold her hand the whole time. Whether Winny, in the confusion of her grief, knew that he did so, nobody but herself can tell. Three or four persons, who knew Winny, had kindly come up to see how the dog was; and the expert amongst them with so much confidence, that he was going to set him on his legs at once. But Rory had taken special charge of him, and would not suffer so premature an experiment, nor the interference of any other doctor.

But here comes the gossoon with the whiskey, like a hare indeed, across the fields, and his middle finger stuck in the neck of the bottle by way of a cork.

Rory took it from him, and claiming the assistance of the expert, whom he had just now repudiated, for a few moments to hold his head, he placed the neck of the bottle in Bully-dhu's mouth. He poured "the least taste in life" down his throat, and with his hand washed his jaws and tongue copiously with the spirits.

With a sort of yelp poor Bully made a struggle and a plunge, and rose to his feet. Winny held out her hand to him, and he staggered over towards her, looking up in her face, and wagging his tail.

"I told you so," said Rory; "get me a handful of salt."

The same cabin which had supplied the "live coal" was applied to by the gossoon (who kept the change,) and it was quickly brought.

Rory then rubbed some into the wounds, in spite of Winny's remonstrances as to the pain, and the dog's own unequivocal objections to the process.

Matters were now really on the mend. Bully-dhu shook himself, looking after the crowd with a growl; and even Winny had no doubt that Rory's prescriptions had been necessary and successful.

"The sooner you get home now with him, Winny, the better," said Rory.

"You are not going to leave us, Rory?" said Winny, doubtingly.

"Certainly not," he replied; "the poor dog is

still very weak, and may require rest if not help, by the way."

He then took a red cotton handkerchief from his pocket, and tying it loosely round the dog's neck, he held the other end of it in his hand, and they all set out together for Rathcash.

The handkerchief, Rory said, would both keep the air from the wounds, and help to sustain the dog on his legs. But he may have had some idea in his mind that it would also serve as an excuse for his accompanying them to the very farthest point possible on their road home.

CHAPTER XX.

For many hundred yards total silence prevailed amongst our pedestrians. Even Kate Mulvey seemed at a loss what first to say, or whether she ought to be the first to say anything.

Winny, seeing that her poor dog was getting on famously, was rather pleased, "since the thing *did* happen," that it had been brought to so satisfactory an end after all; and by whom? Her poor dog might have been killed, and would, undoubtedly, but for Rory of the Hills' fortunate arrival at the last moment, and his prompt and successful assistance. There was poor Bully-dhu now, walking to all appearance almost as well as ever, and tied up in *his* handkerchief. She was glad that the road had become by this time comparatively deserted, for she was timid and frightened, she knew not why. Perhaps she was afraid she might meet her father. She was thinking with herself, too, how far Rory would come with them, and who they might meet who knew them, before he turned back. Rory of the Hills' heart was wishing Kate Mulvey at "*Altha Brashia*," but his head was not sorry that she was one of the party, for common-sense still kept his heart in subjection.

Thus it was that silence prevailed for some time. Bully-dhu was the first to break it. Whether it was that the whiskey had got into his head, or, as the present fashion would say, that he was "screwed," I know not; but he felt so much better, and had so far recovered his strength and spirits, that he had almost pulled the handkerchief from Rory's hand, and cut an awkward sort of a rigadoon round Winny, barking, and looking up *triumphantly* in her face. Could it have been, that while the others had been thinking of these other things, that he had been deluding himself with the notion that he had been the victor in the battle?

"Poor fellow," said Winny, patting him on the head, "I do think there's nothing very bad the matter with you, after all. Rory, I am beginning to believe you."

"I hope you will always believe me, Winny Cavana," was his reply, and he again sunk into silence.

She could not think why he called her Cavana, and "yet her colour rose:" I believe that is the way your experienced novelists would express it in such a case.

A longer silence now ensued. None of the three appeared inclined to talk—Rory less than either. Kate Mulvey, who had always plenty to say for herself, seemed completely dumb [foundered, I was going to add, but I find the word will do as well, perhaps better, in its purity.] But, notwithstanding their silence, they were shortening the road to Rathcash. Winny was framing some pretty little speech of thanks to Rory for the *trouble* he had taken, and for his *kindness;* but she had so often *botched* it to her own mind, that she determined to leave it to chance at the moment of parting. Kate had no such excuse for her silence, and yet she was not without one, which to herself quite justified it.

Some few desultory remarks, however, were made from time to time, followed by the still " awkward pause," until they had now arrived at the turn in sight of Kate Mulvey's house.

Rory was determined to go the whole way to the end of the lane turning up to Winny Cavana's. He had not sought this day's happiness; he had studiously avoided such a chance; but circumstances had so far controlled him, that he could not accuse himself of wilful imprudence. Rory knew very well that if a fair opportunity occurred, he would in all probability betray himself in an unequivocal manner to Winny, and he dreaded the result. Up to the present he was on friendly and familiar terms with her; but once the word was spoken, he feared a barrier would be placed between them, which might put an end to even this calm source of happiness. That he loved Winny with a disinterested but devoted love, he knew too well. How far he might hope that she would ever look upon his love with favour, he had never yet ventured to feel his way; and yet his heart told him there was something about herself, which, if unbiased by circumstances, might bid him not despair. But her rich old father, who had set his heart upon a marriage for his daughter with Tom Murdock, and a union of the farms, he knew would never consent. Neither did he believe that Winny herself would decline so grand a match when it came to the point.

Rory had argued all these matters over and over again in his mind; and the fatal certainty of disappointment, added to a prudent determination to avoid her society as much as possible, had enabled him hitherto to keep his heart under some control.

Kate Mulvey, though "book-sworn" by Winny, if she did not exactly repeat any of the confidential chat she had with her friend about Tom Murdock and himself, felt no hesitation in "letting slip" to Rory, for whom she had a very great regard, a *hint* or two, just casually, as if by accident, that Tom Murdock "was no great favourite" of Winny Cavana's,—that the neighbours "were all astray" in "giving them to one another,"—that if she knew what two and two made, it would all "end in smoke;" and such little gossiping observations. Not by way of *telling* Rory, but just as if in the mere exuberance of her own love of chat. But they had the desired effect, now that Rory was likely to have an opportunity of a few words with Winny alone, for Kate was evidently prepared to turn up to her own house when they came to the little gate.

Rory had heard, even in his rank of life, the aristocratic expression that "faint heart never won fair lady;" and a secret sort of self-esteem prompted him to make the most of the fortuitous circumstances which he had not sought for, and which he therefore argued Providence might have thrown in his way. "What can she do," thought he, "but reject my love? I shall know the worst then; and I can make a start of it. I'm too long hanging about here like a fool; a dumb priest never got a parish; and barring his acres and his cash—if he has any—I'm a better man than ever he was, or ever will be."

These were his thoughts as they approached the gate, and his heart began to tremble, as Kate Mulvey said:

"Winny dear, I must part with you here. I saw my father at the door. He came to it two or three times while we were coming up the road; and he made a sign to me to go in. I'm sure and certain he's half-starved for his dinner, waiting for me."

"Well, Kitty, I suppose I can't expect you to starve him out-and-out, and I'll bid you good-by. I'm all as one as at home now, I may say. Rory— I won't bring you any farther."

"You're not bringing me, Winny; I'm going of my own free will."

"Indeed, Rory, you have been very kind, and I'm entirely obliged to you for all your trouble; but I won't ask you to come any farther now."

Kate's father just then came to the door again; and she, thinking that matters had gone far enough between Rory and her friend in her presence, bid them a final good-by, and turned up to her father, who still stood at the door, and who really did appear to be starving, if one could judge by the position of his hands, and the face he made.

The moment had now arrived when Rory must meet his fate, or call himself a coward and a poltroon for the remainder of his natural life, be it long or short.

He chose the least degrading and the most hopeful alternative—to meet his fate.

As Winny held out her hand to him, and asked him to let out the dog, he said:

"No, Winny; I'll give him up to you at the end of the lane; but not sooner."

Winny saw that remonstrance would be no use. She did not wish to quarrel with Rory, and she knew that at all events that was no time or place to do so.

They had not advanced many yards alone, when Winny stopped again, as if irresolute between her wishes and her fears. She had not yet spoken unkindly to Rory, and she had tact enough to know that the first unkind word would bring out the whole matter, which she dreaded, in a flood from his heart, and which she doubted her own power to withstand.

"Rory," she said, "indeed I will not let you come any farther—don't be angry."

"Winny, you said first you would not ask me,

and now you say you will not let me. Winny Cavana, are you ashamed of *any* one about Rathcash, or Rathcash*more*, seeing you walking with Rory of the Hills?"

"You are very unjust and very unkind, Rory, to say such a thing. I never was ashamed to be seen walking with you; and I'm certain sure the day will never come when you will give me reason to be ashamed of you, Rory of the Hills;—there now, I seldom put the three last words to your name, except when I wish to be kind. But there is a difference between shame and fear, Rory."

"Then you are afraid, Winny?"

"Yes, Rory, but it is only of my father—take that with you now, and be satisfied, but don't fret me by persevering farther. Let the dog go,—and good-by."

All this time she was counting the pebbles on the road with her eyes.

"No, Winny, I'll not fret you willingly; but here or there it is all the same, and the truth must come out. Winny, you have been the woodbine that has twined itself and blossomed round my heart for many a long day. Don't wither it, Winny dear, but say I may water and nourish it with the dew of your love;" and he would have taken her hand.

"Not here, Rory," she said, releasing it; "are you mad? Don't you see we're in sight of the houses, and gracious only knows who may be watching us. Untie your handkerchief and give me the dog. For goodness sake, Rory dear, don't come any farther."

"No, Winny, I'd die before I'd fret you. Here's the dog, handkerchief and all: keep it as a token that I may hope."

"Indeed, Rory, I cannot—don't ask me."

Rory's heart fell, and he stooped to untie the handkerchief in despair, if not in chagrin, at Winny's last words.

But Bully-dhu appeared to know what his mistress ought to have done better than she did herself. It was either that, or Rory's hand shook so, that when endeavouring to untie the knot, the dog got loose, "handkerchief and all," and turning to his mistress, began to bark and jump up on her, with joy that he had gained his liberty, and was so near home. Winny became frightened lest Bully-dhu's barks might bring notice upon them, and she endeavoured to moderate his ecstacy, yet she felt a sort of secret delight that she was in for the handkerchief in spite of herself. She was determined, therefore, not to send poor Rory of the Hills away totally dejected.

"There, Rory dear; for God's sake I say again, be off home. I'll keep it in memory of the day that you saved my poor dog from destruction,—there now, will that do?" and she held out her hand.

"It is enough, Winny dear. This has been the happiest day of my life. May I hope it has only been the first of a long life like it?"

"Now, Rory, don't talk nonsonse, but be off home, if you have any wit; good-by;" and this time she gave him her hand, and let it lie in his.

"God bless you, Winny dearest, I oughtn't to be too hard on you. Sure you have raised my heart up into heaven already, and there is something now worth living for." And he turned away with a quick and steady step.

"She called me 'dear' twice," he soliloquised, after he thought he had fairly turned round. But Winny had heard him, and as she took the handkerchief from Bully-dhu's neck, she patted him upon the head, saying, "And you *are* a dear good fellow, and I'm very fond of you."

Rory heard every part of this little speech except the first word, and Winny managed it to perfection; for though she had used the word "and" in connection with what she had heard Rory say, she was too cunning to let him hear that one small word, which would have calmed his beating heart; and the rest she would fain have it appear had been said to the dog, for which purpose she accompanied the words with those pats upon his head. She spoke somewhat louder, however, than was necessary, if Bully-dhu was alone intended to hear her.

Rory saw the transaction, and heard some of the words—only some. But they were sufficient to make him envy the dog, as he watched them going up the lane, and into the house.

It might be a nice point, in the higher ranks of life, to determine whether, in a "breach of promise" case, the above passages could be relied on as unequivocal evidence on either side of a promise; or whether a young lover would be justified in believing that his suit had been successful upon no other foundation than what had then taken place. But in the rank of life in which Winny Cavana and Rory

Lennon moved, it was as good between them as if they had been "book-sworn"—and they both knew it.

Before Winny went to her bed that night, she had washed and ironed the handkerchief, and she kept it ever after in her pocket, folded up in a piece of newspaper. It had no mark upon it when she got it, but she was not afraid, after some time, to work the letters R. L. in the corner, as no one was ever to see it but herself,—not even Kate Mulvey.

Old Ned Cavana, after returning from prayers, determined to rest himself for some time before taking a tour of the farm, and lay down upon an old black sofa in the parlour. There is no shame in the truth that an old man of his age soon fell fast asleep. The servant-girl looked in once or twice to tell him that the spotted heifer had cut her leg jumping over a wall, as Jamesy Doyle was turning her out of the wheat; but she knew it would not signify; and not wishing, or perhaps not venturing, to disturb him, she quietly shut the door again. He slept so long, that he was only just getting the spotted heifer's leg stuped in the farmyard while the scene already described was passing between Winny and young Lennon upon the road. Were it not for that same heifer's leg he would doubtless have been standing at the window watching his daughter's return,—upon such fortuitous accidents do lovers' chances sometimes hang. This was what Winny in her ignorance of her father's employment had dreaded; and hence alone her anxiety that Rory should "be off home, if he had any wit."

On this point she found, however, that all was right when she entered. Her father was just coming in from the farmyard, "very thankful that it was no worse;" a frame of mind which we would recommend all persons to cultivate under untoward circumstances of any kind.

Of course Winny told her father of the mishap about poor Bully-dhu's battle: she "nothing extenuated, nor set down aught in malice," but told the thing accurately as it had occurred; and did not even hide that young Lennon—she did not call him Rory of the Hills—had ultimately rescued the poor dog from destruction. She did not think it necessary to say how far he had accompanied them on their way home.

"He's a smart young fellow, that Lennon is, an' I'm for ever obliged to him, Winny, for that same turn. There would be no livin' here but for Bully-dhu. I believe it was Rory himself gev him to us, when he was a pup."

"It was, father; and a very fine dog he turned out."

"The sorra betther, Winny. If it wasn't for him, as I say, betune the fox an' the rogues we wouldn't have a goose or a turkey, or a duck, or a cock, or a hen, or so much as a chikin, in the place, nor so much, iv coorse, as a fresh egg for our breakfast. Poor Bully, I hope he's not hurt, Winny;" and he stooped down to examine him. "No, no," he cried, "not much; but I'm sure he's thirsty. Here, Biddy, get Bully a dish of *bonnia-rommer*, and be sure you make him up a good mess afther dinner. That Rory of the Hills, as they call him, is a thundering fine young man; it's a pity the poor fellow is a pauper, I may say."

"No, father, he's *not* a pauper, and never will be; he's well able to earn his living."

"I know that, Winny, for he often worked here; an' there's not a man in the three parishes laves an honester day's work behind him."

"And does not spend it foolishly, father. If you were to see how nicely he was dressed to-day; and— besides all the help he gives his father and mother."

She was about to add a remark that work was just then very slack, as it was the dead time of the year, but that there was always something to be done about the farm; but second thoughts checked the words as they were rising to her lips; and second thoughts, they say, are best.

Old Ned here turned the conversation by "wondering was the dinner near ready."

Winny was not a little surprised, and a good deal delighted, to hear her father talk so familiarly and so kindly of Rory. There never was a time when her father's kind word of him was of more value to her heart. Perhaps it would be an unjust implication of hypocrisy on the old man's part, to suggest that he might have only been "pumping" Winny on the subject. She felt, however, that she had gone far enough for the present in the expression of her opinion, and was not sorry when a touch of the *faire gurtha* put her father in mind of "the dinner."

We, who of course can see much farther than any

L

of our *dramatis personæ*, and who are privileged to be behind the scenes, could tell Winny Cavana—but that we would not wish to fret her—that Tom Murdock was looking on from his own window at the whole scene between her and young Lennon on the road; and that from that moment, although he could not hear a word that was said, he understood the whole thing, and was generating plans of vengeance and destruction against *one* or both.

CHAPTER XXI.

MATTERS were now lying quiet. They were like a line ball at billiards which cannot be played at, and there was nothing "to go out for" by any of the players in this double match. But occasionally something "comes off" in even the most remote locality, which creates some previous excitement, and forms the subject of conversation in all ranks. Sometimes a steeple-chase, "five-sovereigns stakes, with fifty or a hundred added," forms a speculation for the rich; with a farmer's class-race for twenty pounds, without any stakes, for horses *bonâ fide* the property, &c.

A great cricket-match once "came off" not very far from the locality of our story, when Major W—n lived at Mount Campbell, between the officers of the garrison at Boyle and a local club. We belonged to the major's province of constabulary at the time, and, as members, were privileged to take part therein. The thing was rather new in that part of the world at the time, but had been well advertised in the newspapers for the rich, and through the police for the poor; and the consequence was—the weather being very fine—that a concourse of not less than a thousand persons were assembled to witness the game. There can be little doubt that some of the younger portion, at least, of our *dramatis personæ* in this tale were spectators upon the occasion. It was within their county, and not an unreasonable distance from the homes we are now writing of.

January and February had now passed by in the calm monotony of nothing to excite the inhabitants of the Rathcashes. Valentine's-day, indeed, had created a slight stir amongst some of the girls who had bachelors, or thought they had; and many a message was given to those going into C. O. S., to "be sure and ask at the post-office for a letter for me," "and for me," "and for me." A few, very few indeed, got valentines, and many, very many, did not.

It was now March, and even this little anxiety of heart had subsided on the part of the girls; some from self-satisfaction at what they got, and others from disappointment at what they did not.

During this time Tom Murdock had seen Winny Cavana occasionally. It would be quite impossible, with one common lane to both houses, and those houses not more than three hundred yards apart, that any plan of Winny's, less than total seclusion, could have prevented their sometimes "coming across" one another; and total seclusion was a thing that Winny Cavana would not subject herself to on account of any man "that ever stepped in shoe-leather." "What had she to say him, or to be afraid of him for? Let him mind his own business, and she'd mind hers. But for one half hour she'd never shut herself up on his account. Let him let her alone."

Tom Murdock was not without a certain degree of knowledge of the female heart, nor of a certain amount of tact to come round one, in the least objectionable way; at all events so as not to foster any difference which might have taken place. He did not appear to seek her society, nor did he seek to avoid it. When they met, which was really always by accident, he was civil, and sufficiently attentive to show that he harboured no ill-will against her, and respected her enough to make it worth his while not to break with her. He was now certain of a walk home with her on Sundays from Mass. On these occasions her father was generally with her; but this Tom considered rather to be wished for than otherwise, as he could not venture, even if alone, to renew the forbidden subject. But he knew the father had approved of his suit, and his wish was now to establish a constant civility and kindness of manner, which would keep him at least on his side, if it did not help by its quietness to make Winny herself think better of him.

What had passed between Winny and Rory was not likely in a human heart to keep up the constrained indifference which that young man had burdened himself with towards her. He had therefore upon two or three Sundays ventured again to go to the chapel of Rathcash.

It is not very easy to account for, or to explain how, such minor matters fall out, or whether they are instinctively arranged impromptu; but upon each occasion of Rory having reappeared at Rathcash chapel, Tom Murdock's walk home with Winny was spoiled; more particularly if it so happened that her father did not go to prayers.

Rory of the Hills was never devoid of a considerable portion of self-esteem and respect. Though but a daily labourer, his conduct and character were such as to have gained for him the favourable opinion and the good word of every one who knew him; and apart from the innate goodness of his disposition, he would not lose the high position he had attained in the hearts of his neighbours for the consideration of any of those equivocal pleasures generally enjoyed by young men of his class. He felt that he could look old Ned Cavana or old Mick Murdock straight in the face, rich as they were. He felt quite Tom Murdock's equal in every thing mentally and physically. In riches alone he could not compare with him, but these, he thanked God, belonged to neither mind nor body.

Thus far satisfied with himself, he always stopped to have a few words with Winny, when chance—which he sometimes coaxed to be propitious—threw him in her way. Even from Rathcash on Sundays he felt entitled, now perhaps more than ever, to join her as far as his own way home lay along with hers, and this although her father was along with her. If Tom Murdock had joined them, which was only natural, living where he did, Rory was more determined than ever to be of the party, chatting to them all, Tom included; thus showing that he was neither afraid of them nor ashamed of himself.

The first Sunday after the dog-fight was the first that Rory had gone to the chapel of Rathcash for a pretty long time. But as a matter of course he must go there on that day to inquire for poor Bullydhu, and to ascertain if Winny Cavana had recovered her fright and fatigue. We have seen that Winny had told her father sufficient of the transaction of poor Bully's mishap to make it almost a matter of necessity that he should allude to it to Rory, if it were merely to thank him for "the trouble he had taken" in saving the dog. When Winny heard the words her father had used, she thought them cold,—"the trouble he had taken!" her heart suggested that he might have said, and said truly, "the risk he had run."

But, Winny, there had really been no risk; and recollect that you had used the very same word "trouble" to Rory yourself, when you knew no more of his mind than your father does now.

Tom had walked with them on this occasion, and old Ned's civility to "that whelp"—a name he had not forgotten—helped to sour his temper more than anything which had passed between Winny Cavana and him. But all these things he was obliged to bear, and he bore them well, upon "the-long-lane-that-has-no-turning" system.

But now a cause of anticipated excitement began to be spoken of in the neighbourhood; how, or why, or by whom the matter had been set on foot, was a thing not known, and of no consequence at the time. Yet Tom Murdock was at the bottom of it—and for a purpose.

There existed not far from about the centre of the locality of our story a large flat common, where flocks of geese picked the short grass in winter, and over which the pewit curled with a short circular flap, and a timid little hoarse scream in the month of May. It consisted of about sixty acres of hard, level, whitish sod, admirably adapted for short races, athletic sports, and manly exercises of every kind. It formed a sort of amphitheatre, surrounded by low green hills, affording ample space and opportunity for hundreds, aye, thousands of spectators to witness any sport which might be inaugurated upon the level space below.

Upon one or two occasions, but not latterly, hurling-matches had come off upon Glanveigh Common. At one time these hurling-matches were very common in Ireland, and were considered a fair test of the prowess of the young men of different parishes. Many minor matches had come off from time to time, but they were of a mixed nature, got up for the most part upon the spot, and had not been spoken of beforehand—they were mere impromptus amongst the younger lads of the neighbourhood. The love of the game, however, had not died out even amongst those of riper years; and there were very many men, young and old, whose hurls were laid up upon lofts, and who could still handle them in a manner with which few parts of Ireland could compare. Amongst those Tom Murdock was preeminent. He had successfully led the last great match, when not more than twenty years of age, between the parishes of Rathcash and Shanvilla, against a champion called "Big M'Dermott," who led for the latter parish. He was considered the best man in the province to handle a hurl, and his men were good; but Tom Murdock and the boys of Rathcash had beaten them back three times from the very jaws of the goal, and finally conquered. But Shanvilla formally announced that they would seek an early opportunity to retrieve their character. The following Patrick's-day would be three years since they had lost it.

Tom Murdock thought this a good opportunity to forward a portion of his plans. A committee was formed of the best men in Rathcash parish, to send a challenge to the men of Shanvilla to hurl another match on Glanveigh Common upon Patrick's day. Tom Murdock himself was not on the committee; he had too much tact for that. "Big M'Dermott" had emigrated, leaving a younger brother behind him,—a good man no doubt; but as the Shanvilla boys had been latterly bragging of Rory of the Hills as their best man, Tom had no doubt that the challenge would be accepted, and that young Lennon, as a matter of course, would be chosen as their champion. Had he doubted this last circumstance, he might not have cared to originate the match at all. He had not forgotten the poker-and-tongs jig about four months before. His humiliation on that occasion had sunk deeper into his heart than any person who witnessed it was aware of; and although never afterwards adverted to, had still to be avenged. If, then, at the head of his hundred men, he could beat back young Lennon with an equal number twice out of thrice before the assembled parishes, it would in some degree wash out the humiliation of his defeat in the dance.

Upon the acceptance of this challenge not only the character of the Shanvilla boys depended, but their pride and confidence in Rory of the Hills as their best man.

At once upon the posting of the challenge, with the names of the committee, upon the chapel-gate of Rathcash, a counter-committee was formed for Shanvilla, and, taking a leaf from their opponent's book their best man's name was left out.. But he at the same time accepted the leadership of the party, which was unanimously placed upon him.

Thus far matters had tended to the private exultation of Tom Murdock, who was determined to make Patrick's day a day of disgrace to his rival, for since the scene he had witnessed with the dog and the handkerchief, he could no longer doubt the fact.

The whole population of the parishes were sure to be assembled, and Winny Cavana, of course, amongst the rest. What a triumph to degrade him in her eyes before his friends and hers! Surely he would put forth all his energies to attain so glorious a result. He would show before the assembled multitude that, physically at least, "that whelp" was no match for Tom Murdock,—his defeat at the poker-and-tongs jig was a mere mischance.

The preliminaries were now finally settled for this, the greatest hurling-match which for many years had come off, or was likely to come off, in the province. Rathcash had been victorious on the last great occasion of the kind just three years before, when Tom Murdock had led the parish, as a mere stripling, against "Big M'Dermott" and his men. The additional three years had now given more manliness to Tom's heart, in one sense at least, and a greater development to the sinew and muscle of his frame, than he could boast of on that occasion. He was an inch, or an inch and a half, over Rory of the Hills in height, upwards of a stone-weight heavier, and nearly two years his senior in age. His men were on an average as good men, and as well accustomed to the use of the hurl as those of Shanvilla,—their hurls were as well-seasoned and as sound, and their *pluck* was proverbially high. What wonder, then, if Tom Murdock anticipated a certain, if not an easy, victory?

As hurling, however, has gone very much out of fashion since those days, and is now seldom seen—never indeed in the glorious strength of two populous parishes pitted against each other—it may be well for those who have never seen, or perhaps heard of it, to close this chapter with a short description of it.

A large flat field, or common, the larger the better, is selected for the performance. Two large blocks of stone are placed about fifteen or twenty feet apart, towards either end of the field. One pair of these stones forms the goal of one party, and the other pair that of their opponents. They are about four hundred yards distant from each other, and are generally whitewashed, that they may more easily catch the attention of the players. A ball, somewhat larger than a cricket-ball, but pretty much of the same nature, is produced by each party, which will be more fully explained by and by. The hurlers assemble, ranged in two opposing parties in the centre between the goals. The hurls are admirably calculated for the kind of work they are intended to perform—viz. to *puck* the ball towards the respective goals. But they would be very formidable weapons should a fight arise between the contending parties. This ere now, we regret to say, has not unfrequently been the case,—leading sometimes to bloodshed, and on a few occasions to manslaughter, if not to murder. The hurl is invariably made of a piece of well-seasoned ash. It is between three and four feet long, having a flat surface of about four inches broad, and an inch thick, turned at the lower end. Many and close searches in those days have been made through the woods, and in cartmakers' shops, for pieces of ash with the necessary turn, grown by nature in the wood; but failing this fortunate chance, the object was pretty well effected by a process of steaming, and the application of cramps, until the desired shape was attained. But these were never considered as good as those grown *designedly* by nature *for the purpose.*

The contending parties being drawn up, as I have said, in the centre of the ground, the respective leaders step forward and shake hands, like two pugilists, to show that there is no malice. Although this act of the leaders is supposed to guarantee the good feeling of the men as well, yet the example is generally followed by such of the opposing players as are near each other.

"A toss" then takes place, as to which side shall "sky" their ball. These balls are closely inspected by the leaders of the opposite parties, and pronounced upon before the game begins. There is no choice of goals, as the parties generally set them up at the end of the field next the parish they belong to. Whichever side wins "the toss" then "skies" their ball, the leader throwing it from his hand to the full height of his power, and "the game is on." But after this no hand, under any circumstances, is permitted to touch the ball; an apparently unnecessary rule, for it would be a mad act to attempt it, as in all probability the hand would be smashed to pieces. The game then is, to puck the ball through the opponents' goal. Two goal-masters are stationed at either goal, belonging one to each party, and they must be men of well-known experience as such. Their principal duty is to see that the ball is put fairly between the stones; but they are not prohibited from using their hurls in the final struggle at the spot, the one to assist, the other to obstruct, as the state of their party may require.

Sometimes the game is nearly won, when a fortunate young fellow on the losing side slips the ball from the crowd to the open, where one of his party curls it into the air with the flat of his hurl, and the whole assembly—for there is always one—hears the puck it gets, sending it half-way towards the other gaol. The rush to it then is tremendous by both sides, and another crowded clashing of hurls takes place.

When the ball is fairly put through the goal of one party by the other, the game is won, and the shouts of the victors and their friends are deafening.

CHAPTER XXII.

A HURLING match in those days was no light matter, particularly when it was on so extensive a scale as that which we are about to describe—between two large parishes. They were supposed, and intended to be, amicable tests of the prowess and activity of the young men, at a healthy game of recreation, as the cricket-matches of the present day are that of the athletic aristocracy of the land. In all these great matches, numbers of men, women, and children used to collect to look on, and cheer as the success of the game swayed one way or the other; and as most of the players were unmarried men, it is not to be wondered at if there were many young women amongst the crowd with their hearts swaying accordingly.

It had been decided by the committees upon the occasion of this great match, that a sort of distinguishing dress—they would not of course call it uniform—should be worn by the men. To hurl in coats of any kind had never in this or any other parish been thought of. The committee left the choice of the distinguishing colours to their respective leaders, recommending, however, that the same manner should be adopted of exhibiting it. It was agreed that sleeves of different colours should be worn over the shirt-sleeves, with a broad piece of ribbon tied at the throat to match.

Tom Murdock had chosen green for his party, and not only that, but, with a determination to make himself popular, and to throw his rival as far as possible into the back-ground, had purchased a sufficient quantity of calico and ribbon to supply his men gratis with sleeves and neck-ties.

Poor Rory of the Hills could not afford this liberality, and he felt the object with which it had been puffed and paraded on the other side for a whole week previous. He was not afraid, however, that his men would think the less of him on that account. They knew he was only a labouring man depending upon his day's wages; and many of those who would wield the hurl by his side upon the 17th of March were well-to-do sons of comfortable farmers. Many, no doubt, were labouring boys like himself, and many servant-boys to the farming-class.

A deputation of Shanvillas had waited on Rory of the Hills to ascertain his choice of a colour for their sleeves and ribbon.

He thought for a few moments, and then taking a red pocket-handkerchief from his box he said, "Boys, this is the only colour I can think of. It is as good as any."

"I don't like it, Rory," said M'Dermott, the next best man in the parish.

"Why so, Phil?" said another.

"Well, I hardly know why. It is too much the colour of blood. I'd rather have white."

"Don't be superstitious, Phil *awochal*," said Rory; "white is a cowardly colour all over the world, and red is the best contrast we can have to their colour."

"So be it," said Phil.

"So be it," re-choed the rest of the deputation; "sure, Rory has a right to the choice. Lend us the handkerchief, that we may match it as near as possible."

"And welcome, boys; here it is; but take good care of it for me, as it is the only one I have *now*."

The deputation did not know, but the readers do, that he had given the fellow to it—off the same piece—to Winny Cavana with the dog. Hence his emphasis upon the last word.

No time was lost by the deputation when they left Rory. They had scarcely got out of hearing, when Phil M'Dermott said, "Boys, you all know that Tom Murdock has bestowed his men with a pair of sleeves, and half a yard of ribbon each. Now if he was as well liked as he lets on, he needn't have done that; and in my opinion he done it by way of casting a slur upon our man's poverty. Tom Murdock can afford a hundred yards of green calico and fifty yards of tuppenny ribbon very well;—at least he ought to be able to do so. Now I vote, that amongst the best of us we bestow our man with a pair of silk sleeves, and a silk cap and ribbon, for the battle. There's my tenpenny-bit towards it."

"An' I second that vote, boys; there's mine," said another.

"Aisy, boys, an' listen to me," broke in a young Solon, who formed one of the deputation. "There's none of us that wouldn't give a tenpenny-bit, if it was the last he had, to do what you say, Phil; but the whole thing, sleeves, ribbon, and cap,—won't cost more than a couple of crowns; an' many's the one of the Shanvilla boys would like to have part in it. I vote all them can afford it give a fippenny-bit apiece, an' say nothing about it to the boys that can't afford it. If we do, there isn't a man of them but what id want to put in his penny; and I know Rory would not like that. It wouldn't sound well, an' might be laughed at by that rich chap, Murdock. Here's my fippenny, Phil."

There was much good sense in this. It met not only the approbation of the whole deputation, but the pockets of some, and was unanimously adopted. The necessary amount of money was made up before an hour's time; and a smart fellow—the very Solon who had spoken, and who was as smart of limb as he was of mind—was despatched forthwith to C. O. S. for three yards of silk and two yards of ribbon, to match as nearly as possible Rory of the Hills' handkerchief, which was secured in the crown of his cap.

The very next afternoon—for Shanvilla did not sleep on its resolve—there was no lion in the street for them: the same deputation walked up to Rory's house at dinner-hour, when they knew he would be at home. He had just finished, and was on his way out, to continue a job of planting "a few gets" of early potatoes on the hill behind the house, when he met them near the door.

M'Dermott carried a paper parcel in his hand.

"Well, boys," said Rory, "what's the matter now? I thought we settled everything yesterday morning."

"You did, Rory *awochal;* but we had a trifle to do after we left you. I hope you done nothing about your own sleeves as yet."

"No, Phil, I did not; but never fear, I'll be up to time. But I don't wish to change the colour, if that's what brought you."

"The sorra change nor change, Rory; it is late for that now. But some of the boys heerd that Tom Murdock is givin' his men, every man of 'em, sleeves an' ribbon for this match. We don't expect the likes from you, Rory; and we don't mind that fellow's puffery and pride. We think it better that the Shanvilla boys should present their leader with one pair of sleeves than that he should give a hundred pairs to them. We have them here, Rory *awochal;* an' there isn't a boy in the parish of Shanvilla, or a man, woman, or child, that won't cheer to see you win in them."

"An' maybe some one in the parish of Rathcash," whispered Solon to Phil.

Phil M'Dermott then untied his parcel and exhibited the sleeves, finished off in the best style by his sister Peggy. What would fit Phil would fit Rory; and she was at no loss upon that point.

"Here they are, made and all, Rory. Peggy made them on my fit; and we wish you luck to win in them. Faix, if you don't, it won't be your fault nor ours. Here's your hankicher; you see there isn't the differ of a *milthiogue's* wing in the two colours."

Perhaps it was the proximity to Boher-na-milthiogue that had suggested the comparison.

"Indeed, boys, I'm entirely obliged to you, and I don't think we can fail of success. It shall not be my fault if we do, and I'm certain it won't be yours. But I'm sorry"—

"*Bidh a hurst*, Rory; don't say wan word, or I'll choke you. But thry them on."

Rory's coat was forthwith slipped off his back and thrown upon the end of a turf-stack hard by, and Phil M'Dermott drew the sleeves upon his arms, and tied them artistically over his shoulders.

"Dam' the wan, Rory, but they were med for you!" said Phil, smoothing them down towards the wrists.

"Divil a word of lie in *that*, any way, Phil," said Solon. "Tell us something we don't know."

"Well, I may tell them that you have too much wit in your head to have any room for sense," replied M'Dermott, seemingly a little annoyed at the remark.

Solon grinned, and drew in his horns.

"They are, indeed, the very thing," said Rory, turning his head from one to the other and admiring them. He could have wished, however, that it had been a Rathcash girl who had made them instead of Peggy M'Dermott. "But I cannot have everything my own way," sighed he to himself.

M'Dermott then quietly removed Rory's hat with one hand, while with the other he slily placed the silk cap jauntily upon his head. There was a general murmur of approbation at the effect, in which Rory himself could not choose but join. He felt that he was looking the thing.

After a sufficient time had been allowed for the admiration, and verdict of the committee as to their fit and appearance, Phil M'Dermott took them off again, and, folding them up carefully in the paper, handed them to Rory, wishing him on his own part, and that of the whole parish, health to wear and win in them on Patrick's day, "Every man of us will have our own colours ready the day before," he added.

Rory then thanked them heartily, and turned into the house, to show them to his father, and the deputation returned to their homes.

CHAPTER XXIII.

THE long-wished-for day, appointed for this great match, had now arrived, and there was not a man of a hundred in each parish, besides the two leading men, who had not on that morning taken his hurl from the rack before he went to prayers, inspected it, weighed it in his hand, to ascertain if the *set* lay fair to the *swipe*, as he placed it on the ground.

Two o'clock in the afternoon had been appointed for the men to be on the ground, and punctual to the moment they were seen in two compact masses beyond opposite ends of the common. They had assembled outside, and were not permitted to straggle in, in order that their approach towards each other, in two distinct bodies, amidst the inspiring cheers of their respective parties, might have the better effect. This great occasion had been talked of for weeks, and was looked upon, not only by the players themselves, and the two great men at their heads, but it might be said, by the "public at large," as the most important hurling-match which had been projected for years in that, or perhaps any other district. The friends of each party, besides hundreds of neutral spectators, had already occupied the hills round what might be called the arena.

Conspicuous at the head of the Rathcash men as they advanced with their green sleeves amidst the cheers of their friends, Tom Murdock could be seen walking with his head erect, and his hurl sloping over his shoulder. He kept his right hand disengaged that he might fulfil the usual custom of giving it to his opponent, in token of good-will, ere the game began.

He was undoubtedly a splendid handsome-looking fellow "that day." Upwards of six feet high, made in full proportion. His shirt tied at the throat with a broad green ribbon, having the collar turned down nearly to the shoulders, showed a neck of unsullied whiteness, which contrasted remarkably with the dark curled whiskers above it. His men, too, were a splendid set of fellows. Most of them were as tall and as well made as himself, and none were under five feet ten; there was not a small man among them—the picked unmarried men of the parish. Their green sleeves and bare necks, with their hurls across their left shoulders, as in the case of their leader, elicited thunders of applause from the whole population of Rathcash upon the hill to their right.

A deep ditch with a high grass bank lay between the common and the spot where Rory of the Hills and his men had assembled.

Phil M'Dermott was silent. He was not yet reconciled to the colour which their leader had chosen. Of course he could not account for it, but he did not half like it. To him it looked sombre, melancholy, and prophetic. But Phil had sense enough to assume a cheerfulness, if he did not feel it.

Rory himself, though five feet ten and a half inches high, was about the smallest man of his party. In every respect they equalled, if they did not exceed, the Rathcash men.

"Come, boys," said Rory; "Tom Murdock is bringing on his men; we'll have to jump the bank. Shall I lead the way?"

"Of course, Rory; an' bad luck to the man of the hundred will lave a toe on it!"

"No, nor a heel, Phil!" said the wit.

"Stand back, boys, about fifteen yards," said Rory. "Let me at it first; and when I am clean over, go at it as much in a line as you can. Give yourselves plenty of room, and don't crowd."

"Take your time, boys," whispered the prophet, "an' let none of us trip or fall."

"Never fear, Phil!" ran through them all in reply.

Rory then drew back a few yards; and with a light quick run he cleared the bank, giving a slight little steadying-jump on the other side, like a man who had made a summersault from a spring-board.

The Shanvilla population—the whole of which, I may say, was on the surrounding hills—rent the air with their cheers, amidst which the red-sleeves were seen clearing the bank like so many young deer. Not a mistake was made; not a man jumped low or short; not a toe was left upon it, as the prophet had said—nor a heel, as the wit had added. It was an enlivening sight to see the red-sleeves rising by turns about eight feet into the air, and landing steadily on the level sward beyond the bank.

The cheers from Shanvilla were redoubled, and even some of the Rathcash men joined.

The two parties were now closing each other in friendly approach towards the centre of the field, where they halted within about six yards of each other; Tom Murdock and Rory of the Hills a little in advance. They stepped forward, with their right hands a little extended.

"Hallo, Lennon!" said Murdock; "why, you are dressed in silk, man, and have a cap to match; I heard nothing of that. I could not afford silk, and our sleeves are plain calico."

"So are ours, and I could afford silk still less than you could; but my men presented me with these sleeves and this cap, and I shall wear them."

"Of course, of course, Lennon. But I cannot say much for the colour; blue would have looked much better—and, perhaps, have been more appropriate."

"I left that for the girls to wear in their bonnets," replied Lennon, sarcastically. He knew that Winny Cavana's holiday bonnet was trimmed with blue, and thought it not unlikely that Murdock knew it also.

They then shook hands, but it was more formal than cordial; and Murdock took a half-crown from his pocket. He was determined to be down on Rory of the Hills' poverty, for a penny would have done as well; and he said: "Shall I call, or will you?"

"The challenger generally 'skies,' and the other calls," he replied.

"Here, then!" said Murdock, standing out into a clear spot, and curling the half-crown into the air, eighteen or twenty feet above their heads.

"Head!" cried Lennon; and head it was.

It was the usual method on such occasions for the leader who won the toss to throw the ball with all his force as high into the air as possible, and, as a matter of course, as far towards his opponent's goal as he could. The height into the air was as a token to his friends to cheer, and the direction towards his opponent's goal was considered the great advantage of having won the toss.

This was, however, the first occasion in the annals of hurling where this latter point had been questioned. Rory of the Hills and Phil M'Dermott were both experienced hurlers; and previous to their having taken the high bank in such style, from the field outside the common, they had stepped aside from their men, and discussed the matter thus:

"Phil, I hope we'll win the 'toss," said Rory.

"That we may, I pray. You'll put the ball a trifle on its way if we do, Rory."

"No, Phil, that is the very point I want to settle with you. I have always remarked that when the winner of the toss throws the ball towards the other goal, it is always met by some good man, who is on the watch for it; and as none of the opposite party are allowed into their ground until 'the game is on,' he has it all to himself, and generally deals it such a swipe as puts it half-way back, over the others' heads. Now my plan is this: If I win 'the toss,' I'll throw the ball more towards our own goal than towards theirs. Let you be there, Phil, to meet it; and I have little fear that the first puck you give it will send it double as far into our opponent's ground as I could throw it with my hand. Besides, the moment the ball is up, our men can advance all over the ground, and another good man of ours may help it on. What say you, Phil?"

"Well, Rory, there's a grate dale of raison in what you say, now that I think of it; but I never seen it done that way afore."

It had been thus settled between these two best men of Shanvilla; and Rory, having won the toss,

cast his eye over his shoulder and caught a side
glance of Phil M'Dermott in position, with his hurl
poised for action.

Contrary to all experience and all expectation,
Rory of the Hills, instead of casting the ball from
him, towards the other goal, threw it as high as
possible, but unmistakably inclined towards his own.
Here there was a murmur of disappointed surprise
from Shanvilla on the hill. But it was soon explained. Phil M'Dermott had it all his own way
for the first puck, which was considered a great
object. Never had such an expedient (*nunc* dodge)
to secure it been thought of before. M'Dermott had
full room to deal with it. There was no one near
him but his own men, who stood exulting at what
they knew was about to come. M'Dermott with the
underside of his hurl rolled the ball towards him,
and curling it up into the air, about a foot above his
head, met it as it came down with a puck that was
heard all over the hills, and drove it three distances
beyond where Rory could have thrown it from his
hand. The object of the backward cast by the
leader had now been explained to the satisfaction of
Shanvilla, whose cheers of approbation loudly succeeded to their previous murmurs of surprise.

"Be gorrat they're a knowing pair," said one of
the spectators on the hill.

But I cannot attend to the game, which is now
well "on," and tell you what each party said during the struggle.

Of course the ball was met by Rathcash, and put
back; but every man was now at work as best he

might, where and when he could, but not altogether from under a certain sort of discipline and eye to their leaders. Now some fortunate young fellow got an open at the ball, and gave it a puck which sent it spinning through the crowd, until stopped by the other party. Then a close struggle and clashing of hurls, as if life and death depended on the result. Now, again, some fellow gets an open swipe at it, and puck it goes over their heads, while a rush of both parties takes place towards the probable spot it must arrive at; then another crowded struggle, and ultimately another puck, and it is seen like a cannon-ball on the strand at Sandymount. Another rush, another close struggle and clashing of hurls, and—puck—puck—now at the jaws of this goal, now at the jaws of that, while the cheers and counter-cheers re-echo through the surrounding hills.

It is needless to say that Tom Murdock and Rory of the Hills were conspicuous in all these vicissitudes of the game. No man took the ball from either of them if he was likely to get a puck at it *in time;* but no risk of a counter-puck would be run if an opponent was at hand to give it. This was the use of the distinguishing colours, and right curious it was to see the green and red sleeves twisting through each other, and rushing in groups to one spot.

After all Rory's colour "did not look so bad;" and Shanvilla held their own so gallantly as the game went on, that betting—for it was a sort of Derby-day with the parish gamblers—which was six, and even seven, to four on Rathcash at the commencement, was now even for choice. Aye, there is one red-haired fellow with a small eye and a big one, who shoves three thimbles upon a board at races, has offered five fippenny-bits to four upon Shanvilla; and well he may, for Rory and his men had got the ball amongst them, and Rory's orders were to keep it close—not to puck it at all, now that they had it, but to tip it along and keep round it in a body. This was quite fair, and would have been adopted by the other party, had they got the chance. It was like a pugilist "fibbing" his opponent's head, when he gets it under his arm.

They were thus advancing steadily but slowly. The Rathcash men were on the outside, but found it difficult, if not impossible, to enter the solid body of Shanvilla men, who were advancing with the ball in the middle of them towards Rathcash goal.

"To the front, to the front, boys, or the game is lost!" roared Tom Murdock, who was himself then watching for an open to get in at the ball.

Forthwith there was a body of the green-sleeves right before Shanvilla, who came on with their ball, tip by tip, undaunted.

Still Rathcash was on the outside, and could not put a hurl on the ball. It was a piece of generalship upon the part of the Shanvilla leader not often before thought of, and likely to be crowned with success. The cheers from Shanvilla on the hills were now deafening,—the final struggle was evidently at hand. Rathcash on the hills was silent, except a few murmurs of apprehension.

"This will never do, boys!" said Tom Murdock, rushing into the centre of Shanvilla, and endeavouring to hook the ball from amongst them; but they were too solid for that, although he had now made his way within a hurl's length of Rory.

Rory called to his men to stoop in front that he might see the goal, and judge his distance.

"A few yards farther, boys," he cried, "and then open out for me to swipe; I will not miss either the ball or the goal."

"Steady, Rory, steady a bit!" said Phil M'Dermott; "don't you see who is, I may say, alongside you? Keep it close another bit."

"In with you, men! what are you about?" roared Tom Murdock; and half a score of the green-sleeves rushed in amongst the red. Here the clashing of hurls was at its height, and the shouts from both sides on the hill were tremendous. Shanvilla kept and defended their ball in spite of every attempt of Rathcash to pick it from amongst them; but nothing like violence was thought of by either side.

Shanvilla seemed assured of victory, and such of them as were on the outside, and could not get a tip at the ball, kept brandishing their hurls in the air, roaring at the top of their voices: "Good boys, Shanvilla, good boys!" "Through with it—through with it!" "Good boys!"

Rory looked out. Though he did not see the stones, he saw the goal-masters—one red, the other green—ready expecting the final puck, and he knew the spot.

"Give me room now, Phil," he whispered; and his men drew back.

Rory curled the ball into the air about the height of his head, and struck it sure and home. As if from a cannon's mouth it went over the heads of Rathcash, Shanvilla and all, and sped right through the centre of the stones—hop—hop—hop—until it was finally lost sight of in some rushes. But another blow had been struck at the same moment, and Rory of the Hills lay senseless on the ground, his face and neck, shirt and sleeves, all the same colour, and that colour was—blood.

Tom Murdock's hurl had been poised, ready to strike the ball the moment Lennon had curled it into the air. Upon this one blow the whole game depended. Rory was rather sideways to Tom, who was on his left. Both their blows were aimed almost simultaneously at the ball, but Tom's being a second or two late, had no ball to hit; and not being able to restrain the impetus of the blow, his hurl passed on, and took Rory's head above the top of the left ear, raising a scalp of flesh to the skull-bone, about three inches in length, and more than half that breadth.

The cheers of Shanvilla were speedily quashed, and there was a rush of the red-sleeves round their leader. Phil M'Dermott had taken him in his arms, and replaced the loose piece of flesh upon Rory's skull in the most artistic manner, and bound it down with a handkerchief tied under the chin. He could see that no injury had been done to the bone. It was a mere sloping stroke, which had lifted the piece of flesh clean from the skull. But poor Rory still lay insensible, his whole face, neck, and breast covered with blood.

There was some growling amongst the Shanvilla boys, and those from the hill ran down with their sticks, to join their comrades with their hurls; while the Rathcash men closed into a compact body, beckoning to their friends on the hill, who also ran down to defend them in case of need.

This was indeed a critical moment, and one that, if not properly managed, might have led to bloodshed of a more extended kind. But Tom Murdock was equal to the occasion. He gave his hurl to one of his men the moment he had struck the blow, and went forward.

"Good Heaven, boys, I hope he is not much hurt!" he exclaimed. "Rathcash should lose a hundred games before Shanvilla should be hurt."

As he spoke he perceived a scowl of doubt and rising anger in the faces of many of the Shanvilla men, some of whom ground their teeth, and grasped their hurls tighter in their hands. Tom did not lose his presence of mind at even this, although he almost feared the result. He took Rory by the hand, and bid him speak to him. Phil M'Dermott had ordered his men to keep back the crowd to give the sufferer air. Poor Rory's own remedy in another cause had been resorted to. Phil had rubbed his lips and gums with whiskey—on this occasion it was near at hand—and poured a few thimblefuls down his throat. He soon opened his eyes, and looked round him.

"Thank God!" cried Tom Murdock. "Are you much hurt, Lennon?"

The very return to life had already quashed any cordiality towards Rory in Tom's heart.

"Not much, I hope, Tom. I was stunned; that was all. But what about the game? I thought my ear caught the cheers of victory as I fell."

"So they did, Rory," said M'Dermott; "but stop talking, I tell you. The game is ours, and it was you who won it with that last puck."

"Ay, and it was that last puck that nearly lost him his life," continued Tom, knowingly enough. "We both struck at the ball nearly at the same moment; he took it first, and my hurl had nothing to hit until it met the top of his head. I protest before Heaven, Lennon, it was entirely accidental."

"I have not accused you of it's being anything else, Murdock; don't seem to doubt yourself," said Rory, in a very low weak voice. But it was evident he was coming-to.

Still the Shanvilla men were grumbling and whispering. One of them, a big black-haired fellow named Ned Murrican, burst out at last, and brandishing his hurl over his head, cried out:

"Arrah, now, what are we about, boys! Are we going to see our best man murdered before our eyes, an' be satisfied with a piper an' a dance? I say we must have blood for blood!"

"An' why not?" said another. "It was no accident; I'm sure of that."

"What baldherdash!" cried a third! "didn't I see him aim the blow?" And the whole of Shanvilla flourished their hurls and their sticks in the air, clashing them together with the terrific noise of an onslaught.

Tom Murdock's cheeks blanched. He feared that he had opened a floodgate which he could not stop, and that if there had not been, there would soon be murder. His men stood firm in a close body, and not a word was heard to pass amongst them.

"Don't strike a blow, for the life of you, boys!" he cried, at the same time he took back his hurl from the man to whom he had given it to hold, who handed it to him, saying: "Here, Tom, you'll be apt to want this."

The Shanvilla men saw him take the hurl, and thought it an acceptance of a challenge to fight. They now began to jump off the ground, crying, "Whoop, whoop!" a sure sign of prompt action in an Irish row.

At this still more critical moment, Father Farrell, the parish-priest of Shanvilla, who had been sent for in all haste "for the man who was killed," was seen cantering across the common towards the crowd; and more fortunately still, he was accompanied by Father Roche, the parish-priest of Rathcash. They were both known at a glance; Shanvilla on his "strawberry cob," and Rathcash on his "tight little black mare."

It is needless to say that the approach of these two good men calmed to all appearance, if not in reality, the exhibition of angry feeling amongst the two parties.

"Here, your reverence," said one of the Shanvilla men to Father Farrell,—"here's where the man that was hurt is lying; poor Rory of the Hills, your reverence."

Father Farrell turned for a moment and whispered to his companion, "I'll see about the hurt man and do you try and keep the boys quiet. I can see that Shanvilla is ready for a fight. Tell them that I'll be with them in a very few minutes, if the man is not badly hurt. If he is, my friend, I'm afraid we shall have a hard task to keep Shanvilla quiet. Could you not send your men home at once?"

"I'll do what I can; but you can do more with your own men than I can. Rathcash will not strike a blow, I know, until the very last moment."

They then separated, Father Farrell dismounting, and going over to where Rory of the Hills still lay in M'Dermott's arms; and Father Roche rode up towards the Rathcash men.

"Boys," said he, addressing them, "this is a sad ending to the day's sport; but, thank God, from what I hear, the man is not much hurt. Be steady, at all events. Indeed, you had better go home at once, every man of you. Won't you take your priest's advice?"

"An' why not, your reverence? to be sure we will, if it comes to that; but, plaise God, it won't. At worst it was only an accident, an' we're tould it won't signify. We'll stan' our ground another while, your reverence, until we hear how the boy is. Sure, there's two barrels of beer an' a dance to the fore, by an' by."

"Well, lads, be very steady, and keep yourselves quiet. I'll visit the first man of you that strikes a blow with condign—"

"We'll strike no blow, your reverence, if we hant struck first. Let Father Farrell look to that."

"And so he will, you may depend upon it," said Father Roche.

The Shanvilla men had great confidence in Father Farrell in every respect, and there was not a man in the parish who would not almost die at his bidding from pure love of the man, apart from his religious influence. They knew him to be a good physician in a literal, as well as a moral, point of view; and he had been proving himself the good Samaritan for the last seventeen years to every one in the parish, whether they fell among thieves or not. He had commenced life as a medical student, but had (prudently, perhaps) preferred the Church. In memory, however, of his early predilections, he kept a sort of little private dispensary behind his kitchen; and so numerous were the cures which nature had effected under his mild advice and harmless prescriptions, that he had established a reputation for infallibility almost equal to that subsequently attained by Holloway or Morrison. Never, however, was his medical knowledge of more use as well as value than on the present occasion.

Shanville grounded their weapons at his approach, and waited for his report. Father Farrell of course first felt the young man's pulse. He was not pedantic or affected enough to hold his watch in his other hand while he did so; but like all good physicians, he held his tongue. He then untied the handkerchief and gently examined the wound so far as possible without disturbing the work which Phil M'Dermott had so promptly and judiciously performed. His last test of the state of his patient was his voice; and upon this, in his own mind, he laid no inconsiderable stress. In reply to his questions as to whether he felt sick or giddy, Rory replied, much more stoutly than was expected, that he felt neither the one nor the other. Father Farrell was now fully satisfied that there was nothing seriously wrong with him, and that giving him the rites of the Church, or even remaining longer with him then, might have an unfavourable effect upon the already excited minds of the Shanvilla men. He, therefore, said, smiling, "Thank God, Rory, you want no further doctoring just now; and I'll leave you for a few minutes while I tell Shanvilla that nothing serious has befallen you."

He then left him, and hastened over towards his parishioners, who eagerly met him half-way as he approached.

"Well, your reverence?" "Well, your reverence?" ran through the foremost of them.

"It is well, and very well, boys," he replied; "I bless God it is nothing but a scalp wound, which will not signify. Put by your hurls, and go and ask the Rathcash girls to dance."

"Three cheers for Father Farrell!" shouted Ned Murrican of the black curly head. They were given heartily, and peace was restored.

Father Farrell then remounted his strawberry

cob, and rode over towards where Father Roche was with the Rathcash men. They were, "in a manner," as anxious to hear his opinion of Rory of the Hills as his own men had been. They knew nothing; or, if they did, they cared nothing for any private cause of ill-will on their leader's part towards Rory of the Hills. They were not about to espouse his quarrel, if he had one; and, as they had said, they would not have struck a blow unless in self-defence.

Father Farrell now assured them there was nothing of any consequence "upon" Rory: it was a mere tip of the flesh, and would be quite well in a few days. "But, Tom *awochal*," he added, laughing, "you don't often aim at a crow and hit a pigeon."

"I was awkward and unfortunate enough to do so this time, Father Farrell," he replied. And he then entered into a full, and apparently a candid, detail of how it had happened.

Father Farrell listened with much attention, bowing at him now and then, like the foreman of a jury to a judge's charge, to show that he understood him. When he had ended, Father Farrell placed his hand upon his shoulder, and bending down towards him, whispered in his ear,—"O Tom Murdock, but you are the fortunate man this day! for if the blow had been one inch and a-half lower, all the priests and doctors in Connaught would not save you from being tried for manslaughter."

"Or murder," whispered Tom's heart to himself.

By this time Rory of the Hills, with M'Dermott's help, had risen to his feet; and leaning on him and big Ned Murrican, crept feebly along towards the boreen which formed the entrance to the common.

Father Farrell, perceiving the move, rode after him, and said, as he passed, that he would trot on and send for a horse and cart to fetch him home, as he would not allow him to walk any farther than the end of the lane. Indeed, it was not his intention to do so; for he was still scarcely able to stand, and that not without help.

Before he and his assistants, however, had reached the end of the lane, Father Farrell came cantering back, saying, "All right, my good lads; there is a jennet and cart coming up the lane for him."

Rory cocked his ear at the word jennet: he knew who owned the only one for miles around. And there indeed it was; and the sight of it went well-nigh to cure Rory, better than any doctoring he could get.

CHAPTER XXIV.

THE moment it had been ascertained that Rory of the Hills had been so seriously hurt, *somebody* thought—oh! the thoughtfulness of some people—that some conveyance would be required, and she was determined to take time by the forelock. Jamesy Doyle it was who had been despatched for the jennet and cart, with a token to the only servant-woman in the house to put a hair-mattress—she knew *where* to get it—over plenty of straw in the cart, and to make no delay.

Jamesy Doyle was the very fellow to make no mistake, and to do as he was bid; and sure enough there he was now, coming up the boreen with everything as correct as possible. Phil M'Dermott and Ned Murrican led poor Rory to the end of the lane just as Jamesy Doyle came up.

"This is for you, my poor fellow," said he, addressing Rory. "An' I'm to lave you every foot at your own doore—them's my ordhers from th' ould masther himsel'."

Rory was about to speak, or to endeavour to do so; but M'Dermott stopped him.

"Don't be desthroyin' yourself, Rory, strivin' to speak; but let us lift you into the cart—an' hould your tongue."

Rory of the Hills smiled; but it was a happy smile.

Of course there was a crowd round him; and many a whispered observation passed through them as poor Rory was lifted in, fixed in a reclining position, and Jamesy Doyle desired to "go on," while Phil M'Dermott and big Ned Murrican gave him an escort, walking one on each side.

"It was herself sent Jamesy Doyle for the jinnet, Judy; I heerd her tellin' him to put plenty of straw into the cart."

"Aye, Peggy, an' I heerd her tellin' him to get a hair-matt*rass*, an' put it a top of it. Isn't it well for the likes of her that has hair-matt*rass*es to spare?"

"Aye, Nelly Gaffeny, an' didn't I hear her tellin' him to dhrive for his life?"

"In troth an' you didn't, Nancy; what she said was, 'to make no delay;' wasn't I as near her as I am to you this minute?"

"Whist, girls!" broke in (as Lever would say) a sensible old woman,—"it was ould Ned Cavana himself sent Jamesy off; wasn't I lookin' at him givin' him the kay of the barn to get the sthraw? Dear me, how pleasant ye all are!"

"Thrue for you, Katty avrone; but wasn't it Winny that put him up to it, an' the tears coming up in her eyes as she axed him? an' be the same token, the hankicher she had in her hand was for all the world the very colour of Rory of the Hill's cap an' sleeves."

There was a good deal of truth, but some exaggeration in the above gossip.

It was old Ned Cavana himself who had despatched Jamesy Doyle for the jennet and cart, and he had also given him the key of the barn—old Katty was quite right so far.

Now let it be known that there was not a man in the parish of Rathcash who was the owner of a horse and cart, who would not have cheerfully sent for it to bring Rory of the Hills home, when the proper time arrived to do so—and Winny Cavana knew that; she knew that her father would be all life for the purpose, the moment it was mentioned to him; and she was determined that her father should be "first in the field." There was nothing extraordinary in the fact itself; it was the relative positions of the parties that rendered it food for the gossip which we have been listening to. But old Ned never thought of the gossip in his willingness to serve a neighbour. Winny had thought of it, but braved it, rather than lose the chance. It was she who had suggested to her father to send Jamesy for the jennet, and to give him the key of the barn where the *dry* straw was. If the gossips had known this little turn of the transaction, doubtless it would not have escaped their comments.

But we must return to the common, and see how matters are going on there.

Tom Murdock had witnessed from no great distance the arrival of the jennet and cart; and of course he knew them. He did not know, however, that it was Winny Cavana who had sent for them—he only guessed that. He saw "that —— whelp" —he put this shameful addition to it in his anger— lifted into it; and if he had a regret as to the accident, it was that the blow had not been the inch-and-a-half lower which Father Farrell had blessed his stars had not been the case. This was the second time his eyes had seen the preference he had always dreaded. He had not forgotten the scene with the dog on the road. He had not been so far that he could not see, nor so careless that he did not remark, the handkerchief; nor was he so stupid as not to divine the purport of the amicable little battle which apparently took place between them about it. The colour of Lennon's cap and sleeves now also recurred to his mind, and jealousy suggested that it was *she* who made them.

But his business was by no means finished on the common. He could not, as it were, abscond, deserting his friends; and ill as his humour was for what was before him, he must go through with it. It would help to keep him from thinking for a while, at all events. Besides, the sooner he saw Winny Cavana now, the better. He would explain the accident to her as if it had happened to any other person, not as to one in whom he believed there was a particular interest on her part. To be silent on the subject altogether, he felt would betray the very thing he wished to avoid.

The hurling-match over, it had been arranged that the evening should conclude with a dance, to crown the amicable feelings with which the two contending parishes had met in the strife of hurls. The boys and girls of Rathcash and Shanvilla, whichever side won, were to mingle in the mazy dance, to the enlivening lilts of blind Murrin the piper, who, as he could not see the game, had been the whole afternoon squealing, and droning, and hopping the brass end of his pipes upon a square polished-leather patch, stitched upon the knee of his breeches.

There now appeared to be some sort of a hitch as to the dance coming off at all, in consequence of the "untoward event" which had already considerably marred the harmony of the meeting; for it would be idle to deny that dissatisfaction and doubt still lingered in the hearts of Shanvilla. Both sides had brought a barrel of beer for the occasion, which by this time it was almost necessary to put upon "the stoop;" Tom Murdock superintending the distribution of that from Rathcash, and a brother of big Ned Murrican's that from Shanvilla.

Blind Murrin heard some of the talk which was passing round him about the postponement of the dance. Like all blind pipers he was sharp of hearing, and somewhat cranky, if put at all out of tune.

"Arra, what would they put it off for?" said he, *looking* up, and closing his elbow on the bellows to silence the pipes. "Is it because wan man got a cut on the head? I heerd Father Farrell say there wouldn't be a haporth on him agen Sunda' eight days; an' I heerd him, more be token, tellin' the boys to go an' ask the Rathcash girls to dance. Arra, what do ye mane? Isn't the counthry gotthered now; an' the day as fine as summer, an' the grass brave an' dhry, an' lashin's of beer at both sides, an' didn't I come eleven miles this mornin' a purpose, an' what the diowl would they go an' put off the dance for? Do you mane to say they're *onshioughs* or *aumadhawns*, or—what?"

"No, Billy," said a Shanvilla girl, with good legs, neat feet, black boots, and stockings as white as snow,—"no, Billy; but neither the Shanvilla boys nor girls have any heart to dance, after Rory of the Hills bein' kilt an' sent home."

"There won't be a haporth on him, I tell you, agen Sunda'. Didn't I hear Father Farrell say so, over an' over again? arra *badhershin*, Kitty, to be sure they'll dance!"

While blind Murrin was "letting off" thus, Phil M'Dermott was seen returning by a short cut across the fields towards them.

"Here's news of Rory, any way; he's aither

better or worse," continued Kitty Reilly; and some dread that it was unfavourable crept through the Shanvillas.

"Well, Phil, how is he? well, Phil, how is he?" greeted M'Dermott from several quarters as he came up.

"All right, girls. He's much better, and he sent me back for fear I'd lose the first dance—for he knew I was engaged;" and he winked at a very pretty Rathcash girl with soft blue eyes and bright auburn hair, who was not far off.

"Arra, didn't I know they'd dance?" said Murrin, giving two or three dumb squeezes with his elbow before the music came, like the three or four first pulls at a pump before the water flows.

It then ran like lightning through the crowd that the dance was going to begin, and old Murrin blew up in earnest at the top of his power. He had, with the help of some of the best dancers amongst the girls on both sides, selected that spot for the purpose, before the game had commenced; and he had kept his ground patiently all through, playing all the planxties in Carolan's catalogue. But not without wetting his whistle; for as he belonged to neither party, he had been supplied with beer alternately by both.

Phil M'Dermott whispered a few words to the pretty Rathcash girl, and left her apparently in haste. But she was "heerd" by one of our gossips to say, "Of course, Phil; but I will not say 'with all my heart;' sure, it is only a pleasure postponed for a little,—now mind, Phil."

"Never fear, Sally." And he was off through the crowd, with his head up.

Phil's expedition was to look for Winny Cavana, to whom Rory of the Hills had been engaged for the first dance; and as he knew where the bonnet trimmed with broad blue ribbon could be seen all day, he made for the spot. As he came within a few perches of it, he saw Tom Murdock in seemingly earnest conversation with the object of his search, and he hung back for a few minutes unperceived.

Tom Murdock, we have seen, was not a man to be easily taken aback by circumstances, or to stand self-accused by any apparent consciousness of guilt. Guilty or not, he always braved the matter out, whatever it might be, as an innocent man would, and ought. As the dance was now about to begin, and old Murrin's pipes were getting loud and impatient, Tom made up to Winny. He had watched an opportunity when she was partly disengaged from those around her; and indeed, to do them justice, they "made themselves scarce" as he approached.

"They are going to dance, Winny; will you allow me to lead you out?" he said.

Winny had been pondering in her own mind the possibility of what had now taken place; and after turning and twisting her answer into twenty different shapes, had selected one as the safest and best she could give, with a decided refusal. Now, when the anticipated moment had arrived, and she was obliged to speak, she was almost dumb. Not a single word of any one of the replies she had shaped out—and least of all the one she had rehearsed so often as the best—came to her aid.

"Will you not even answer me, Winny?" he added, after an unusually long pause.

"I heard," she said hesitatingly, "that as a proof of the good-will which was supposed to exist between the parishes, that the Rathcash men were to ask the Shanvilla girls, and Shanvilla the Rathcash."

"That may be carried out too; but surely such an arrangement is not to prohibit a person from the privilege of asking a near neighbour."

"No; but you had better begin, as leader, by setting the example yourself. You were head of the Rathcash men all day, and they will be likely to take pattern by you."

"Well, I shall *begin* so, Winny; but say that you will dance with me by and by."

"No, Tom, I shall not say any such thing, for I do not intend to do so. I don't think I shall dance at all; but if I do, it shall be but once,—and that with a Shanvilla man."

"Do you mean to say, Winny, that you came here to-day intending to dance but once?"

"I mean to say," she replied rather haughtily, "that you have no right to do more than ask me to dance. That is a right I can no more deny you than you can deny me the right to refuse. But you have no right to cross-question me."

"If," he continued, "it is in consequence of that unfortunate accident, I protest—"

"Here, father," said Winny, interrupting him

and turning from him; "shall we go up towards the piper? I see they are at it."

Tom stood disconcerted, as if riveted to the spot; and as old Ned and his daughter walked away, he saw Phil M'Dermott come towards them. He watched, and saw them enter into conversation.

The first question old Ned asked, knowing that Phil had gone a piece of the way home with him, was of course to know how Rory was.

"So much better," said Phil, "that he had a mind to come back in the cart an' look on at the dancin'; but of course we would not let him do so foolish a turn. He then sent me back, afeard Miss Winny here would be engaged afore I got as far as her. He tould me, Miss Winny, that he was to take you out for the first dance yourself; an' although Phil M'Dermott is a poor excuse for Rory of the Hills in a dance, or anywhere else, for that matther, I hope, Miss Winny, you will dance with me."

"*Ceade mille a faltha*, Phil, for your own sake as well as for his," said Winny, putting her arm through his, and walking up to where they were " at it," as she had said.

Tom Murdock had kept his eye upon her, and had seen this transaction. Winny, although she did not know it, felt conscious that he was watching her; and it was with a sort of savage triumph she had thrust her arm through Phil M'Dermott's, and walked off with him.

"Surely," said Tom to himself, "it is not possible that she's going to dance with Phil M'Dermott, the greatest clout of a fellow in all Shanvilla,—and that's a bold word. Nothing but a bellows-blower to his father—a common nailor at the cross-roads. Thank God, I put Rory, as she calls him, from dancing with her, any way. He would be bad enough; but he is always clean at all events, that's one thing—*neen han an shin*. See! by the devil, there she's out with him, sure enough. I think the girl is mad."

Now Tom Murdock's ill-humour and vexation had led him, though only to himself, to give an underestimate of Phil M'Dermott in more respects than one. In the first place, Phil's father, so far from being a common nailor, was a most excellent smith of all work. He made ploughs, harrows, and all sorts of machinery, and was unequivocally the best horse-shoer in the whole country. People were in the habit of sending their horses five, aye ten, miles to Bryan M'Dermott's forge,—" establishment" it might almost be called,—and Tom Murdock himself, when he kept the race-mare, had sent her past half-a-dozen forges to get her "properly fitted" at Phil M'Dermott's.

Phil himself had served his time to his father, and was no less an adept in all matters belonging to his trade; and as to "driving a nail," there never was a man wore an apron could put on a shoe so safely. A nail, too, except for the above purpose, was never made in their forge. If sometimes Phil threw up his bare hairy arm to pull down the handle of the bellows, it was only what his father himself would do, if the regular blower was out of the way.

In fact, "Bryan M'Dermott and Son, Smiths," might have very justly figured over their forge-door; but they were so well known, that a signboard of any kind was superfluous.

Then as to being a *clout*, Phil was the very farthest from it in the world, if it can have any meaning with reference to a man at all. There are *nails* called *clouts;* and perhaps as a nailor was uppermost in Tom's cantankerous mind, it had suggested the epithet.

We have now only to deal with the dirt—the *neen han an shin* of his spite.

That Phil M'Dermott was very often dirty was the necessary result of his calling, at which the excellence of his knowledge kept him constantly employed. But on this occasion, as on all Sundays and holidays, Phil M'Dermott's person could vie with even Tom Murdock's, "or any other man's," in scrupulous cleanliness. Now indeed if there were some streaks and blotches of blood upon the breast of his shirt, he might thank Tom Murdock's handiwork for that same.

Such as he was, however, bloody shirt and all, Winny Cavana went out to dance with him before the whole assembly of Rathcash boys, speckless as they were.

Kate Mulvey had been endeavouring to carry on her own tactics privately all the morning, and had refused two or three Shanvilla boys, saying that she heard there would be no dance, but that if there was, she would dance with them before it was over. She now *accidentally* stood not very far from where

Tom had been snubbed and turned away from by her bosom friend, Winny Cavana. Tom Murdock saw her, and saw that she was alone as far as a partner was concerned.

Determined to let Winny see that there were "as good fish in the sea as ever were caught," and that she had not the power to upset his enjoyment, Tom made up to Kate, and assuming the most amiable smile which the wicked confusion of his mind permitted, he asked her to dance.

"How is it that you are not dancing, Kate? Will you allow me to lead you out?"

"I would, Tom, with the greatest possible pleasure; but I heard the Rathcash boys were to dance with the Shanvilla girls, and so by the others with Rathcash girls."

"That's the old story, Kate. It was thrown up to me just now; but there is no such restriction upon any of us at either side. And I'll tell you what it is, Kate Mulvey,—not a Shanvilla girl I'll dance with this day, if I never struck a foot under me!"

Kate was not sorry to find him in this humour. If she could soothe round his feelings on her own account now, all would be right. Under any phase of beauty, Kate's expression of countenance was more amiable than Winny Cavana's, although perhaps not so regularly handsome, and she felt that she was now looking her best.

"Fie, fie, Tom; you should not let that little accident put you through other like that, to be making you angry. I heard that was the rule; and I refused

o

a couple of the Rathcash boys. But if you tell me there is no such rule, sure I'll go out with you, Tom, afore any man in the parish."

"Thank you, Kate; and if you wish to know the truth, there's not a girl in Rathcash, or Shanvilla either, that I'd so soon dance with."

"Ah! *na boklish*, Tom; you'll hardly make me b'lieve that."

"Time will tell, Kate dear," said he; and he led her to the ring.

Kate made herself as agreeable as possible; amiable she always was. She rallied her partner upon his ill-humour. "It is a great shame for you, Tom," she said, "to let trifles annoy you—"

"They are not trifles, Kate."

"The way you do, where you have so much to make you happy; plenty of money and property, and everybody fond of you."

"No, not everybody."

"And you can do just as you like."

"No, I can't."

"And there won't be a pin's-worth the matter with young Lennon in a few days; and sure, Tom, everyone knows it was an accident."

"No, not *every* one," thought Tom to himself. The other interruptions were aloud to Kate; but she kept never minding him, and finished what she had to say.

"It is not that all out, Kate," said Tom.

"Oh! I see. I suppose Winny has vexed you; I saw her laying down the law."

"She'd vex a saint, Kate."

"Faix, an' you're not one, Tom, I'm afeerd."

"Nor never will, *I'm afeerd*," said he, forgetting his manners, and pronouncing the last word as she had done, although he knew better.

She saw he was greatly vexed, but she did not mind it.

"If I were you, Tom," she continued, "I would not be losing my time and my thoughts on the likes of her."

This last expression was not very complimentary to her friend; but Kate knew she would excuse it (for she intended to tell her), as it was only helping her out.

"You are her bosom friend, Kate," he went on, "and could tell me a great deal about her, if you liked."

"I don't like, then; and the sorra word I'll tell you, Tom. If you're not able to find out all you want yourself, what good's in you?"

"Well, keep it to yourself, Kate; I think I know enough about her already."

"See that, now; an' you strivin' to pick more out of me! This much I'll tell you, any way, for you're apt to find it out yourself,—that she's as stubborn a lass as any in the province of Connaught. What she says she won't do, she *won't*."

"And what I say I will do, I *will;* and I'll take that one's pride down a peg or two, as sure as my name is Tom Murdock, and that before Easter Monday."

"Whist, Tom agra; she's not worth putting yourself in a passion about; and she's likely enough to bring her own pride low enough. But betune you an' me, I don't think she has very much. Whisper me this, Tom; did she ever let on to you?"

"Never, Kate; I won't belie her."

"Answer me another question now, Tom; did she ever do th'other thing?"

"You are sifting me very close, Kate. Do you mean, did she ever refuse me?"

"I do just; and what I'm saying to you, Tom, is for your good. I'm afeer'd its for her money you care, and not much for herself. Now, Thomas Murdock, I always thought, an' more than myself thought the same thing, that the joining of them two farms in holy wedlock was a bad plan, and that *one* of you would find it a dear bargain in the end."

"Which of us, Kate?"

"Not a word you'll tell Tom, avic. There's the floore idle; come out for another dance;" and she gave him one of her most beautiful looks. He was glad, however, that her volubility prevented her from observing that he had not answered her *other* question.

Kate succeeded during this second dance in putting Tom into somewhat better humour with himself. He had never thought her so handsome before, nor had he until now even drawn a comparison between herself and Winny Cavana, as to beauty of either face or figure, neither of which it now struck him were much, if at all, inferior to that celebrated beauty; and he certainly never found her so agreeable. He listened with a new pleasure to her full rich voice, and looked occasionally, unperceived (as he thought), into her soft swimming eyes, and were it not for pure spite towards "that whelp, Lennon," and indeed towards that "proud hussy" Winny Cavana herself, he would, after that second dance, have transferred his whole mind and body to the said Kate Mulvey on the spot. He considered at all events that he had Kate Mulvey hooked, however slightly it might be. But he would play her gently, not handle her too roughly, and thus keep her on his line in case he might find it desirable to put the landing-net under her at any time. He never thought she was so fine a girl.

But then he thought again: to be cut out, and hunted out of the field with all his money, by such a fellow as that, a common day-labourer, was what he could not reconcile himself to. As for any real love for Winny Cavana, if it had ever existed in his heart towards her, it had that day been crushed, and for ever; yet, notwithstanding the favourable circumstances for its growth, it had not yet sprung up for another. A firm resolve, then, to see his spite out, at any cost to himself, to her, and to "that whelp," was the final determination of his heart after the day closed.

Winny Cavana, having danced with Phil M'Dermott until they were both tired, sat down beside her father on a *furrum*. Several of the Shanvilla, and some of the Rathcash boys "made up" to her, but she refused to dance any more, pleading fatigue, which by-the-by none of them believed, for it was not easy to tire the same Winny Cavana dancing. After sitting some time to cool, and look on at the neighbours "footing it," she proposed to her father to go home; and he, poor old man, thought "it was an angel spoke." He would have proposed it to Winny himself long before, but that he did not wish to interfere with her enjoyment. He thought she would have danced more, but was now glad of the reprieve; for to say the truth, it was one to him. He, and Winny, and Bully-dhu, who had been curled up at his feet all day, then stood up, and went down the boreen together; Bully careering and barking round them with his usual activity.

We need not remain much longer at the dance ourselves. In another half hour it was "getting late," the beer was all out, Murrin's pipes were getting confused, and Rathcash and Shanvilla were seen straggling over the hills in twos and threes and small parties towards their respective homes.

We cannot do better than end this chapter with a hearty Irish wish—"God send them safe!"

CHAPTER XXV.

THIS great hurling-match, although much spoken of before it came off, was so universally believed to be a mere amicable, a *bonâ-fide* piece of holiday recreation, and not an ostensible excuse for the ulterior purposes of Ribbonism, or a fight, that no precautions had been deemed necessary by the police to detect the one, or to prevent the other. The sub-inspector (then called chief-constable) had merely reported the fact that it would take place to the *resident* magistrate—*lucos à non*. But "in the absence of sworn informations" of an intended row, he would neither attend himself, nor give orders for the police to do so, leaving the responsibility, if such existed, entirely to the judgment and discretion of the chief in question; who, wishing to enjoy the day otherwise himself, was satisfied with the report he had made, and did not interfere by his own presence or that of his men with the game. Thus, as "in the absence of sworn informations" the resident magistrate would not attend, and in the absence of the resident magistrate the chief would not attend, Rathcash and Shanvilla had it all to themselves. Perhaps it was so best for the *dénouement* of this story; for had the police been present, the whole thing from that point might have ended very differently.

But although it had not been thought necessary that a police-party should put a stop to the day's sport on the common, it is not to be supposed that they could hear of a man "having been murdered" on the occasion, without being instantly all zeal and activity. Like the three black crows, the real fact had been exaggerated, and so distorted as to frighten both the chief and the resident magistrate, but principally the latter, as the intended assembly had been reported to him. However, "better late than never." They heard that the man was not yet dead, and away they started on the same jarvey, to visit him, on the morning after the occurrence.

Their whole discussion during the drive—if an explanation by the magistrate could be called a discussion—was on the safest and the most legal method of taking a dying man's depositions, and wondering if he knew who struck the fatal blow in this instance, and if the police had him in custody, &c.

They soon arrived at the house, but saw no sign of a crowd, or of police, whom the chief would have backed at any odds to have met on the road with a prisoner.

"Is he still alive?" whispered the resident magistrate to the father, who came to the door.

"Oh! yes, your honour, blessed be God! an' will soon be as well as ever," he replied. "It was a mere scratch, an' there won't be a haporth on him in a day or two. He wanted to go back to look at them dancin', but I kep' him lying on the bed."

"Does he know you?" said the magistrate, believing that the man wanted to make light of it, as is generally the case.

"Does he know me, is it? athen why wouldn't he know his own father?"

"Oh! he is sensible, then."

"Arrah, why wouldn't he be sensible? the boy was never anything else."

"That's right. Does he know who struck the blow?"

"Ochone, doesn't everyone know that, your honour? Sure, wasn't it Tom Murdock? an' isn't his heart bruck about it?"

Here the constable and two men of the nearest police-station came up at "the double," wiping their faces, to make inquiries for report; so that they were not so remiss after all, for it was still early in the morning.

Old Lennon was annoyed at all this parade and show about the place, and continued:—"Athen, your honour, what do ye's all want here, an' these gentlemen?" inclining his head towards the police; "sure there's nothing the matther."

"We heard the man was killed," said the chief.

"And we heard the same thing not an hour ago," said the constable.

"Arrah, God give ye sinse, gentlemen! Go home, an' don't be making a show of our little place. I tell you there's not a pin's-worth upon the boy, and the tip he did get was all accidents."

"I must see him, nevertheless, my good man; and you need not be uncivil, at all events."

"I ax your honour's pardon; I didn't mane it. To be sure you can see him; but there's no harm done, and what harm was done was an accident. Sure Rory will tell you the whole thing how it was himself."

"That is the very thing I want. Let me see him."

Lennon then led the way into the room where Rory was sitting up in the bed; for he had heard the buzz of the discussion outside, and caught some of its meaning.

Lennon took care "to draw" the police into the kitchen; for there was nothing annoyed him more—and that he knew would annoy his son—than that they should be seen about the place. He had taken his cue from Rory, who did not wish the matter to be made a blowing-horn of.

A very few words with the young man sufficed to show the magistrate and the chief that their discussion upon the subject of taking a dying man's depositions had been unnecessary in this instance, however profitable it might prove on some future occasion. Rory, except that his head was still tied with a handkerchief, showed no symptom whatever of having received an injury. He cheerfully explained how the matter had happened, untied the handkerchief promptly at the request of the magistrate, and showed him "the tip," as he called it, he had received from Tom Murdock's hurl. There was no mystery or hesitation in Rory's manner of describing the matter. Murdock himself had been the very first to admit and to apologise for the accident; and they did not wish that any fuss should be made about it. As to prosecuting him for the blow—which had been casually asked—he might as well think of prosecuting a man who had accidentally jostled him in the street.

All this was a great relief to the magistrate, who at once took the sensible view of the case, and said he was delighted to find that the whole matter had been exaggerated both as to facts and extent, and congratulated both himself and the police upon this happy termination to their zeal.

The magistrate then spoke of the propriety of "the doctor" seeing young Lennon, saying that these sort of "tips" sometimes required medical care, and occasionally turned out more serious than might at first be anticipated. But Rory told him that Father Farrell, who was an experienced doctor himself, had examined the wound, and declared that it would not signify.

The fact was that the magistrate, in his justifiable fright, had on the first report of the "murder" sent off four miles for the dispensary doctor, in case "the man might not be yet dead," and he expected his arrival every moment, as the point at which his valuable aid would be required was plainly to be explained to him by the messenger.

Finding that matters were much less serious than rumour had made them, and perceiving that the Lennons were far from gratified at the exhibition already made, he was not anxious that it should appear he had sent for the doctor to raise, as it were, young Lennon from the dead. He was therefore determined to watch his approach, and to pretend he was passing by on other business, and that it was as well to bring him in. But the doctor had not been at home when the messenger called; he had been at a *real* case—not of murder, but of birth; and the magistrate and chief could not now await his arrival without awkwardness for the delay.

The magistrate was annoyed; but the chief soon set him to rights by telling him that the doctor could not come there except by the road by which they should go home, and that if on his way they must meet him. And so they did—*powdhering* on his pony, truly as if for life or death.

"I suppose it is all over, and that I am late," he said, pulling up.

"No, you are time enough," said the chief. "It is nothing but a scratch, and was a mere accident."

"And there is nothing then for me to do," said the doctor.

"Nothing but to go '*bock again*,' like the Scotchman."

"No trepanning, nor 'post-mortem,' doctor," added the R. M. He was a droll fellow was the R. M.

It was a great satisfaction to each of these officials, as they secretly considered their positions in this affair, that no person had been seriously hurt, and that the slight injury which had really taken place was entirely accidental. The R. M. felt relieved upon the grounds that the intended assembly had been officially reported to him, and that he had declined to attend, or to give any directions to the chief to use any precautions to preserve the peace. But then he reconciled himself with the burden of his excuse upon all such occasions, that, "in the absence of sworn informations," he would have been safe under any circumstances. Still he was better pleased as it was.

The chief was relieved, because he had some idea that merely having reported the intended assembly to the resident magistrate might have been deemed insufficient, had a real homicide taken place; and that he should upon his own responsibility have had a party of police in attendance. These officials were therefore both ready to accept, without much suspicion, the statement of young Lennon, that the blow was purely accidental, and that the consequence would be of a trifling nature. But they were "dark" to each other as to the grounds upon which their satisfaction rested.

The doctor, finding that there was no chance of

earning a fee from the coroner, turned his horse's head round, and followed the car at a much easier pace than he had met it. He of all the officials—for he was constab. doc.—was least gratified with the favourable position of affairs. He had not only started without his own breakfast, but had brought his horse out without a feed; and they had galloped four miles upon two empty stomachs. No wonder that he was dissatisfied as compared with the magistrate and the chief. But we must recollect that there was no responsibility upon him, beyond his skill, involved in the affair: with its origin, or the fact of its having been permitted to occur at all, he had nothing to do. There were therefore no points of congratulation for him to muse upon, and he was vexed accordingly. From his experience of himself in the treatment of broken heads in the district, he had no doubt that his attendance would have "ended in recovery," and that at least three pounds would have come down, "approved" by the government upon the chief's report, which would be much better than the coroner's one-pound note. The disappointment had completely taken away his own hunger, but he forgot that his horse did not understand these things, so he grumbled slowly home.

A contemplative silence of some minutes ensued between the two executives on the car, which was ultimately broken by the magistrate. He, like the doctor, had had no breakfast, so certain was he of a murder; but the whole thing being a bottle of smoke, he was now both hungry and cross. It was the chief's car they were on, and he was driving,—the

R. M. "knocked that much out of him, at all events,"—so there was no driver to damp the familiarity of conversation.

"It was fortunate for you, my young friend, that nothing more serious occurred at this same hurling-match," said the magistrate.

(Certainly he was no prig in his choice of language. He was of course much older than the chief, and considered that he could carry a high hand with "a mere boy" without any experience.)

"I am extremely glad," replied the chief, "for *both* our sakes, that it was a mere trifle and an accident."

"For both our sakes! Oh! you know, my dear young friend, that, in the absence of sworn informations, I was not concerned in the matter at all. I conceive that the whole responsibility—if there be any—in a mere casual meeting of the kind, where there is admittedly no apprehension of a breach of the peace, rests entirely upon your own judgment and discretion. To be plain with you, except where a breach of the peace may be fairly anticipated, and sworn informations lodged to that effect, I do not think the magistrate's time should be interfered with. I might have lost a petty-sessions to-day, inquiring into a mere accident."

"But it might not have been one; and we could not have known until we saw the injured man and made inquiries. But the absence of sworn informations, and the fact that there was no apprehension of a row, would have exonerated me from all blame as well as you. Besides, I so far took the precaution of reporting the intended assembly to you, with its professed object, and I took your instructions upon the subject."

"No, you didn't; for I did not give you any."

"Well, I reported the meeting to you, and asked for instructions."

"That is the very thing which I object to—making reports without sufficient grounds. I should decline to act again under similar circumstances."

"That you would do so, I have no doubt; but that you *should* do so, I have some."

"I am right, young sir, as well in my grammar as in my view of the case; *ought* is the word you *should* have used, to have properly expressed what you intended."

The chief was nettled. He was not quite certain that the R. M. was not right, and merely replied:

"Perhaps so, sir; but it really was not of *Lindley Murray* I was thinking at the time."

The magistrate was softened. He felt that he had been sparring rather sharply with a lad not much more than one-third of his age.

"Well, I really beg your pardon," he said; "I did not intend to be so sharp."

"Granted," said the chief, laughing; for he was not an ill-tempered fellow. "But here we are at my box; come in and have some breakfast, and I'll drive you to petty-sessions after."

"Thank you very much. I'll take breakfast; for I came away in a horrid fuss without saying a word as to when I should be back again. I will not trespass upon you, however, to do more than you have already done in the driving way. I had some fears when we started that we should have breakfasted at dinner, some time this evening, after a coroner's inquest. But this is better."

They then gave "the trap" to the "private orderly," and proceeded to punish the tea, toast, eggs, and cold ham in a most exemplary manner.

CHAPTER XXVI.

Young Lennon's wound was neither so slight nor so insignificant as had at first been supposed. At least it did not mend as rapidly as Father Farrell had prognosticated. As long as the wound was fresh he did not feel much inconvenience from it; but each day it became sorer and more sore, accompanied by a sort of confused recollection of the exact manner in which it had occurred; and he began to fear that it *would* signify. The police-constable had received private instructions from the chief, as quietly as possible, without making any fuss about it, to find out how young Lennon was going on; for even in his short experience he had already known "a mere tip" of the kind to have ended most seriously. The constable reported on the fifth day that young Lennon, believing himself to be much better, had gone out to assist his father in planting some potatoes on the hill behind his house, and that he had fallen forward on his face, and was obliged to return to his bed again, and was much worse; that he could not recollect a word of what had taken place; that Father Farrell had heard of it, and had been to see him, but that he, the constable, had not seen Father Farrell since.

The chief was well aware of the reputation which the priest had obtained through the parish for medical skill, and was himself convinced of how well he deserved it. Indeed, had the alternative rested in any case between Father Farrell and the dispensary doctor, there was not a parishioner who would not have preferred his pastor's medical as well as spiritual aid.

The chief, therefore, instead of ordering off the dispensary doctor to see young Lennon upon this rumour of the constable, who had not heard it from any of the family, went quietly to Father Farrell, who must know the truth, and be able to give good advice as to what steps, if any, were necessary to adopt.

The matter turned out to be another black-crow story. Father Farrell had also heard it in its exaggerated form, and had not lost a moment in proceeding to the spot. Young Lennon had gone out to assist his father in planting some potatoes— so far the rumour was correct. But he had been premature in his own opinion of his convalescence. The very first stoop he made he felt quite giddy; and although he did not fall forward on his face, he was obliged to lean upon his father for support for a few moments. This little experiment served to keep him quiet for a while longer; but Father Farrell assured the chief that matters were no worse than they had been—he might make his mind easy;

there was no injury beyond the flesh, which, of course, had become much sorer, and must do so for a few days still. He had given young Lennon strict orders to remain quiet for some days, and not again expose himself to labour before he was perfectly recovered.

The chief, however, suggested the prudence, if not the necessity, of having a medical man to see him. "Not," said he, "but that I have as much, if not more, confidence in your own skill and experience than in any which is available in this wild district."

"That is rather an equivocal compliment; but perhaps it is fully as much as I deserve," said the priest.

"Well, I don't mean it as such, Father Farrell; but you know a great responsibility would rest upon me, should anything unfortunate occur."

"I see. It would not do in a court of justice to put a priest upon the table in a medical position. I certainly could not produce a diploma. You are quite right, my dear sir; you would be held responsible. However, I can go the length to assure you that at present there is not the slightest necessity for medical aid, particularly—between you and me—under existing circumstances, which I understand very well. Call in the dispensary doctor now, and what will be the result? Why he will make a fortnight or three weeks' 'constant attendance indispensably necessary;' at the end of which time the young man will not be better, if he be as well as he is this moment. Of course the doctor must make out a case for compensation, and for which you yourself will be obliged to certify,—sure I understand these things very well, my dear sir. Then look further into the thing in this light. The matter was a mere accident I am fully persuaded. But, supposing for a moment that it was not, I know young Lennon since he was a child running to school in his bare feet, with 'his turf and his read-a-ma-daisy;' and I am convinced that no power on earth would induce him to prosecute Tom Murdock."

"Why, are they such friends?"

"No; quite the reverse, and that is the very reason. But ask me no more about it. Another objection I see to calling in the dispensary doctor is this—that I am aware of an ill-feeling existing between him and Tom Murdock about a prize at a coursing-match, which the doctor thinks was unfairly given to Tom Murdock through his influence with the judge; and the doctor was heard to say in reference to it, 'that it was a long lane that had no turning.' Now here would be an open for the doctor to put a turn on the lane, however straight it might be in fact. He would not certify that Lennon's life was out of danger,—you would have to arrest Tom Murdock; young Lennon would go distracted, and the two parishes would be in an uproar. Ill-will would be engendered between all the young men of opposite sides, and all for nothing; for young Lennon will be as well as ever he was in ten days. These are my views of the case. But if your official responsibility obliges you to differ with me, I am ready to hear you further."

This was a great oration of Father Farrell's, but it was both sensible and true from beginning to end, and it convinced the chief of the propriety of "resting on his oars" for a few days longer at all events.

The result proved at least that there was more luck in leisure than danger in delay. Rory of the Hills grew better, but it was by degrees. He could not yet venture to attend to his usual daily labour by which he so materially contributed to the support of the family. The weather was fine, and "the spring business" was going forward rapidly in all directions. Poor Rory fretted that he was not able to add his accustomed portion to the weekly earnings; but Father Farrell watched him too closely. Once or twice he stole out to do some of their own work, and let his father earn some of the high wages which was just then to be had; but his own good sense told him that he was still unable for the effort. At the end of an hour's work the old idea haunted him that an attempt had been made to murder him, and if he had been made a merchant-prince for it, he could not recollect how it had happened. The only thing he did recollect distinctly about it was, that Shanvilla won the day, and that he had been sent home in Winny Cavana's cart and jennet—*that*, if he were in a raging fever, he could never forget.

But it was a sad loss to the family, Rory's incapacity to work. He had been now three weeks ill; and although the wound in his head was in a fair way of being healed, there was still a confused idea in his mind about the whole affair which he could not get rid of. At times, as he endeavoured to review the matter as it had actually occurred, he could not persuade himself but that it was really an accident; and while under this impression he felt quite well, and able for his ordinary labour. But there were moments when a sudden thought would cross his mind that it had been a secret and premeditated attempt upon his life; and then it was that the confusion ensued which rendered him unable to recollect. What if it were really this attempt— supposing that positive proof could be adduced of the fact—what then? Would he prosecute Tom Murdock? Oh! no. Father Farrell was right; but he had not formed his opinion upon the true foundation. Rory of the Hills would not prosecute, even if he could do so to conviction. He would deal with Tom Murdock himself if ever a fair opportunity should arise; and if not, he might yet be in a position more thoroughly to despise him.

In the mean time Lennon's family had not been improving in circumstances. Rory was losing all the high wages of the spring's work. Upon one or two occasions, when he stealthily endeavoured to do a little on his own land, while his father was catching the ready penny abroad, he found, before he was two hours at work, the haunting idea press upon his brain; and he returned to the house and threw himself upon the bed confused and sad. In spite of this, however, the wound in his head was now progressing more favourably, and returning strength renewed a more cheerful spirit within him. He fought hard against the idea which at times forced itself upon him. At one time it was so vivid before his mind, that Father Farrell, who was a constant and careful visitor, could not but perceive there was something which depressed him; and he rallied him upon the subject, assuring him that he had progressed most favourably, and would in a few days be perfectly able to resume his usual occupations.

Rory was silent. He was not going to tell even Father Farrell the idea by which he was sometimes haunted.

The priest saw that all was not yet right. He took Rory kindly by the hand and said: "My dear young friend, do you not feel as well as your outward condition would indicate that you ought to be?"

"Yes, Father Farrell, I thank God I feel my strength almost perfectly restored. I shall be able, I hope, to give my poor father the usual help in a few days. The worst of it is that the throng of the spring work is over, and wages are now down a third from what they were a month or three weeks ago."

A thought had struck Father Farrell. He could not shut his ears, priest and all as he was, to some of the gossip which was abroad.

"If *that* be all that is fretting you, Rory, cheer up, for there is plenty of work still to be had; and if the wages are not quite so high as they were a while back, you shall have constant work for some time, which will be better than high wages for a start. I can myself afford to make up for some of the loss this unfortunate blow has caused you. You must accept this." And he pulled a pound-note from his breeches-pocket.

If occasionally there were moments when Rory's ideas were somewhat confused, they were never clearer or sharper than as Father Farrell said this. It so happened that he was thinking of Winny Cavana at the moment; indeed, it would be hard to hit upon the moment when he was not. Shanvilla was proverbially a poor parish; and Father Farrell's continual and expressed regret was, that he was not able personally to do more for the poor of his flock. Rory was sharp enough, and stout enough, to speak his mind even to his priest, when he found it necessary.

He looked inquiringly into Father Farrell's face. "No! Father Farrell, you *cannot* afford it," he said. "It is your kindness leads you to say so; and if you could afford it there are—and no man knows it better than you do—many still poorer families than ours in the parish requiring your aid. But under no circumstances shall I touch *that* pound."

The priest was found out, and became disconcerted; but the matter was coming to a point, and he might as well have it out.

"Why do you lay such an emphasis upon the word *that?*" said he. "It is a very good one," he added, laughing.

"Well, Father Farrell, I am always ready and willing to answer you any questions you may choose to ask me, for you are always discreet and considerate. Of course I must always answer any questions you have a right to ask; but you have no right to probe me now."

"Certainly not, Rory, but you know a counsel's no command."

"Your counsel, Father Farrell, is always good, and almost amounts to a command. I beg your pardon, if I have spoken hastily."

There was a melancholy tremor in Rory's voice as he turned his face a little to one side from his companion.

"Rory, my good young friend, and, I will add, my dear young friend, I do not wish to probe you upon any subject you are not bound to give me your confidence upon; but why did you lay such an emphasis just now on the word *that?* If you do not wish to answer me, you need not do so. But you must take *this* pound-note. You see I can lay an emphasis as well as you, when I think it is required."

"No, Father Farrell. If the note was your own, I might take the loan of it, and work it in with you, or pay you when I earned it. But I do not think it is: there is the truth for you, Father Farrell."

"I see how it is, Rory, and you are very proud. However, the truth is, the pound was sent to me anonymously for you from a friend."

"She might as well have signed her name in full," said Rory, sadly, "for any loss that I can be at upon the subject—or perhaps you yourself, Father Farrell."

"Well, I was at no loss, I confess. But you were to know nothing about it, Rory; only you were so sharp. There is no fear that your intellects have been injured by the blow, at all events. It was meant kindly, Rory, and I think you ought to take it—here."

"You think so, Father Farrell?"

"I do; indeed, I do, Rory."

"Give it me, then," he said, taking it; and before Father Farrell's face, he pressed it to his lips. He then got a pen and ink and wrote something upon it. It was nothing but the date; he wanted no memorandum of anything else respecting it. But he would hardly have written even that, had he intended to make use of it.

The priest stood up to leave. He knew more than he chose to tell Rory of the Hills. But there was an amicable smile upon his lips as he held out his hand to bid him good-by.

Oh! the suspicion of a heart that loves!

"Father Farrell," he said, still holding the priest's hand, "is this the note, the very note, the identical note, she sent me?"

"Yes, Rory; I would not deceive you about it. It is the very note,—which, I fear," he added, "is not likely to be of much use to you."

"Why do you say that, Father Farrell? You shall one day see the contrary."

"Because you seem to me rather inclined to 'huxter it up,' as we say, than to make use of it. Believe me, that was not the intention it was sent with; oh! no, Rory; it was sent with the hope that it might be of some use, and not to be hoarded up through any morbid sentimentality."

"Give me one instead of it, Father Farrell, and keep this one until I can redeem it."

"I have not got another, Rory; pounds are not so plenty with me."

"And yet you would have persuaded me just now that it was your own, and that you could afford to bestow it upon me."

"Pardon me, Rory, I would not have persuaded you; I was merely silent upon the subject until your suspicions made you cross-examine me. I was then plain enough with you. I used no deceit; and I now tell you plainly that if you take this pound-note, you ought to use it, otherwise you will give her who sent it very just cause for annoyance."

"Then it shall be as she wishes and as you advise, Father Farrell. I cannot err under your guidance. I shall use it freely and with gratitude; but you need not tell her that I know who sent it."

"*Badhershin!* do you think that I am an *aumadhawn*, Rory? The very thing she was anxious to avoid herself. I shall never speak to her, perhaps, upon the subject."

The priest then left him with a genuine and hearty blessing, which could not fail of a beneficial influence.

CHAPTER XXVII.

The priest had been a true prophet and a good doctor, and perhaps it was well for all parties concerned that the dispensary M.D. had been dispensed with. Rory now recovered his strength every day more and more. The wound in his head had completely healed.

There was scarcely a mark left of where it had been, unless you blew his beautiful soft hair aside, when a slight hard ridge was just perceptible. Father Farrell had procured him a permanent job of some weeks, at rather an increase of wages from what was "going" at the time, for the spring business was now over, and work was slack. But a gentleman who had recently purchased a small property in that part of the country, and intended to reside, had commenced alterations in the laying-out of the grounds about his "mansion;" and meeting Father Farrell one day, asked him if he could recommend a smart handy man for a tolerably long job. There would be a good deal of "skinning" and cutting of sods, levelling hillocks, and filling-up hollows, and wheeling of clay. For the latter portion of the work, the man should have help. What he wanted was a tasty, handy fellow, who would understand quickly what was required as it was explained to him.

Father Farrell, as the gentleman said all this, thought that he must have actually had Rory of the Hills in his mind's eye. He was the very man on every account, and the priest at once recommended him. This job would soon make up for all the time poor Rory had lost with his broken head. And for his intelligence and taste, Father Farrell had gone bail. Thus it was that Rory after all had not broken the pound-note, but, in spite of the priest, had hoarded it as a trophy of Winny's love.

Rory would have had a rather long walk every morning to his work, and the same in the evening after it was over. But Mr. D——, on the very first interview with young Lennon, was sharp enough to find out his value as a rural engineer, and for his own sake as well as Lennon's, he made arrangements that he should stop at a tenant's house not far from the scene of his landscape gardening, which was likely to last for some time. Mr. D—— was not a man who measured a day's work by its external extent. He looked rather to the manner of its accomplishment, and would not allow the thing to be "run over." He did not care for the expense; what he wanted was to have the thing well done; and he gave Father Farrell great credit for his choice in a workman. If he liked the job when it was finished, he did not say but that he would give Lennon a permanent situation, as overseer at a fixed salary.

Rory had now fallen on his feet, instead of his head. But up to this he had not seen, nor even heard, of Winny Cavana, except what had been implied to his heart by the priest's pound-note. He was farther now from Rathcash chapel than ever; nevertheless, he would show himself there, "God willing," next Sunday. He was neither afraid nor ashamed to do so.

What was Tom Murdock's surprise and chagrin on the following Sunday to observe "that *confounded* whelp" on the road before him, as he went to prayers —looking, too, better dressed, and as well and handsome as ever! He thought he had "put a spoke in his wheel" for the whole summer at least; and before that was over, he had determined to have matters irrevocably *clinched*, if not *settled*, with Miss Winifred Cavana. After what manner this was to be accomplished was only known to himself and three others, associates of his villany.

The matter had been already discussed in all its bearings. All the arguments in favour of, and opposed to its success had been exhausted, and the final result was, that the thing should be done, and was only waiting a favourable opportunity to be put in practice. Some matters of detail, however, had to be arranged, which would take some time; but as the business was kept "dark," there was no hurry. Tom Murdock's secret was safe in the keeping of his coadjutors, whose "oath of brotherhood" bound them not only to inviolable silence, but to their assistance in carrying out his nefarious designs.

The sight of young Lennon once more upon the scene, gave a spur to Tom's plans and determination. He had hoped that that "accidental tip" which he had given him would at least have had the effect of reducing him in circumstances and appearance, and have kept him in his own parish. He knew that Lennon was depending upon his day's wages for even the sustenance of life; that there was a family of at least four besides himself to support; and he gloated himself over the idea that a month or six weeks' sick idleness, recovering at best when there was no work to be had, would have left "that whelp" in a condition almost unpresentable even at his own parish chapel. What was his mortification, therefore, when he now beheld young Lennon before him on the road!

"By the table of war," he said in his heart, "this must hasten my plans! I cannot permit an intimacy to be renewed in that quarter. I must see my friends at once."

Winny Cavana, although she had not seen Rory of the Hills since the accident, had taken care to learn through her peculiar resources how "the poor fellow was getting on." Her friend Kate Mulvey was one of these resources.

Although it has not yet oozed out in this story, it is necessary that it should now do so; Phil M'Dermott, then, was a grand admirer of Kate Mulvey. He was one of those who advocated an interchange of parishioners in the courting line. He did not think it fair that "exclusive dealing" should be observed in such cases. There were many pretty girls in the parish of Shanvilla, and let the Rathcash boys look after them; and *vice versâ*, Phil would have said, had he known Latin, but his method of expressing it was, "and so by Shanvilla with Rathcash."

Now useless as it was, and forlorn as had been hitherto the hope, Phil M'Dermott, like all true lovers, could not keep away from his cold-hearted Kate. It was a satisfaction to him at all events to be looking at her;" and somehow since Rory's accident she seemed more friendly and condescending in her manner to poor Phil. It will be remembered that Phil M'Dermott was a great friend of Rory of the Hills', and it may now be said that he was a near neighbour. It was natural, then, that Kate Mulvey should find out all about Rory from him, and "have word" for Winny when they met. This was one resource, and Father Farrell, as he sometimes passed Kate's door, was another. Father

Farrell could guess very well, notwithstanding Kate's careless manner of asking, that his information would not rest in her own breast, and gave it as fully and satisfactorily as he could. Rory of the Hills, we know, was a great favourite of Father Farrell's.

Kate Mulvey, however, "would not for the world" say a word to either Phil M'Dermott or Father Farrell which could be construed as coming from Winny Cavana to Rory of the Hills; she had Winny's strict orders to that effect. But Kate felt quite at liberty to make any remarks she chose, as coming from herself. In that respect no person had a right to impose a restriction.

Poor Rory, upon this his first occasion of, it may be said, appearing in public after his accident, was greeted, after prayers were over, with a genuine cordiality by the Rathcash boys, none of whom partook of the feeling which existed in Tom Murdock's heart towards him. Their anxiety to see him and have a talk with him was very gratifying to him; but to a certain degree just then it annoyed him, as the shaking of hands and kind inquiries several times interfered with his object in "getting speech" of Winny Cavana, who was some distance in advance in consequence of these delays.

But Winny was not the girl to be frustrated by any unnecessary prudery on such an occasion. Why should she not openly delay until she too had an opportunity to congratulate Rory on his recovery? She saw no reason why she should not do so, and she felt that there was one why she should.

"Father," she said, "there's Rory at our chapel

to-day for the first time since he was hurt. Let us not be behindhand with the neighbours to congratulate him on his recovery. I see all the Rathcash people are glad to see him."

"And so they ought, Winny; I'm glad you told me he was here, for I did not happen to see him. Stand where you are until he comes up." And the old man stood patiently for some minutes while Rory's friends were expressing their pleasure at his reappearance.

Winny had kept as clear as possible of Tom Murdock since the accident at the hurling-match; so much so, that he could not but know it was intentional. She had latterly contracted a serious meditative cast of countenance while going about her household affairs, and if ever she happened to meet Tom, she scarcely did more than formally acknowledge his forced attempt at a cordial greeting.

Tom had remarked during prayers that Winny's countenance had brightened up wonderfully when young Lennon came into the chapel, and took a quiet place not far inside the door; for he had been kept outside by the kind inquiries of friends, until the congregation had become pretty throng. He had observed, too, for he was on the watch, that Winny's eyes had often wandered in the direction of the door up to the time when "that whelp" had entered; but from that moment, when he had observed the bright smile light up her face, she had never turned them from the officiating priest and the altar.

Tom had not ventured to walk home with Winny

from the chapel for some Sundays past, nor would he to-day. What puzzled him not a little was, what his line of conduct ought to be with respect to Lennon, whom he had not seen since the accident. His course was, however, taken after a few moments' reflection. He did not forget that on the occasion of the blow he had exhibited much sympathy with the sufferer, and had declared it to have been purely accidental. He should keep up that character of the affair now, or make a liar of himself, both as to the past and his feelings.

"Besides," thought he, "I may so delay him, that Miss Winifred cannot have the face to delay for him so long."

Just then as Rory had emancipated himself from the cordiality of three or four young men, and was about to step-out quickly to where he saw Winny and her father standing on the road, Tom came up.

"Ah! Lennon," he said, stretching out his hand, "I am glad to see you in this part of the country again. I hope you are quite recovered."

"Quite, thank God," said Rory pushing by without taking his hand. "But I see Winny and her father waiting on the road, and I cannot stop to talk to you;" and he strode on. Rory left out the "Cavana" in the above sentence on purpose, because he knew the familiarity its omission created would vex Tom Murdock.

"Bad luck to your impudence, you conceited cub, you!" was Murdock's mental ejaculation as he watched the cordial greeting between him and

Winny Cavana, to say nothing of her father, who appeared equally glad to see him.

Phil M'Dermott had come for company that day with Rory, and had managed to join Kate Mulvey as they came out of chapel. She had her eyes about her, and saw very well how matters had gone so far. For the first time in her life she noticed the scowl on Tom Murdock's brow as she came towards him.

"God between us and harm, but he looks wicked this morning!" thought she; and she was almost not sorry when he turned suddenly round and walked off without waiting for her so much as to "bid him the time of day."

"That's more of it," said Tom to himself. "There is that one now taking up with that tinker."

He felt something like the little boy who said, "What! will nobody come and play with me?" But Tom did not, like him, become a good boy after that.

He watched the Cavanas and Lennon, who had not left the spot where Lennon came up with them until they were joined by Kate and Phil M'Dermott, when they all walked on together, chatting and laughing as if nobody in the world was wicked or unhappy.

He dodged them at some distance, and was not a little surprised to see the whole party—"the whelp," "the tinker," and all—turn up the lane, and go into Cavana's house.

"*That will do*," said he; "I must see my friends this very night, and before this day fortnight we'll see who'll win the trick."

Rory of the Hills and Phil M'Dermott actually paid a visit at old Ned Cavana's that Sunday. Tom Murdock had seen them going in, and he minuted them by his silver hunting-watch—for he had one. His eye wandered from the door to his watch, and from his watch to the door, as if he were feeling the pulse of their visit. He thought he had never seen Kate Mulvey looking so handsome, or Phil M'Dermott so clean or so well-dressed. It is astonishing what an improvement a good-looking well-dressed fellow will make, not only in the looks of a young girl to whom he may be talking, but in the opinion of any other young fellow who has been in the habit of flirting with the same girl, though perhaps doubting her pretensions to beauty at the time. Let another fellow seem to think her handsome, and from that moment the other has no doubt of it either; his wavering opinion becomes fixed in her favour. But it mattered not. If Kate was a Venus, Tom will carry out his plans with respect to Winny, and let Phil M'Dermott work his own point in that other quarter. Not that he cared much for Winny herself, but he wanted her farm, and he *hated " that whelp Lennon."*

They remained just twenty-five minutes in old Cavana's; this for Kate Mulvey was nothing very wonderful, but for two young men—neither of whom had ever darkened his doors before—Tom thought it rather a long visit.

There they were now, going down the lane together, laughing and chatting, all three seemingly in good-humour.

Cranky and out of temper as he was, Tom's observation was correct in more matters than one. Phil M'Dermott was particularly well-dressed on this occasion, his first visit to Rathcash chapel. Perhaps after to-day he may be oftener there than at his own. He had never heard Father Roche preach before, and he thought somehow that he was better than his own poor Father Farrell, good a man as he was.

But we must account for his dress.

Phil M'Dermott's father was growing old; a little bit beyond his work, for the business of "the firm" had latterly increased to a wonderful extent. They were obliged to engage two journeymen, who had constant sledging and hammering and fitting and filing in every department of agricultural implements, besides a separate forge for horse-shoeing, with special men for that purpose. The result of all this was, that Phil M'Dermott was making a comfortable independence for himself, and supporting his good old father handsomely, who had given up the whole business to his son. The signboard now was, "Philip M'Dermott, agricultural-implement maker. Horses carefully fitted and neatly shod."

Thus this "tinker," as Tom Murdock called him, had thriven apace, and was now making an independence which might one day vie with the remnant of Tom's ill-spent wealth.

Phil, as he walked beside Kate, thought her less cold and less reserved than usual, and he of course became more familiar in his manner with her. She thought, almost every moment, that she had never seen Phil M'Dermott to so much advantage. The fact was, the scowl she had caught on Tom Murdock's face for the first time, and the rude manner in which he had turned away from her, had set her a thinking. She had never seen such a look upon M'Dermott's face as *that*. *He* had never turned away from her in that rude sour manner as she approached to speak to him. She had heard too that Tom Murdock had latterly "got greatly into debt." Some had said that he would soon be smashed—"horse, foot, and dragoons." Report, on the other hand, had it that Phil M'Dermott was the rising man of the country; that he was "making a fortune" at "his profession," Kate called it, though report had only said "hammer and anvil." These in a few words were the first and second-class passengers who had arrived by a long train of thought at the terminus of Kate Mulvey's mind, which had started for a Sunday-excursion trip.

Having left Kate safe at her own door the two young men went on their way together.

Taking a metaphor from Phil M'Dermott's "profession," as Kate had called it, we would advise him to "strike while the iron is hot."

CHAPTER XXVIII.

PERHAPS there was nothing extraordinary, after the encouragement which Rory had met with upon his first appearance at Rathcash chapel after "the accident," if he found it pleasanter to "overtake Mass" there, than to come in quietly at Shanvilla. The walk did him good. Be this as it may, he was now a regular attendant at a chapel which was a mile and a half farther from his home than his own.

Two Sundays had now come round since Tom Murdock had seen the reception which "that whelp" had met with from the Cavanas, not only as he came out of the chapel, but in asking him up to the house, and, he supposed, giving him luncheon; for the visits had been repeated each successive Sunday. Then that fellow M'Dermott had also come to their chapel, and he and Kate Mulvey had also gone up with the Cavanas. This was now the third Sunday on which this had taken place; and not only Winny herself, but her father seemed to acquiesce in bringing it about.

Tom's fortnight had passed by, and he had not "won the trick," as he had threatened to do. "Well," thought he, "it cannot be done in a minute. I have been dealing the cards, and, contrary to custom, the dealer shall lead besides; and that soon."

Winny's happy smile was now so continuous and

so gratifying to her father's heart, that if he had not become altogether reconciled to an increased intimacy with Rory of the Hills, he had at all events become a convert to her dislike to Tom Murdock, and no mistake.

In spite of all his caution, one or two matters had crept out as to his doings, and had come to old Ned's ears in such a way that no doubt could remain on his mind of their veracity. He began to give Winny credit for more sharpness than he had been inclined to do; and it crossed his mind once that, if Winny was not mistaken about Tom Murdock's villany, she might not be mistaken either about *any body else's worth*. The thought had not individualised itself as yet. In the meantime young Lennon's quiet and natural manner, his unvarying attention and respect for the old man himself, and his apparent carelessness for Winny's private company, grew upon old Ned insensibly; and it was now almost as a fixed rule that he paid a Sunday visit after Mass at Rathcash, the old man putting his hand upon his shoulder, and facing him towards the house at the end of the lane, saying, "Come, Rory Lennon, the *murphys* will be teemed by the time we get up, and no one can fault our bacon or our butter."

"*My* butter, Rory," said Winny on one occasion, at a venture.

Her father looked at her. But there was never another word about it.

All this was anything but pleasing to Tom Murdock, who always sulkily dogged them at some distance behind.

Now we shall not believe that Rory of the Hills was such a muff, or Winny Cavana such a prude, as to suppose that no little opportunity was seized upon for a kind soft word between them *unknown*. Nor shall we suppose that Kate Mulvey, who was always of the party, was such a marplot as to obstruct such a happy casualty, should it occur, particularly if Phil was to the fore.

Rory's careless loud laugh along the road, as he escorted Kate to her own door, gave evidence that his heart was light, and that (as Kate thought, though she did not question him,) matters were on the right road for him. Winny too, when they met, was so happy, and so different from what for a while she had been, that Kate, although she did not question her either, guessed that all was right with her too.

Matters, as they now seemed to progress, and he watched them close, were daggers to Tom Murdock's heart. He had seen Winny Cavana, on more than one evening, leave the house and take the turn towards Kate Mulvey's. On these occasions he had the meanness and want of spirit to watch her movements; and although he could not satisfy himself that young Lennon came to meet her, he was not quite satisfied that he did not.

Winny invariably turned into Kate Mulvey's, and remained for a long visit. Might not "that hound" be there?—Tom sometimes varied his epithets;— might it not be a place of assignation? This was but the suspicion of a low mean mind like Tom Murdock's.

These visits were mere visits of cordiality from Winny to her friend, and were as often reciprocated by Kate to Rathcash house,—where young Lennon could certainly not have been "concealed," as Tom Murdock called it. Besides, on more than one occasion the girls had come out together for a walk, and turned their backs towards Shanvilla altogether, when Tom was obliged to sneak behind some hedge, to hide his creditable character of a spy upon two innocent and unconscious females.

The fact is, since Tom's threat about "winning the trick" he had been rather idle. His game was not one which could be played out by correspondence,—he was too cunning for that,—and the means which he would be obliged to adopt were not exactly ready at his hand. He saw that matters were not pressing in another quarter, yet, if ever they should press, and he would "ride a waiting race," and win unexpectedly. Thus the simile of Tom's thoughts still took their tone from the racecourse, and he would "hold hard" for another bit. Circumstances however soon occurred which made him "push forward towards the front," if he had any hope "to come in first."

Rory Lennon having finished his "landscape gardening" at Mr. D—'s, and the overseership being held over for the present, had got another rather long job, on the far part of old Ned Cavana's farm, in laying-out and cutting drains, where the land required reclaiming. He had shown so much taste and intelligence in both planning and performing, that old Ned was quite delighted with him, and began to regret "that he had not known his value as an agricultural labourer long before." There was one other at least—if not two—who sympathised in that regret. At all events there he was now every day up to his hips in dirty red clay, scooping it up from the bottom of little drains more than three feet deep, in a long iron scoop with a crooked handle. This job was at the far end of Ned's farm, and in coming to his work, Lennon need hardly come within sight of the house, for the work lay in the direction of Shanvilla. Rory did not "quit work," until it was late; he was then in anything but visiting trim, if such a thing were even possible. He therefore saw no more of Winny on account of the job than if he had been at work upon the Giant's Causeway. But a grand object had been attained, nevertheless—he was working for Ned Cavana, and had given him more than satisfaction in the performance of the job, and on one occasion old Ned had called him "Rory awochal," a term of great familiarity.

This was a great change for the better. If young Lennon had been as well acquainted with racing phraseology as Tom Murdock, he also would have thought that he would "make a waiting race of it." But the expression of *his* thoughts was, that he "would bide his time."

The Sundays, however, were still available, and Rory did not lose the chance. He now became so regular an attendant at Rathcash chapel, and went up so regularly with old Ned and his daughter after prayers, that it was no wonder if people began to talk.

"I donna what Tom Murdock says to all this, Bill," said Tim Fahy to a neighbour, on the road from the chapel.

"The sorra wan of me knows, Tim, but I hear he isn't overwell plaised."

"Arrah, what id he be plaised at? Is it to see a Shanvilla boy, without a cross, intherlopin' betune him an' his bachelor?"

"Well, they say he needn't be a bit afeared. Lennon is a very good workman, an' undherstan's dhrainin', an' ould Ned's cute enough to get a job well done; but he'd no more give his daughter with her fine fortin' to that chap, than he'd throw her an' it into the say—b'lieve you me."

"There's some very heavy cloud upon Tom this while back, any way; and though he keeps it very close, there's people thinks it's what she refused him."

"The sorra fear iv her, Tim; she has more sinse nor that."

"Well, riddle me this, Bill. What brings that chap here Sunda' afther Sunda', an' what takes him up to old Ned Cavana's every Sunda' afther Mass? He is a very good-lookin' young fellow, an' knows a sheep's head from a sow's ear, or Tim Fahy's a fool."

"*Och, badhershin*, doesn't he go up to walk home wid Kate Mulvey, for she's always iv the party?"

"And *badhershin* yourself, Bill, isn't Phil M'Dermott always to the fore for Kate?—another intherloper from Shanvilla! I donna what the sorra the Ruthcash boys are about."

Other confabs of a similar nature were carried on by different sets as they returned from prayers, and saw the Cavanas with their company turn up the lane towards the house. The young girls of the district too had their chats upon the subject; but they were so voluble, and some of them so ill-natured, that I forbear to give the reader any specimen of their remarks.

It were idle to deny that "the footing" which young Lennon had somehow established for himself at Rathcash house, although he still prudently confined the indulgence of it to Sundays, became the subject of general surprise and conversation in the parish. One or two intimate associates of Tom ventured to quiz him—*chaff*, I believe is the present word; but I am writing of what took place five-and-thirty years ago,—to quiz him upon the state of affairs. Now none but a very intimate friend indeed of Tom's should have ventured, under the circumstances, to have touched upon so sore a subject, and those who did, intimate as they were, did not venture to repeat the joke. No, it was no joke; and that they soon found out. To one friend who had quizzed him privately he said, "Suspend your judgment,"—taking the expression from the letter of a jockey who had been accused of foul play in riding a race, and had appealed to the public through the press,—"Suspend your judgment, Denis; and if I don't prove myself more than a match for that half-bred *kiout*, then condemn me."

But to another, who had quizzed him before some bystanders in rather a ridiculous point of view, he turned like a bull-terrier, while his face assumed a scowl of a peculiarly unpleasant character.

"It is no business of yours," he said, "and I advise you to mind your own affairs, or perhaps I'll make you."

The man drew in his horns, and sneaked off, of course; and from that moment they all guessed that the business had gone against Tom, and they left off quizzing.

Tom felt that he had been wrong, and had only helped to betray himself. His game now was, to prevent, if possible, any talk about the matter one way or the other, until his plans should be matured, when he doubted not that success would gain him the approbation of every one, no matter what the means.

One of Tom's maxims was, that to be successful was to be right.

The preface to his plans was, to spread a report that he had gone back to Armagh, to get married to a girl with an immense fortune, and he indorsed the report by the fact of his leaving home; but whether to Armagh or not, was never clearly known.

Young Lennon went on with his job, at which old Ned told him to take his time, an' do it well. "It was not," he said, "like digging a plot, which had to be dug every year, or maybe twice. When it was wance finished and covered up, there it was; worse nor the first day, if it was not done right; so don't hurry it over, Rory awochal. I don't mind the expense; ground can't be dhrained for nothin', an' it id be a bad job if we were obliged to be openin' any of the dhrains a second time, an' maybe not know where the stoppage lay: so take your time, and don't blame me if you botch it."

"You need not fear, sir," said Lennon. (He always said 'sir,' as yet.) "You need not fear; if every drain of them does not run like the stream from Tubbernaltha, never give me a day's work again."

"As far as you have gone, Rory, I think they are complate; we'll have forty carts of stones in afore Saturda' night. I hope you have help enough, boy."

"Plenty, sir, until we begin to cover in."

"Wouldn't you be able for that yourself? or couldn't you bring your father with you? I'd wish to put whatever I could in your way?"

"Thank you, sir, very much. I will do so if I want more help; but for the lucre of keeping up his wages and mine, I would not recommend you to lose this fine weather in covering in the drains. It is a great matter to get the scraws turned down dry, and the earth dry over them. I think when we are ready you should turn in half-a-dozen men at once, and finish them off. Thanks be to God, my father and I can get plenty of work when this job is finished,—thanks to you, Mr. Cavana, all the same. I only speak for your own good, and for the credit of the work I may leave after me."

"You are an honest boy, Rory, and I like your way of talkin', as well as workin'; plaise God we won't see you or your father idle."

Up to this time it will be seen that Rory was not idle in any sense of the word. He was ingratiating himself, but honestly, into the good graces of old Ned: "if he was not fishing, he was mending his nets;" and the above conversation will show that he was not a dunce at that same.

It happened, upon one or two occasions, that old Ned was with Rory at leaving off work in the evening, and he asked him to "cum" up to the house and have a dhrink of beer, or whiskey-and-wather, his choice."

But Rory excused himself, saying he was no fit figure to go into any decent man's parlour in that trim, and indeed his appearance did not belie his words; for he was spotted and striped with yellow clay, from his head and face to his feet, and the clothes he brought to the work were worth nothing.

"Well, you'll not be always so, Rory, when you're done wid the scoopin'," said old Ned; and he added, laughing, "the divil a wan o' me'd know you to be the same boy I seen cummin' out o' Mass a Sunda'."

Rory had heard, as everybody else had heard, that Tom Murdock had left home, and he felt as if an incubus had been lifted off his heart. Not that he feared Tom in any one way; but he knew that his absence would be a relief to Winny, and as such, a relief to himself.

Rory was now as happy as his position and his hopes permitted him to be; but there can be little doubt but this happiness arose from an understanding between himself and Winny; but how, when, or where that understanding had been confirmed, it would be hard to say. We have seen that it was only originated at the scene of the handkerchief with which Bully-dhu ran away. We cannot believe either, that although Rory's own sound judgment and proper feeling prompted his respectful conduct towards old Ned, yet that his course was shaped by advice from one who knew every twist and turn of the old man's mind better than any other being upon earth. So far, however, it had met with a reception beyond his most sanguine expectations.

Old Ned's remarks to his daughter respecting young Lennon were "nuts and apples" to her. She knew the day would come, and perhaps at no far distant time, when she must openly avow, not only a preference for Rory, but declare an absolute determination to cast her lot with his, and ask her father's blessing upon them. She was aware that this could not, that it ought not, to be hurried. She hoped—oh! how fervently she hoped—that the report of Tom Murdock's marriage might be true; that of his absence from home she knew to be so. In the meantime it kept the happy smile for ever on her lips to know that Rory was daily creeping into the good opinion of her father. Oh! how could Rory, her own Rory, fail, not only to creep, but to rush into the good opinion, the very heart, of all who knew him! Poor enthusiastic Winny! But she was right. With the solitary exception of Tom Murdock, there was not a human being who knew him, who did not love Rory Lennon. But where is the man with Tom Murdock's heart, and in Tom Murdock's place, who would not have hated him as he did?

CHAPTER XXIX.

It would be futile to expect or suppose that any reader of common experience in the unravelling of the mysteries of a plot, though our plot really has no mysteries, could even approach a certain portion of this chapter without at once detecting the performers and the plans. We may therefore prepare them plainly for one of the principal incidents in it, by saying that Tom Murdock, seeing that his hopes by fair means were completely at an end, and that matters were likely to progress in another quarter at a rate which made it advisable not to let the leading horse get too far ahead, determined to make a rush to the front, no matter whether he went the wrong side of a post or not—let that be settled after. These were as usual the shape his thoughts took.

He had left home, as we have seen, and left a report behind him, which he took care to have industriously circulated, that he had gone to Armagh, and was about to be married to "a young lady" with a large fortune, and that he would visit the metropolis, Fermanagh, and perhaps Sligo, before he returned. But as far as we can ascertain, and it is now difficult to do so, he did not go farther than an obscure public-house in a small village in the lower part of the county of Cavan. There he met the materials for carrying out his plan. The object of it was shortly this—to carry away Winny Cavana by force, and bring her to a *friend's* house in the mountains behind the village adverted to. Here he was to have an old buckle-beggar at hand to marry them the moment Winny's spirit was broken to consent. This man, a degraded clergyman, as the report went, wandered about the country in green spectacles and a short black cloak, always ready and willing to perform such a job; doubly willing and ready for this particular one from the reward which Tom had promised him. If even the marriage ceremony should fail, either through Winny's obstinacy or the clergyman's want of spirit to go through with it in the face of opposition, still he would keep her for ten days or a fortnight at this *friend's* house, stopping there himself too; and at the end of that time, should he fail in obtaining her consent, he would quit the country for a while, and allow her to return home "so blasted in character" that even "that whelp" would disown her. There was a pretty specimen of a lover—a husband!

Not only Easter Monday, but the greater part of the summer, had now passed by, and Tom had not taken "that one's pride down a peg yet." But he must be fairly on for it at last, if he did not intend to be "distanced."

It was now the end of June. The weather had been dry for some time, and the nights were clear and mild; the stars shone brightly, and the early

dawn would soon present a heavy dew hanging on
the bushes and the grass. Some people said that
"there was frost" every night. The moon was on
the wane; but at a later hour of the night it was
conspicuous in the heaven, adding a stronger light
to that given by the clearness of the sky and the
brilliancy of the stars.

Rathcash and Rathcashmore were sunk in still
repose; and if silence could be echoed, it was echoed
by the stillness of the mountains behind Shanvilla
and beyond them. The inhabitants of the whole
district had long since retired to rest, and now lay
buried in sleep, some of them in confused dreams of
pleasure and delight.

The angel of the dawn was scarcely yet awake,
or he might have heard the sound of muffled horses'
feet and muffled wheels creeping along the road
towards the lane turning up to Rathcash house,
about two hours before day; and he must have seen
a man with a dark mask mounted on another muffled
horse at a little distance from the cart.

Presently Tom Murdock—there is no use in simu-
lating mystery where none exists—took charge of the
horse and cart to prevent them from moving, while
three men stole up towards the house. Aye, there
is Bully-dhu's deep bark, and they are already at
the door.

"That dog! he'll betray us, boys," said one of
the men.

"I'd blow his brains out if this pistol was loaded,"
said another; "and I wanted Tom to give me a
cartridge."

"He wouldn't let any one load but himself, and he was right; a shot would be twice as bad as the dog; besides, he's in the back-yard, and cannot get out. Never heed him, but to work as fast as possible."

Old Ned Cavana and Winny heard not only the dog, but the voices. Winny's heart foretold the whole thing in a moment, and she braced her nerves for the scene.

The door was now smashed-in, and the three men entered. By this time old Ned had drawn on his trousers; and as he was throwing his coat over his head to get his arms into the sleeves he was seized, and ere you could count ten he was pinioned, with his arms behind him and his legs tied at the ankles, and a handkerchief tied across his mouth. Thus rendered perfectly powerless he was thrown back upon the bed, and the room-door locked. Jamesy Doyle, who slept in the barn, had heard the crash of the door, dressed himself in "less than no time," let Bully-dhu out of the yard, and brought him to the front-door, in at which he rushed like a tiger. But Jamesy Doyle did not go in. That was not his game; but he peeped-in at the window. No light had been struck, so he could make nothing of the state of affairs inside, except from the voices; and from what he heard he could make no mistake as to the object of this attack. He could not tell whether Tom Murdock was in the house or not, but he did not hear his voice. One man said, "Come, now, be quick, Larry; the sooner we're off with her the better."

Jamesy waited for no more; he turned to the lane as the shortest way, but at a glance he saw the horse and cart and the man on horseback on the road outside; and turning again he darted off across the fields as fast as his legs could carry him.

Bully-dhu, having gained access to the house, showed no disposition to compromise the matter. "No quarter!" was his cry, as he flew at the nearest man to him, and seizing him by the throat brought him to the ground with a *sough*, where in spite of his struggles, he held him fast with a silent deadly grip. He had learned this much, at least, by his encounter with the mastiff on New-year's day.

Careless of their companion's strait, who, they thought, ought to be able to defend himself, the other two fellows—and powerful fellows they were —proceeded to the bedroom to their left; they had locked the door to their right, leaving poor old Ned tied and insensible on the bed. Winny was now dressed, and met them at the door.

"Are you come to commit murder," she cried, as they stopped her in the doorway; "or have you done it already? Let me to my father's room."

"The sorra harm on him, Miss, nor the sorra take the hair of his head we'll hurt no more nor your own. Come, put on your bonnet an' cloak, an' come along wid us; them's our ordhers."

"You have a master then. Where is he? where is Tom Murdock?—I knew Tom *Murder* should have been his name. Where is he, I say?"

"Come, come, no talk; but on wid your bonnet and cloak at wanst."

"Never; nor shall I ever leave this house, except torn from it by the most brutal force. Where is your master, I say? Is he afraid of the rope himself, which he would thus put round your necks?"

"Come, come, on wid your bonnet an' cloak, or, be the powers, we'll take you away as you are."

"Never; where is your master, I say?"

"Come, Larry, we won't put up with any more of her pillaver; out with the worsted."

Here Biddy Murtagh rushed in to her mistress's aid; but she was soon overpowered, and tied "neck and heels," as they called it, and thrown upon Winny's bed. They had the precaution to gag her also with a handkerchief, that she might not give the alarm, and they locked the door like that at the other end of the house.

Larry, whoever he was, then pulled a couple of skeins of coarse worsted from his pocket, while his companion seized Winny round the waist, outside her arms; and the other fellow, who seemed expert, soon tied her feet together, and then her hands. A thick handkerchief was then tied across her mouth.

"Take care to lave plenty of braithin' room out iv her nose, Larry," said the other ruffian; and thus rendered unable to move or scream they carried her to the road, and laid her on the car. The horseman in the mask asked them where the third man was, and they replied that he must have "made off" from the dog, for that they neither saw nor heard him after the dog flew at him.

This was likely enough. He was the only man of

the party in whom Tom Murdock could not place the most unbounded confidence.

"The cowardly rascal," he said. "We must do without him."

But he had *not* made off from the dog.

The cart was well provided—*to do Tom Murdock ustice*—with a feather-bed over plenty of straw, and plenty of good covering to keep out the night-air. They started at a brisk trot, still keeping the horses' feet and the wheels muffled; and they passed down the road where the reader was once caught at a dog-fight.

But we shall not accompany them at present. We will take a short cut, and after a little, perhaps we may come across them again.

We must first return, however, for a few minutes to Rathcash house. Bully-dhu was worth a score of old Ned Cavana, even supposing him to have been at liberty, and free of the cords by which he was bound. The poor old man had worked the handkerchief by which he had been gagged off his mouth, by rubbing it against the bed-post. He had then rolled himself to the door; but further than that he was powerless, except to ascertain, by placing his chin to the thumb-latch, for he had got upon his feet, that it was fastened outside. He then set up a lamentable demand for help,—upon Winny, upon Biddy Murtagh, and upon Bully-dhu. The dog was the only one who answered him, with a smothered growl, for he still held fast by the grip he had taken of the man's throat. Poor Bully! you need not have been so pertinacious of that grip—the man has been *dead* for the last ten minutes! That fearful grip has choked him! Finding that it was indeed so, from the perfect stillness of the man, Bully-dhu released his hold, and lay licking his paws and keeping up an angry growl, in answer to the old man's cries.

Bully-dhu, you have taken the law into your own hands, and I hope you may not suffer for it—at all events you ought not; for at worst it was nothing but "justifiable homicide." Fate, however, made one great mistake—Tom Murdock should have been the man.

But we must now leave Bully-dhu licking his paws, and watching the dead man, ready to pounce upon him again if he moved hand or foot, for we cannot say if Bully-dhu was sure whether he was dead or not. We have seen a terrier return some distance to give a dead rat another shake, by way of making assurance doubly sure. But Bully-dhu did no such thing; and we may therefore suppose that he was fully aware of the extent of his performances, and that he was only now calmly waiting to "give himself up."

We must also leave poor old Ned, who had roared himself hoarse for help without avail, and had subsided into a course of broken sobs, with an odd jump against the door with both his feet, for he could not kick. We must leave them, I say, and follow Jamesy Doyle across the fields, and see if it was cowardice made him run so fast from the scene of danger.

Ah! no. Jamesy was not that sort of a chap at

all. He was plucky as well as true to the heart's core. Nor was his intelligence and judgment at fault for a moment as to the best course for him to adopt. Seeing the fearful odds of three stout men against him, he knew that he could do better than to remain there, to be tied "neck and crop" like the poor old man and Biddy. So having brought Bully-dhu round and given him his cue, he started off, and never drew breath until he found himself outside Rory of the Hill's window at Shanvilla, on his way to the nearest police-station.

"Are you there, Rory?" said he, tapping at it.

"Yes," Rory replied from his bed; "who are you, or what do you want?"

"Jamesy Doyle from Rathcash house. Get up at wanst! They have taken away Miss Winny."

"Great Heaven! do you say so? Here, father, get up in a jiffy, and dress yourself. They have taken away Winny Cavana, and we must be off to the rescue like a shot. Come in, Jamesy, my boy." And while they were "drawing on" their clothes, they questioned him as to the particulars.

But Jamesy had few such to give them, as the reader knows; for, like a sensible boy, he was off for help without waiting for particulars.

The principal point, however, was to know what road they had taken. Upon this Jamesy was able to answer with some certainty, for ere he had started finally off, he had watched them, and he had seen the cart move on under the smothered cries of Winny; and he heard the horseman say, "Now, boys, through the pass between 'the sisters.'"

"They took the road to the left from the end of the lane, that's all I know; so let you cut across the country as fast as you can, an' you'll be at Boher before them. Don't delay me now, for I must go on to the police-station an' hurry out the sargent and his men; if you can clog them at the bridge tal I cum' up with the police, all will be right, an' we'll have her back wid us. I know very well if I had a word with Miss Winny unknown to the men, she would have sent me for the police; but I took you in my way,—it wasn't twenty perches of a round."

"Thank you, Jamesy, a thousand times! There, be off to the serjeant as fast as you can; tell him you called here, and that I have calculated everything in my mind, and for him and his men to make for Boher-na-Milthiogue bridge as fast as possible."

"There, be off, Jamesy, and I'll give you a pound-note if the police are at the bridge before Tom Murdock comes through the pass with the cart."

"You may keep your pound, man! I'd do more nor that for Miss Winny." And he was out of sight in a moment.

The father and son were now dressed, and arming themselves with two stout sticks, they did not "let the grass grow under their feet." They hurried on until they came to the road turning down to where we have indicated that our readers were once caught at a dog-fight. Here Rory examined the road as well as he could by the dim light which prevailed, and found the fresh marks of wheels. He could scarcely understand them. They were not like the tracks of any wheels he had ever seen before, and there were no tracks of horses' feet at all, although Jamesy had said there was a horseman besides the horse and cart.

Rory soon put down these unusual appearances—and he could not well define them for want of light—to some cunning device of Tom Murdock; and how right he was!

"Come on, father," said he. "I am quite certain they have gone down here. I know Tom Murdock has plenty of associates in the county Cavan, and the pass between 'the sisters' is the shortest way he can take. Besides, Jamesy heard him say the words. Our plan must be to cut across the country and get to Milthiogue bridge, before they get through the pass and so escape us. What say you, father,—are you able and willing to push on, and to stand by me? Recollect the odds that are against us, and count the cost."

"Rory, I'll count nothing; but I'll—"

"Here, father, in here at this gap, and across by the point of Mullagh hill beyond; we must get to Boher before them."

"I'll count no cost, Rory, I was going to tell you. I'm both able and willing, thank God, to stand by you. You deserve it well of me, and so do the Cavanas. God forbid I should renague my duty to you and them! Aren't ye all as wan as the same thing to me now."

Rory now knew that his father knew all about Winny and him.

"Father," said he, "that is a desperate man, and he'll stop at nothing."

"Is it sthrivin' to cow me you are, Rory?"

"No, father; but you saw the state my mother was in as we left."

"Yes, I did, and why wouldn't she? But shure that should not stop us when we have right on our side; an' God knows what hoult or distress that poor girl is in, or what that villain may do to her; an' what state would your mother be in if you were left a desolate madman all your life through that man's wickedness."

These were stout words of his father, and almost assured Rory that all would be well.

"Father," he continued, "if we get to the bridge before them, and can hold it for half an hour, or less, the police will be up with Jamesy Doyle, and we shall be all right."

The conversation was now so frequently interrupted in getting over ditches and through hedges, and they had said so much of what they had to say, that they were nearly quite silent for the rest of the way, except where Rory pointed out to his father the easiest place to get over a ditch, or through a hedge, or up the face of a hill. Both their hearts were evidently in their journey. No less the father's than the son's: the will made the way.

The dappled specks of red had still an hour to slumber ere the dawn awoke, and they had reached the spot: there was the bridge, the Boher-na-Milthiogue of our first chapter, within a stone's throw of them. They crept to the battlement and peered into the pass. As yet no sound of horse or cart, or whispered word, reached their ears.

"They must be some distance off yet, father," said Rory; "thank God! The police will have the more time to be up."

"Should we not hide, Rory?"

"Certainly; and if the police come up before they do, they should hide also. That villain is mounted; and if a strong defence of the pass was shown too soon, he would turn and put spurs to his horse."

As they spoke a distant noise was heard of horses' feet and unmuffled wheels. The muffling had all been taken off as soon as they had reached the far end of the pass between the mountains, and they were now hastening their speed.

"The odds will be fearfully against us, father," said Rory, who now felt more than ever the dangerous position he had placed his father in, and the fearful desolation his loss would cause in his mother's heart and in his home. He felt no fear for himself. "You had better leave Tom himself to me, father. I know he will be the man on horseback. Let you lay hold of the horse's head under the cart, and knock one of the men, or both, down like lightning, if you can. You have your knife ready to cut the cords that tie her."

"I have, Rory; and don't you fear me; one of them shall tumble at all events, almost before they know that we are on them. I hope I may kill him out an' out; we might then be able for the other two. Do you think Tom is armed?" he added, turning pale. But it was so dark Rory did not see it.

R

"I am not sure, but I think not. He cannot have expected any opposition."

"God grant it, Rory! I don't want to hould you back, but don't be 'fool-hardy,' dear boy."

"Do you want to cow me, father, as you said yourself just now?"

"No, Rory. But stoop, stoop! here they are."

Crouching behind the battlements of the bridge, these two resolute men waited the approach of the cavalcade. As they came to the mouth of the pass the elder Lennon sprang to the head of the horse under the cart, and, seizing him with his left hand, struck the man who drove, such a blow as felled him from the shaft upon which he sat. Rory had already seized the bridle of the horseman who still wore the mask, and, pushing the horse backward on his haunches, he made a fierce blow at the rider's head with his stick. But he had darted his heels—spurs he had none—into his horse's sides, which made him plunge forward, rolling Rory on the ground. Forward to the cart the rider then rushed, crying out, "On, on with the cart!" But Lennon's father was still fastened on the horse's head with his left hand, while with his right he was alternately defending himself against the two men, for the first had somewhat recovered, who were in charge of it.

Tom Murdock would have ridden him down also, and turned the battle in favour of a passage through; but Rory had regained his feet, and was again fastened in the horse's bridle, pushing him back on his haunches, hoping to get at the rider's head, for hitherto his blows had only fallen upon his arms and chest. Here Tom Murdock felt the want of the spurs, for his horse did not spring forward with life and force enough upon his assailant.

A fearful struggle now ensued between them. The men at the cart had not yet cleared their way from the desperate opposition given them by old Lennon, who defended himself ably, and at the same time attacked them furiously. He had not time however to cut the cords by which Winny was bound. A single pause in the use of his stick for that purpose would have been fatal. Neither had he been successful in getting beyond his first position at the horse's head. During the whole of this confused attack and defence, poor Winny Cavana, who had managed to shove herself up into a sitting posture in the cart, continued to cry out, "O Tom Murdock, Tom Murdock! even now give me up to to these friends and begone, and I swear there shall never be a word more about it."

But Tom Murdock was not the man either to yield to entreaties, or to be baffled in his purpose. He had *whaled* Rory Lennon with the butt end of his whip about the head and shoulders, as well as he could across his horse's head, which Lennon had judiciously kept between them, at times making a jump up, and striking at Tom with his stick.

Matters had now been interrupted too long to please Tom Murdock, and darting his heels once more into his horse's sides, he sprang forward, rolling young Lennon on the road again.

"All right now, lads!" he cried; "on, on with the cart!" and he rode at old Lennon, who still held his ground against both his antagonists manfully.

But all was not right. A cry of "The police, the police!" issued from one of the men at the cart, and Jamesy Doyle with four policemen were seen hurrying up the boreen from the lower road.

Perhaps it would be unjust to accuse Tom Murdock of cowardice even then—it was not one of his faults—if upon seeing an accession of four armed policemen he turned to fly, leaving his companions in for it. One of them fled too; but Pat Lennon held the other tightly.

As Tom turned to traverse the mountain-pass back again at full speed, young Lennon, who had recovered himself, sprang like a tiger once more at the horse's head. Now or never he must stay his progress.

Tom Murdock tore the mask from his face, and pulling a loaded pistol from his breast, he said: "Lennon, it was not my intention to injure you when I saw you first spring up from the bridge to-night; nor will I do so now, if your own obstinacy and fool-hardy madness does not bring your doom upon yourself. Let go my horse, or by hell I'll blow your brains out! this shall be no mere tip of a hurl, mind you." And he levelled the pistol at his head, not more than a foot from his face.

"Never with life!" cried Lennon; and he aimed a blow at Tom's pistol-arm. Ah! fatal and unhappy chance. His stick had been raised to strike Tom Murdock down, and he had not time to alter its direction. Had he struck the pistol-arm upward, it might have been otherwise; but the blow of necessity descended. Tom Murdock fired at the same moment, and the only difference it made was, that instead of his brains having been blown out, the ball entered a little to one side of his left breast.

Lennon jumped three feet from the ground, with a short sudden shout, and rolled convulsively upon the road, where soon a pool of bloody mud attested the murderous work which had been done.

The angel of the dawn now awoke, as he heard the report of the pistol echoing and reverberating through every recess in the many hearts of Slievedhu and Slieve-bawn. Tom Murdock fled at full gallop; and the hearts of the policemen fell as they heard the clattering of his horse's feet dying away in quadruple regularity through the mountain-pass.

Jamesy Doyle, who was light of foot and without shoe or stocking, rushed forward, saying, "Sergeant, I'll follow him to the end of the pass, an' see what road he'll take." And he sped onward like a deer.

"Come, Maher," said the sergeant, "we'll pursue, however hopeless. Cotter, let you stop with the prisoner we have, and the young woman; and let Donovan stop with the wounded man, and stop the blood if he can."

Sergeant Driscoll and Maher then started at the top of their speed, in the track of Jamesy Doyle, in full pursuit.

There were many turns and twists in the pass between the mountains. It was like a dozen large letter S's strung together.

Driscoll stopped for a moment to listen. Jamesy was beyond their ken, round one or two of the turns, and they could not hear the horse galloping now.

"All's lost," said the sergeant; "he's clean gone. Let us hasten on until we meet the boy; perhaps he knows which road he took."

Jamesy had been stooping now and then, and peering into the coming light, to keep well in view the man whom he pursued. Aye, there he was, sure enough; he saw him, almost plainly, galloping at the top of his speed. Suddenly he heard a crash, and horse and rider rolled upon the ground.

"He's down, thank God!" cried James, still rushing forward with some hope, and peering into the distance. Presently he saw the horse trot on with his head and tail in the air, without his rider, while a dark mass lay in the centre of the road.

"You couldn't have betther luck, you bloodthirsty ruffian, you!" said Jamesy, who thought that it was Heaven's lightning that, in justice, had struck down Tom Murdock; and he maintained the same opinion ever afterwards. At present, however, he had not time to philosophise upon the thought, but rushed on.

Soon he came to the dark mass upon the road. It was Tom Murdock who lay there stunned and insensible, but not seriously hurt by the fall. There was nothing of Heaven's light in the matter at all. It was the common come-down of a stumbling horse upon a bad mountain-road; but the result was the same.

Jamesy was proceeding to thank God again, and to tie his legs, when Tom came to.

Jamesy was sorry the man's *thrance* did not last a little longer, that he might have tied him, legs and arms, with his own handkerchief and suspenders. But he was late now, and not quite sure that Tom Murdock would not murder him also, and "make off afoot."

Here Jamesy thought he heard the hurried step of the police coming round the last turn towards him, and as Tom was struggling to his feet, a bright thought struck him. He "whipt" out a penknife he had in his pocket; and before Tom had sufficiently recovered to know what he was about, he had cut his suspenders, and given the waist-band of his trousers a *slip* of the knife, opening it more than a foot down the back.

Tom had now sufficiently recovered to understand what had happened, and to know the strait he was in. He had a short time before seen a man named Wolff play Richard III. in a barn in C. O. S.; and if he did not roar lustily, "A horse, a horse! my kingdom for a horse!" he thought it. But his horse was nearly half a mile away, where a green spot upon the road-side tempted him to delay a little his journey home.

Tom was not yet aware of the approach of the police. He made a desperate swipe of his whip, which he still held in his hand, at the boy, and sprung to his feet. But Jamesy avoided the blow by a side jump, and kept roaring, "Police, police!" at the top of his voice. Tom now found that he had been outwitted by this young boy. He was so hampered by his loose trousers about his heels, that he could make no run for it, and soon became the prisoner of Sergeant Driscoll and his companion. Well done, Jamesy!

CHAPTER XXX.

WHILE the above exploits were being performed by Jamesy Doyle and the police, a sad scene indeed was being enacted at the bridge. Winny Cavana, whose bonds had been loosed, had rushed to where Rory lay with his head in his father's lap, while the two policemen, Cotter and Donovan, moved up with their prisoner. They not only handcuffed him, but had tied his legs together, and threw him on the side of the road, "to wait their convenience," while they rendered any assistance they could to the wounded man.

The father had succeeded in staunching the blood, which at first had poured so freely from the wound. With the assistance of one of the police, while the other was tying the prisoner, he had drawn his son up into a sitting posture and leaned him against the bank at the side of the road, and got his arm round him to sustain him. He was not shot dead; but was evidently very badly wounded. He was now, however, recovering strength and consciousness, as the blood ceased to flow.

"Open your eyes, Rory dear, if you are not dead, and look at your own Winny," she said; "your mad Winny Cavana who brought you here to be murdered! Open your eyes, Rory, if you are not dead! I don't ask you to speak."

Rory not only opened his eyes, but turned his face, and looked upon her. Oh! the ghastly smile he tried to hide.

"Don't speak, Rory; but tell me with your eyes that you are not dying. No, no, Rory,—Rory of the Hills! demon as he is, he could not murder you. Heaven would not permit so much wickedness!"

Rory looked at her again. A faint but beautiful smile—beautiful now, for the colour had returned to his cheeks—beamed upon his lips, as he shook his head.

"Yes, yes, he has murdered him," sobbed the distracted father; "and I pity you, Winny Cavana, as I hope you will pity his poor mother; to say nothing of myself."

"No, no; do not say so! He will not die, he *shall* not die!" And she pressed her burning lips to his marble forehead. It was smooth as alabaster, cold as ice.

"Win—ny Ca—va—na, good-bye," he faintly breathed in her ear. "My days, my hours, my very moments are numbered. I feel death trembling in every vein, in every nerve. I could—could—have —lived for you,—Winny; but even—to—die for you—is—a blessing, because—successful. One last request,—Winny, my best beloved, is—all—I have —to ask: spare me—a spot in—Rathcash—chapel-yard, in the space allotted to—the—Cavanas. I feel some wonderful strength given me just now. It is

a special mercy that I may speak with you before I
go. But, Winny, my own precious, dearest love,
do not deceive yourself. If I reach home to receive
my mother's blessing before I die, it is the most—"
And he leaned his head against his father's breast.

"No more delay!" cried Winny energetically.
"Time is too precious to be lost; bring the cart
here, and let us take him home at once, and send
for the doctor. Oh! policeman, one of you is enough
to remain with the prisoner here; do, like a good,
good man, leave your gun and belts here, and run
off across the fields as fast as you can, and bring Dr.
Sweeny to Rathcash house—"

"To Shanvilla," faintly murmured the wounded
man; and bring Father Farrell."

"Yes, yes, to Shanvilla, to be sure," repeated
Winny; "my selfish heart had forgotten his poor
mother."

Rory opened his eyes at the word mother, and
smiled. It was a smile of thanks; and he closed
them again.

The policeman had obeyed her request in a
moment; and, stripped of all encumbrances, he was
clearing the hedges, ditches, and drains towards
Dr. Sweeny's.

They then placed Lennon, as gently as if he were
made of wax, into the cart, his head lying in Winny's
lap, and his hand clasped in hers, while the distracted father led the horse more like an automaton
than a human being. They proceeded at a very
gentle pace, for the cart had no springs, and Winny
knew that a jolt might be fatal if it burst the blood

forth afresh. The policeman followed with his prisoner at some distance; and ere long, for the dawn had become clear, he saw his comrades coming on behind him, a long way off. But there was evidently a man besides themselves and Jamesy Doyle. He sat down by the side of the road until they came up.

How matters stood was then explained to Sergeant Driscoll aside. Cotter told him he had no hopes that Lennon would ever reach home alive; that Donovan had gone off across the country for the doctor and the priest, and his *carabine* and belts were on the cart.

"We will take that prisoner from you, Cotter," said Driscoll, "and do you get on to the cart as fast as you can, you may be of use. I don't like to bring this villain Murdock in sight of them; you need not say we have got him at all. We will go on straight to the barrack by the lower road, and let you go up to Lennon's with the cart. But see here, Cotter,—do not speak to the wounded man at all, and don't let anybody else speak to him either. We won't want a word from him; sure we all saw it as plain as possible."

Cotter then hastened on, and soon overtook the cart. He merely said in explanation of being by himself, that his comrades had come up, and that he had given his prisoner to them, and hastened on to see if he could be of any use.

Winny soon suggested a use for the kind-hearted man,—to help poor Pat Lennon into the cart, and to lead the horse. This was done without stirring hand or foot of the poor sufferer; and the father lay at Rory's other side, scarcely less like death than he was himself.

When they came to the end of the road which turned to Rathcash and Shanvilla, Winny, as was natural, could have wished to go to Rathcash. She knew not how her poor father had been left, or what might be his fate. She could not put any confidence in the assurance of such ruffians, that a hair of his head should not be hurt; and did not one of the villains remain in the house? Yes, Winny, one of them *did remain* in the house, but he *did no harm to your father!*

With all her affection and anxiety on her father's account, Winny could not choose but to go on to Shanvilla. The less moving poor Rory got, the better; and to get from under his head now and settle him afresh would be cruel and might be fatal. Winny, therefore, sat silent as Cotter turned the horse's head towards Shanvilla, where, ere another half hour had added to the increasing light, they had arrived.

It is not to be supposed that Pat Lennon and his son had been awakened out of their sleep about midnight, had dressed hurriedly, and left the house without a word, and not have left Mrs. Lennon in a state of anxiety and suspense which she had never experienced before. She had got up and dressed herself, and spent the remainder of the night alternately sitting on the side of the bed and going to the door to listen.

Winny Cavana, who knew what a scene must ensue when they came to the door, had sent on

Cotter to the house; the father again taking his place at the horse's head. He was to tell Mrs. Lennon that an accident had happened—no, no, not *that*; but that Rory had been hurt; and that they were bringing him home quietly for fear of exciting him.

All precautions were of no use. Mrs. Lennon had waited but for the word "hurt," which she understood at once as imparting something serious. She rushed from the house like a mad woman, and stood upon the road gazing up and down. Fortunately Winny had the forethought to stop the cart out of sight of the house to give Cotter time to execute his mission, and calm Mrs. Lennon as much as possible. It was a lucky thought, and Cotter, who was a very intelligent man, was equal to the emergency.

As Mrs. Lennon looked round her in doubt, Cotter cried out, "Oh! don't go that road, Mrs. Lennon, for God's sake!" and he pointed in the direction in which the car was *not*. It was enough; the ruse had succeeded; and Mrs. Lennon started off at full speed, clapping her hands and crying out: "O Rory, Rory, have they killed you at last? Have they killed you? O Rory, Rory, my boy, my boy!" And she clapped her hands, and ran the faster. She was soon out of sight and hearing.

"Now is your time," said Cotter, running back to the cart; "she is gone off in another direction, and we'll have him on his bed before she comes back."

They then brought the cart to the door, and in the most gentle and scientific manner lifted poor Rory into the house and laid him on his bed.

"God bless you, Winny!" he said, stretching out his hand. "Don't, like a good girl, stop here now. Return to your poor father, who must be distracted about you. I'm better and stronger, thank God, and will be able to see you again before I—"

"Whist, whist, Rory mavourneen, don't talk that way; you are better, blessed be God! I must indeed go home, Rory, as you say, for my heart is torn about my poor father. God bless you, Rory, my own Rory!" And she stooped down and kissed his pale lips.

Cotter and she then left the house and made all the speed they could towards Rathcash. They had not gone very far when Cotter heard Mrs. Lennon coming back along the road, and they saw her turn in towards her own house.

Winny, poor soul, distracted as she was on her own account, and the suspense about her father, felt for the poor broken-hearted mother who was now closing perhaps the death-bed of her darling son. Cotter and she pursued their way in silence. There was no room in Winny's thoughts for conversation, and Cotter pitied her too much to intrude a word.

As they came to Kate Mulvey's door—which, if the reader has followed the geography of our story, he must know they had to pass—Captain was barking incessantly in the rear of the house, where he was chained up. He had been set a-going by what soon after broke upon their ears still farther on, though until now they had not heard it.

Bully-dhu having satisfied himself that nothing further was to be apprehended from the senseless form of a man upon the kitchen-floor, and finding it impossible to burst open the door where his master was confined, thought the next best thing that he could do was to bemoan the state of affairs outside the house, in hope of drawing some help to the spot. Accordingly he took his post immediately at the house-door, still determined to be on the safe side, for fear the man was scheming. Here he set up a long dismal and melancholy howl, something in the style of the complaining whistle of a railway-engine in distress, only of a deeper tone. It was an original thought of poor Bully-dhu's, however, for such a thing as the whistle of an engine had never been heard in that part of the world then or since.

"My father is dead," said Winny; "there is the Banshee."

"Not at all, Miss Winny; that is a dog."

"It is all the same; Bully-dhu would not cry that way for nothing; there is somebody dead, I'm sure."

"It is because he knew you were gone, Miss Winny, and he did not know where to look for you; that's all, you may depend."

"Thank you, Cotter; the dog might indeed do that same. God grant it is nothing worse!"

The moment they entered the lane turning to the house, poor Bully seemed as if a weight had been lifted off his heart. He knew Winny in a moment, of course; but, strange to say, there was no whine of delight at her approach, nor did he bound with his accustomed joy to meet her. He did not even wag his huge tail nor stir from the door. He stood up from his sitting posture and stretched out his fore-legs until his breast touched the ground, and then drew his hind-legs up after them into their proper place.

"There is death in that house, Mr. Cotter, depend upon it. O my God!" said Winny.

"Not at all, Miss Winny; don't be frightened. Shall I go in first?"

"Yes do, Cotter; but I'll be at your heels: I'll wait for no report."

By this time they were at the door, and Cotter followed Bully-dhu into the house. Winny, without looking right or left, rushed to her father's room. She found it locked, but quickly turning the key, she burst in. It was now broad daylight, and she saw at a glance her father stretched upon the bed, still bound hand and foot. She flew to the table, and taking his razor cut the cords. The poor old man was quite exhausted from suspense, excitement, and the fruitless physical efforts he had been making to free himself.

"Thank God, father!" she exclaimed; "I hope you are not hurt."

"No, dear. Give me a sup of milk, or I will choke."

Poor Winny, in the ignorance of her past habits, called out to Biddy to bring her some.

Biddy answered with a smothered cry from the inner room. Cotter flew to the door and unlocked it. In another moment he had set her free from her cords, and she darted across the kitchen to minister to the old man's wants at Winny's directions.

Poor Bully-dhu then pointed out to Cotter the share he had taken in the night's work, and it might almost be said quietly "gave himself up." At least he showed no disposition to escape. He lay down at the dead man's head, sweeping the floor with an odd wag of his bushy tail, rather proud than frightened at what he had done. That it was his work, Cotter could not for a moment doubt. The man's throat had by this time turned almost black, and there were the marks of the dog's teeth sunk deep at each side of the windpipe, where the choking grip of death had prevailed.

Cotter then brought a quilt from the room where he had released Biddy Murtagh, and spread it over the corpse, and was bringing Bully-dhu out to the yard, when he met Jamesy Doyle at the door. Jamesy took charge of him at once, and brought him round to the yard, where for the present he shut him up in his wooden house; but he did not intend to neglect him.

Jamesy told Cotter that Sergeant Driscoll and his men had taken their prisoners safe to the barracks, and desired him to tell Cotter to join them as soon as possible.

"I cannot join them yet awhile, Jamesy; we have a corpse in the house."

"God's mercy! an' shure it's not the poor ould masther?" said Jamesy.

"No; I don't know who he is. He must have been one of the depredators."

"An' th' ould masther done for him!—God be praised! More power to his elbow!"

"No, Jamesy, it was not the old master. It was Bully-dhu that choked him—see here;" and he turned down the quilt.

"The devil a word of lie you're tellin', sir; dear me, but he gev' him the tusks in style. Be gorra, Bully, I'll give you my own dinner to-day, an' to-morrow, an' next day for that. See, Mr. Cotter, how the Lord overtakes the guilty at wanst, sometimes. Didn't he strike down Tom Murdock wid lightning, an' he batin' me out a horseback? an' I'd never have cum up wid him only for that."

Cotter could not help smiling at Jamesy's enthusiasm.

"What are you laughin' at, Mr. Cotter? Maybe it's what you don't give in to me; but I tell you I seen the flash of lightning take him down ov the horse, as plain as the daylight. Where's Miss Winny?"

"Whist, whist, boy, don't be talking that way. Never heed Miss Winny; she's with her father. I would not like her to see this dead man here; don't be talking so loud. Is there any place we could draw him into, until we find out who he is?"

"An' I'd like to show him to Miss Winny, for Bully-dhu's sake. Will I call her?"

"If you do, I'll stick you with this, Jamesy," said Cotter, getting angry, and tapping his bayonet with his finger.

"Be gorra, an' that's not the way to get me to do anything, I can tell you; for I—"

"Well, there's a good boy, James; you have proved yourself one to-night; and now for God's sake don't fret poor Miss Winny worse than what she is already, and it would nearly kill her to see this dead man here now—it would make her think of some one else dead, Jamesy,—*thigum thu?*"

"*Thau*, begorra—you're right enough."

"Where can we bring him to? is there any out-house or place?"

"To be sure there is; there's the barn where I sleep; cum out wid him at wanst. I'll take him by the heels, an' let you dhraw him along the floore by his shoulders."

There was a coolness and intrepidity about all Jamesy's actions and expressions which surprised Cotter. With all his experience he had never seen the same in so young a boy—except in a hardened villain; and he had known Jamesy for the last four years to be the very contrary. Cotter, however, was not philosopher enough to know that an excess of principle, and a total want of it, might produce the same intrepidity of character.

But I must not begin to philosophise myself at the end of a chapter.

Cotter took the dead man under the shoulders and drew him along, while Jamesy took him by the feet and pushed him. Winny and Biddy Murtagh were both too busy in the poor old man's room to hear the noise they made, and in a few minutes the dead man, whoever he was, lay stretched in the barn.

Neither Winny, nor Biddy, nor the old man knew a word about this part of the performance. Jamesy saw the propriety of keeping it to himself for the present. Cotter locked the barn-door, and took away the key with him. He told Jamesy that he would find out from the other prisoner "who the corpse was," and that he would call again with instructions in the course of the day. He then hastened to the barrack, and Jamesy went in to see Miss Winny and the ould masther. The message which Cotter had sent her by Jamesy was this— "To keep up her heart, and to hold herself in readiness for a visit from the resident magistrate before the day was over."

CHAPTER XXXI.

It was still very early. The generality of the inhabitants were not yet up, and Winny sighed at the long sad day which was before her. She had first made her father tell her how the ruffians had served him, and after hearing the particulars she detailed everything which had befallen herself. She described the battle at the bridge, as well as her sobs would permit her, from the moment the Lennons sprung up from behind the battlement to their rescue, until the fatal arrival of the police, as she called it, upon the approach of whom "that demon fired his pistol at my poor Rory, as close as I am to you, father."

"Well, well, Winny, don't lave the blame upon the police; he would have fired at Lennon whether they cum up or not, for Rory would never have let go his holt."

"True enough, father. I do not lay it upon them

at all. Rory would have clung to his horse for miles if he had not shot him down."

"Besides, Jamesy says the police has him fast enough. Isn't that a mercy at all events, Winny?"

"It is only the mercy of revenge, father; God forgive me for the thought; the law will call it justice."

"And a just revenge is all fair an' right, Winny. He had no pity on an innocent boy, an' why should you have pity on a guilty villain?"

"Pity! No, father; I have no pity for him. But I wish I did not feel so vengeful."

"But how did the police hear of it, Winny, or find out which way they went; and what brought Jamesy Doyle up with them?"

"We must ask Jamesy himself about that, father," she said; and she desired Biddy to call him in, for he was with Bully-dhu.

Jamesy was soon in attendance again, and they made him sit down, for with all his pluck he looked weary and fatigued. They then asked him to tell everything, from the moment he first heard the men smashing the door.

Jamesy Doyle's description of the whole thing was short and decisive, told in his own graphic style, with many "begorras," in spite of Winny's remonstrances. The reader is already aware of Jamesy's exploits, and the promptness with which he carried them out. We will not, therefore, weary him with a repetition of them in Jamesy's own words. One sentence, however, was so characteristic of the boy that we will venture to repeat it as a fair specimen of the whole detail, which the reader cannot fail to recognise.

"Begorra, Miss Winny, I tould Bully-dhu what they were up to, an' I let him in at the hall-doore, an' when I seen him tumble the fust man he met, and stick in his windpipe without so much as a growl, I knew there was one man wouldn't lave that easy, any way; an' I med off for the polis as fast as my legs an' feet could carry me."

"And how did—how—did—poor Rory hear of it?" sighed Winny.

"Arra blur-an-ages, Miss Winny, didn't I cut across by Shanvilla, an' tould him every haporth? Why, miss, he'd murdher me af I let him lie there dhramin', an' they carryin' you off, Miss Winny."

It was to Jamesy, then, that Winny owed her rescue, after all; and it was to Jamesy that faithful uncompromising young fellow Rory would owe his death.

"O Jamesy, why did you not go straight for the police and never mind Rory of the Hills?" she said.

"Ah! Winny dear," said her father, "remember that there was nearly half-an-hour's battle at the bridge before the police came up; and had your persecutor that half hour's law where and what would you be now?"

"I did not care. I would have fought my battle alone against twenty Tom Murdocks. They might have ill-used me, and then murdered me, but what of that? Rory of the Hills would live,—perhaps to avenge me,—but now—now—O father, father!"

I wish he had murdered me along with Rory. But, God forgive me, indeed I am very sinful; I forgot you, father dear. Here, Biddy, get the kettle boiling; we all want a cup of tea;" and she put her handkerchief to her swimming eyes.

She soon straightened herself up, and pushing the dark bands of damp hair off her face she rolled them in thick curls behind her ears, and set about getting some breakfast for her poor father and herself.

Biddy was not long blowing up the fire, and the kettle was soon boiling. A "raking" pot of tea was then made for the whole party—for which of them did not need refreshment?

Winny persuaded her father to eat some bread and butter, by setting him the example; and when this early breakfast was over she made him go again to bed. She closed the window-shutter, and as the poor old man was not tied, and could turn as he liked, fatigue soon found him in a sound sleep.

Biddy Murtagh and Jamesy Doyle both lay down also, and both soon slept. Jamesy had thrown himself in his clothes on some empty sacks in a corner of the kitchen, saying, "Miss Winny, I'm tired enough to sleep anywhere, an' I'll lie down here."

"Hadn't you better go to your own bed in the barn, Jamesy, where you can take off your clothes? I am sure you would be more comfortable."

"No, Miss Winny, I'm sure I would not. Besides, the policeman tuck—" Jamesy stopped himself. "What the mischief have I said?" thought he.

"The policeman took what, Jamesy?" said Winny.

"He tuck the key, Miss. He said no one should g'win there tal he cum back."

"Oh! very well, Jamesy; lie down, and let me throw this quilt over you. I wonder what brought it here. But, God's mercy, if here is not a pool of blood! Oh! am I doomed to see nothing but blood —blood? What is this, Jamesy? do you know?"

"I do, Miss. It was Bully-dhu that cut one of the men when they cum in; an' the devil's cure to him, Miss Winny!"

"Fie, Jamesy, don't say that, but he must have cut him severely, the whole floor is covered with blood."

"Cut him is it? Begorra, Miss Winny, he kilt him out-an'-out: I may as well tell you the thruth at wanst."

"For Heaven's sake, you do not mean to say that he actually killed him, Jamesy?"

"That's just what I do mane, Miss Winny, an' I may as well tell you, for Mr. Cotter will be here by-an'-bye with the coroner and a jury to hould an inquest. Isn't he lyin' there abroad in the barn as stiff as a crowbar, an' as ugly as if he was bespoke, Miss? Didn't I help Mr. Cotter to carry him out, or rather to dhrag him, for begorra he was as heavy as if he was made of led?"

"Fie, fie, James, you should not talk that way of any poor fellow-being—for shame!"

"An' a bad fellow-bein' he was, to cum here to carry you away, Miss Winny, an' maybe to murdher you in the mountain—or maybe worse. My blessin' on you, Bully-dhu!"

Winny was shocked at the cool manner in which Jamesy spoke of such a frightful occurrence. She was afraid she would never make a Christian of him.

Now Jamesy was quite as good a Christian as she was herself, but he had a different way of showing it.

The day wore on slowly enough until the afternoon. Reports had to be made to the magistrate and to the chief. The coroner had to be sent for, and summonses had to be filled in. It was therefore late in the afternoon before any further interruption occurred at Rathcash house.

Cotter and a comrade now returned, and took charge of the body until the coroner should arrive. They had served summonses upon twelve or fourteen of the most respectable neighbours—good men and true. They had ascertained that the deceased was a man named John Fahy, from the county of Cavan, a reputed Ribbonman. The cart had belonged to him, but of course there was no name upon it. The news of the whole affair had already spread like fire the moment the people began to get about; and two brothers of Fahy's arrived to claim the body before the inquest was over.

Jamesy Doyle was the principal witness "before the fact." His evidence was like himself all over. Having been sworn by the coroner, he did not think that sufficient, but began his statement with another oath of his own—the reader knows by this time what it was. The coroner checked him, and reminded him that he was already on his solemn oath, and that light swearing of that kind was very unseemly, and could not be permitted—he advised him to be cautious.

Jamesy had sense enough to take his advice, although he seldom took Winny's upon the same subject.

"When I first heered the *rookawn*, I got up, an' dhrew on my clothes, an' cum round the corner of the house. I seen three men stannin' at the doore, an' I heered wan of 'em ordher it to be bruck in. I knew there was but two women an' wan ould man, the masther, in the house, an' I knew there was no use in goin' in to be murdhered, an' that I could be of more use a grate dale outside. Bully-dhu was roarin' like a lion in the back-yard, an' couldn't get out. I knew Bully was well able for wan of 'em any way, if not two; an' I let him out, an' brought him to the hall-doore. The minnit ever I let him out iv the yard he was as silent as the grave, an' I knew what that meant. Well, I brought him to the doore, an' pointed to the disceased, for he was the first man I seen in from me. Well, without with your lave or by your lave, Bully had him tumbled on the floore, an' his four big teeth stuck in his windpipe. 'That'll do,' says I, 'as far as wan of ye goes, any way;' an' I med off for the police. I wasn't much out about Bully, your worship, for the man never left that antil Mr. Cotter an' I helped him out into the barn."

The rest of what Jamesy had to say did not touch upon the death of Fahy, and he was told he might keep it for the magistrate.

Cotter was then examined. His evidence was

"that he had found the deceased lying dead on the kitchen-floor; that the dog on entering lay down at his head and put his paw upon his breast, as if pointing out what he had done." That was all he knew about it.

The doctor was then examined,—surgeon perhaps we should call him on this occasion,—and swore "that he had carefully examined the deceased; that he had been choked; and that the wounds in the throat indicated that they had been inflicted by the teeth of a large powerful dog: no cat, nor other animal known in this country, could have done it."

This closed the evidence. The coroner made a short charge to the jury, and the verdict was, "that the deceased, John Fahy, as they believed him to be, had come by his death by being suffocated *and choked* by a large black dog called Bully-dhu, belonging to one Edward Cavana of Rathcash, in the parish, &c. &c.; but that inasmuch as he, the said deceased, was in the act of committing a felony at the time, for which, if convicted in a court of law, he would have forfeited his life, they would not recommend the dog to be destroyed."

The coroner said, "he thought this was a very elaborate verdict upon so simple a case, and disagreed with the jury upon the latter part of the verdict. The dog could not have known that, and it was evident he was a ferocious animal, and he thought he ought to be destroyed."

"He did know it, your honour," vociferated Jamesy Doyle. "Didn't I tell him, and wasn't it I pointed out the deceased to him, and tould him to hould him? If it was th'ould masther or myself kilt him, you couldn't say a haporth to aidher of us, let alone the dog."

If this was not logic for the coroner, it was for the jury, who refused to change their verdict. But the tack to the verdict, exonerating poor Bully-dhu, was almost unnecessary, where he had such a friend in court as Jamesy Doyle; for he, anticipating some such attempt, had provided for poor Bully's safety. His first act after Cotter had left in the morning was to get a chum of his, who lived not far off, to take the dog in his collar and strap to an uncle's son, a first cousin of his, about seven miles away, to tell him what had happened, and to take care of the dog until the thing "blew over," and that "Miss Winny would never forget it to him."

It would almost appear that Bully-dhu was aware of what all this was for. He trotted along with his guide, with no more than a slight whistle now and then as he clambered over some ditch or wall. Billy Brennan delivered the dog and the message safely: "he'd do more nor that for Miss Winny;" or for that matter for the dog himself, for they were great play-fellows in the dry grass of a summer's day. Now it was a strange fact, and deserves to be recorded for the curious in such things, that although Bully-dhu had never seen Jamesy's cousin in his life, and that although he was a surly distant dog to strangers, he took up with young Barney Foley the moment he saw him. He never stirred from his side, and did not appear inclined to leave the place. But he was quite silent and never wagged his tail.

He showed every sign and token that he was "on his keeping;" and that he knew it. But his banishment to this strange place did not last long. Jamesy, although he was on the safe side in sending him "out of the way," could not bear, now that he was "acquitted by the jury," to be a moment longer without him than could be helped; and Billy Brennan was to get another tenpenny-bit to start again before day, and bring him back. Billy had got one already for leaving him beyond; and these two tenpenny-bits were out of a little tin porringer, where Jamesy kept his private bank. Winny would no doubt indorse Jamesy's liberality with her own, when she *found out* the truth; but Jamesy would not tell her.

Before the inquest had closed its proceedings, the two brothers of the deceased man adverted to, had arrived to take away the body. It was well for poor Bully-dhu, after all, that Jamesy had been so thoughtful, although it was quite another source of danger he had apprehended. The two Fahys searched high and low for the dog, one of them armed secretly with a loaded pistol, but both openly with huge crab-tree sticks, to beat his brains out, in spite of coroner, magistrate, police, or jury. But they searched in vain. They offered Jamesy, not knowing the stuff he was made of, a pound-note "to show them where the big black dog was." His answer, though mute, was just like him. He put his left thumb to the tip of his nose, his right thumb to the little finger of the left hand, and began to play the bag-pipes in the air with his fingers.

They pressed it upon him and he got vexed.

"Begorra," said he, "af ye cum here to-night afther midnight to take Miss Winny away, I'll show him to you, an' maybe it wouldn't be worth the coroner's while to go home."

"He may stay where he is, for that matther," said one of the brothers. "He'll have work enough to-morrow or next day at Shanvilla;" and they turned away.

"Aye, and the hangman from the county of *Cavan* will have something to do soon afther," shouted Jamesy after them, who was never at a loss for an answer. He had the last word here, and it was a sore one.

As the brothers Fahy failed in their search for Bully, they had nothing further that they dare vent their grief and indignation upon. It was no use in bemoaning the matter there amongst unsympathising strangers; so they fetched the cart to the barn-door and laid the corpse into it, covering it with a white sheet which they had brought for the purpose.

"Will I lind you a hand, boys?" said Jamesy, as they were struggling with the weight of the dead man at the barn-door.

The scowl he got from one of the brothers would have discomfited a boy less plucky or self-possessed than Jamesy Doyle; but he had not said it in irony. No one there appeared inclined to give any help, and Jamesy actually did get under the corpse, and "*helped* him into the cart," as he said himself.

The unfortunate men then left, walking one at each side of their dead brother. And who is there, except perhaps Jamesy Doyle, who would not pity them as they rumbled their melancholy way down the boreen to the road?

CHAPTER XXXII.

About two hours later in the day, "the chief" arrived to "visit the scene," as he was bound to do before he made his report.

He was received courteously and with respect by Winny Cavana, who showed him into the parlour. He considerately began by regretting the unfortunate and melancholy occurrence which had taken place; but of course added, the satisfaction it was to him, indeed that it must be to everyone, that the perpetrators had been secured, particularly the principal mover in the sad event.

Winny made no remark, and "the chief" then requested her to state in detail what had occurred from the time the men broke into the house until the shot was fired which wounded the man. She seemed at first disinclined to do so; but upon that gentleman explaining that she would be required to do so on her oath, when the magistrate called to take her information, she merely sighed, and said.

"I suppose so; indeed I do not see why I should not."

She then gave him a plain and succinct account as far as their conduct to herself was concerned, and referred him to her father and the servants for the share they had taken towards them.

He soon obtained from old Cavana, Biddy Murtagh, and Jamesy Doyle what they knew of the transaction; and thus fully primed and loaded for his report, he left, telling Winny Cavana "the stipendiary magistrate had left home the day before, but that he would be back the next day; and she might expect an official visit from him, as he would make arrangements with him that she should not be brought from her home, when no doubt the prisoners would be remanded for the doctor's report of the wounded man."

There was no *local* magistrate within miles of the place, and as the stipendiary had been written for, there was no doubt of his speedy return. "The chief" had no choice under the circumstances but to detain the prisoners in the police-barrack until he could get them finally committed for trial. The temporary absence of the magistrate saved much trouble, after all. Had he been on the spot the day after the occurrence he would have only committed the prisoners for further examination, and it would have been necessary to bring them up again. Now it was otherwise; the *one* committal and transmission was all that was required.

The morning after "the chief" had been at Rathcash house, Winny Cavana, almost immediately after breakfast, told Jamesy Doyle to get ready, and come with her to Shanvilla. She was anxious to ascertain from personal knowledge how poor Rory was going on. She was distracted by the contradictory reports which Biddy Murtagh brought in from time to time from the passers-by upon the road. Winny had little, if any, hope at all that Rory Lennon would survive. She had been assured by Father Farrell, in whose truth and experience she placed the greatest confidence, that it was *impossible*, although he might linger for a few days. The doctor too had pronounced the same solemn doom. Her thoughts as she hastened towards Shanvilla were full of awe and *determination*. She had spent the night, the entire night, for she had never closed an eye, in laying down a broad short map of her future life, and it was already engraven on her mind. She had been clever in drawing such things at the school where she had been educated, and her thoughts now took that form.

Her poor father while he lived; herself before and after his death; the Lennons one and all; Kate Mulvey, Phil M'Dermott, Jamesy Doyle, Biddy Murtagh, and Bully-dhu were the only spots marked upon the map; but they were conspicuous, like the capital towns of counties. There was but one river on the map, and it could be traced by Winny's tears. It was the great river of "the Past," and rose in the distant mountains of her memory which hemmed-in this map of her fancy. It flowed first round old Ned and the Lennons, who were bounded by Winny on the north, south, east, and west. It passed by Kate Mulvey and Phil M'Dermott, and thence passing by Jamesy Doyle, Biddy Murtagh, and Bully-dhu, it emptied itself into the Irish ocean of Winny's affectionate heart.

Winny knew that she would meet Father Farrell at Rory's bedside; he scarcely ever left it; and she knew that he would not deceive her as to his real state. She knew too that he would not refuse her a sincere Christian advice and counsel upon the sudden resolve which had taken possession of her heart.

Father Farrell saw her coming from Rory's window, and went to meet her at the door. They stood in the kitchen alone. The poor father and mother had been kept out of Rory's room by the priest, and were bewailing their fate in their own room.

"I am glad you are come, Winny dear," said he. "The poor fellow has not ceased to speak of you, and pray for you from the first, when he does transgress his orders not to speak at all."

"How is he, oh! how is he, Father Farrell?"

"Stronger just now, but dying, Winny Cavana. Let nothing tempt you to deceive yourself. He has been so much stronger for the last hour or so, that I was just going to send my gig for you. He said it would soothe his death-bed, which he knows he is on, Winny, to see you and have your blessing."

"He shall have my blessing, and I shall claim every right to give it to him. Father Farrell," she added solemnly, but with a full untrembling tone, "will you marry me to Rory Lennon?"

The priest almost staggered back from her for a moment.

"Yes, Father Farrell, you have heard aright, and I solemnly and sincerely repeat the question. Listen: you must know that never on this earth shall I wed any other. . I shall devote myself, and the greater portion of any wealth I may possess, to the Church for charitable purposes, after Rory Lennon, my future husband—future here and hereafter—is dead. I wish to call him husband by that precious right which death will so soon rob me of. Even so, Father Farrell; give me that right, short though it be. It will enable me legally to provide for his honest stout-hearted father and his broken-hearted mother, without the lying lips of slander doubting the motive. O Father Farrell, it is the only consolation left me now to hope for, or in your power to bestow."

The priest was struck dumb. Her eyes, her breath, pleaded almost more than her words.

Father Farrell sat down upon a form.

"Winny Cavana," he said, "do not press me—that is, I mean do not hurry me. The matter admits of serious consideration, and may not be altogether so unreasonable or extraordinary as it might at first appear. But I say that it requires consideration. Walk abroad for a few minutes, and let me think."

"No, father. You may remain here for a few minutes and think. Let me go in and see my poor Rory."

"Yes, yes, you shall; but I must go in along with you, Winny. I can come out again if I find that more consideration is necessary."

Winny saw that she had gained her point. They then entered the room, and Rory cast such a look of gratitude and love upon Winny as calmed every doubt upon the priest's mind, for he was afraid that Rory himself would object, and that the scene would injure him.

Winny was soon at Rory's side with his hand clasped in hers.

"You are come, Winny dear, to bid me a final good-bye—in this world," he murmured. "God bless you for your goodness, and your love for me!"

"I am come, Rory dear, to fulfil that love in the presence of Heaven, and with Father Farrell's sanction—am I not, Father Farrell?"

"I never doubted it, Winny dear."

"And you shall not doubt it now. You shall die declaring it. Rory—Rory, my own Rory of the Hills, I am come to claim the promise you gave me to make me your wife."

"Great God! Winny, are you mad?—is she not mad, Father Farrell?"

"No, Rory dear, she really is not mad. She will devote herself and her whole future life to charity and the love of a better world than this. She can do that not only as well, but better in some respects as your widow than otherwise. I have considered the matter, and I cannot see that there are any just reasons to deny her request."

"Then I shall die happy, though it be this very night. But, O Winny, Winny, think of what you are about: time will soften your grief, and you may yet be happy with ano—"

"Stop, Rory dear—not another word; for here, before Heaven and Father Farrell, I swear never shall I marry any one in this world but you! Here, Father Farrell, begin; here is a ring you gave me yourself, Rory, and although not a wedding-ring it will do very well—we will make one of it."

Father Farrell then brought in Rory's father and mother, and married Winny Cavana to the dying man.

She stooped down, and kissed his pallid lips. Big drops of sweat burst out upon his forehead, and Father Farrell saw that the last moment was at hand. Winny held his hand between both hers, and said, "Rory, you are now mine—mine, by divine right, and I resign you to the Lord." And she looked up to Heaven through the roof, while the big tears rolled down her pale cheeks.

"Winny," said Rory, in a solemn but distinct voice, "I now die happy. For this I have lived, and for this I die. I cannot count on even hours now; my very moments are numbered. I feel death trembling round my heart. But you have calmed its approach, Winny dear. Your love and devotion at a moment like this is the happiest pang that softens my passage to the grave. I can now claim a right to what you promised me as a favour—my portion of your space in Rathcash chapel-yard. God bless you, Winny dear!—good-bye—my—wife!"

Yes, Rory had lived and had died for the love of her who was *now his widow*.

As Rory had ceased to speak, a bright smile broke over his whole countenance, and he rendered his last sigh into the safe keeping of his guardian angel until the last great day.

Winny knew that he was dead, though his breath had passed so gently forth, that he might have been only falling asleep. She continued to hold his hand, and to gaze upon his still features, while Father

Farrell's lips moved in silent prayer, more for the living than the dead.

"Come, Winny," he said at last, "you cannot remain here just at present. Come along with me, and I will bring you in my gig to your father's house, where I will tell him all myself."

"O, thank you, thank you, Father Farrell," she said, turning resignedly with him. "Tell poor Pat Lennon what has happened; their pity for me as a companion in their grief may help to soften their own. Tell him, of course, Father Farrell, that I shall take all the arrangements of the funeral upon myself—God help them and me!"

As they came from the dead man's room they met Pat Lennon in the kitchen, and Winny, throwing her arms round his neck, caught the big salt tears which were rolling down his face upon her quivering lips.

"I have a right to call you father now," she exclaimed. "You have lost a son, but I will be your daughter." And she kissed him again and again.

Of course the keening and clapping of hands now rang through the house and around it. But Father Farrell, whose quiet old horse had been standing at the door all this time, hurried poor Winny into the gig, and drove her home.

CHAPTER XXXIII.

On their way to Rathcash, Winny in the first instance told the priest that "of course her poor husband should be buried in Rathcash chapel-yard, and, as a matter in which she could not interfere, by Father Roche." Here she stopped, but the kind-hearted priest took her up at once.

"Of course, my dear child," he said, "that will be quite right. Indeed, Winny, I should not wish to be the person so soon to add that sad ceremony to the still sadder one I was engaged in to-day."

"Before God or man, Father Farrell, you will never have cause to regret that act. It was my own choosing after deliberate consideration, and I was the best judge of my own feeling. I *can* be happy now. I never *could* be happy if it were otherwise."

"God grant it, my love," said the priest.

"But still, Father Farrell," she continued, "I have something more for you to do for me. Will you not, like a good man, take all the arrangement of the funeral upon yourself. I will pay every penny of the expenses, and let them not be niggardly. Thank God, Father Farrell, I can do so now without reproach."

The kind sympathising priest engaged to do everything which was requisite in the most-approved-of manner. The more he reflected upon what he had done, the less fault he had to find with himself.

There was a calm resigned tone about all that Winny now said very different from what he might have anticipated from his knowledge of her temper and disposition, had the fatal moment taken place when the shot was fired, or even subsequently before she became Rory Lennon's wife. Bitter revenge, he thought, would have seized her soul towards the man who had deprived her of all hope or source of happiness in this world. Now the only time she trusted her tongue to speak of him was an exclamation,—" May God forgive him!"

But even now could Father Farrell hope that *she* had done so? Oh! no, no, Father Farrell had read human nature too attentively to hope it. He believed, however, that she had subdued the feeling of revenge in her heart, if not that of exultation at Murdock's arrest. That Winny was hot-tempered and determined he knew from her own pastor, Father Roche, and that she sometimes, when under excitement or provocation, was in the habit of uttering hasty exclamations of resolve which were not creditable or consistent with her calmer moments. But he had it from Father Roche also that it was only necessary to point out the impropriety of these exclamations, or any imprudence in the resolves themselves, to gain, not only her prompt and cordial acquiescence in the proper view of the case, but a sincere promise to refrain from such hasty and objectionable exclamations for the future. But Father Farrell knew right well that this resolve of Winny's with respect to young Lennon was no hasty or inconsiderate ebullition of feeling. He believed it to be a well-digested plan for praiseworthy and important purposes, which Winny's character would never alter or give up. He, on his part, had given the matter his most serious and well-intentioned consideration; and to do the good man no more than justice, it was not because he sympathised in some of Winny's intentions towards the Church, that he saw nothing wrong in yielding to her entreaties.

The thing was done, however, and Father Farrell did not regret it.

They soon arrived at Rathcash house, where Father Farrell paid a long visit to old Ned Cavana. His kindness quite gained upon the old man, although he was not *his own* priest; and before he left, he acquainted him with the facts of his daughter's position and the death of her husband.

The old man sat silent for some time after the truth had been made known to him. Winny stood hoping for a look of encouragement and forgiveness; but the old man gave it not. At length, with that impatience habitual to her disposition, she rushed into his arms, and wept upon his breast.

"O father," she exclaimed, "I could never be the wife of any man living after poor Rory's death in defence of my life; aye, more than my life, of my honour."

"But, O Winny, Winny! to sacrifice yourself for a man so near the grave! There was no hope for him, I heered."

"None, father. I was aware of that. Had there been, I should have waited patiently. I told Father Farrell here my plans, and the same thing as swore that I would not alter them. He will now tell them to you, father dear; and I shall lie down for a couple of hours, for indeed I want rest of both body and mind."

She then kissed her father again and again. and blessed him, or rather she prayed to God to do so, and went to her room.

Father Farrell then explained all Winny's views to her distracted father, observing, as he had been enjoined to do, the tenderest love and respect for the old man; taking nothing "for granted;" but at the same time showing the utmost confidence that all matters would still be arranged for his daughter in the same manner he had often explained to her to be his intention. "One step she was determined on," Father Farrell said; "and that was to join a religious sisterhood of charity in the North. Nothing should ever tempt her to marry."

"I'll sell this place at wance," said old Ned, "It's not a month since I had a rattlin' bid for it; but my landlord—and he's member for the county, you know—tould me with his own lips, that if ever I had a mind to part with it, he'd give me a hundred pounds more for it than anyone else."

"That was Winny's wish, Ned; and that you should remove with her to the North, where she would settle you comfortably, and where she could see you almost every day in the week."

"Almost," repeated old Ned sorrowfully.

"Well, perhaps every day, Ned, for that matter."

"Well, Father Farrell, I would not wish to stay

here any longer afther what has happened. I'll sell the place out an' out at wance. I have nothing to do but to write to my landlord. I could not bear to be lookin' across at Mick Murdock's afther what tuck place. I think my poor Winny is right; an' that it was the Lord put it all into her head. Athen, Father Farrell, maybe it was yourself laid it down for the little girl?"

"No, Ned; she laid it all down for me. I was going to reason with her at first, but she put her hand upon my mouth, and told me to stop, and as good as swore that nothing should alter her plans. I considered her words, Ned, for a while, and I gave in; not on account of her determination, but because I thought she was right. And I think so still; even to the marrying of Rory on his death-bed."

"Indeed, Father Farrell, you have aised my mind. Glory be to God, that guided her!"

"Amen," said the priest.

Father Farrell had now in the kindest manner dealt with old Ned Cavana, according to Winny's wishes and instructions; so that it was an easy matter for Winny herself on that evening, when she had joined her father after a refreshing sleep, to explain more in detail her intentions as regarded herself, and her wishes as regarded her friends,—those capitals of counties which were marked on the map of her imagination.

Old Ned was like a child in her hands; and no mother ever handled her first-born babe more fondly than Winny dealt with her poor old father.

"Ducks an' dhrakes iv it, Winny asthore; ducks

an' dhrakes iv it, Winny dear! Isn't it all your own; what do I want with it, mavrone, but to see you happy; an' haven't you laid out a plan for both yourself an' myself that can't be bet—can't be bet, Winny mavourneen?"

The old man was perfectly satisfied with the map, and studied it so well, that he had it by heart before he went to bed, and could have told you the boundaries of all Winny's wishes to the breadth of a hair, as he kissed her for the last time that night.

I will spare the reader a detail of the melancholy *cortège* of poor Rory of the Hills' funeral, which proceeded from Shanvilla to Rathcash chapel-yard the day but one after.

Winny had expressed a wish to attend it, but had yielded to the joint advice of Father Farrell and Father Roche to resist the impulse. She might well and truly plead, or rather they might plead for her, prostration of mind and body, should any observation be made upon the subject.

So large—or, what in Ireland is thought so much of, so *decent*—a funeral had not passed into Rathcash chapel-yard for years. The whole population of the two parishes, joining at different points, moved slowly along; nor was there a light or irreverent smile on the lips of a single individual in the crowd, nor a word spoken upon indifferent affairs.

Rory of the Hills had been well and truly loved in life and was now sincerely regretted in death. Father Farrell, at the head of the procession, was met by Father Roche bare-headed at the chapel-gate of Rathcash; and the melancholy ceremony was performed amidst the silent grief of the immense crowd around.

Poor Rory's "last wish was complied with;" and he now occupied his last resting-place with the Cavanas of Rathcash.

CHAPTER XXXIV.

The stipendiary had hastened home upon the receipt of "the chief's" letter. It was too important a case to be absent from the inquiry and management of. They had driven in the first instance to the police-barrack, where the prisoners were still detained. Pat Lennon as a "material witness" had been sent for, and had soon arrived. The magistrate then had the prisoners brought into the day-room, and told them what they were charged with, and proceeded to take down in their presence the informations of the policemen who were present when the shot was fired. He also took the informations of Pat Lennon. He next proceeded to Rathcash house, to take the informations of the inmates there, where the first attack and abduction were made, both as a distinct offence in itself, as well as a stepping-stone to the murder which had been subsequently committed.

It was still about an hour after noon, when Winny beheld from the parlour-window at which she stood a very exciting cavalcade upon the road, slowly approaching the house. At once she became acquainted with the whole concern. "The chief" had forewarned her that she might expect a visit from the magistrate the moment he returned; and her intelligence at once recognised the addition of the police and prisoners some distance in rear of the car.

Winny's heart beat quick and high as she saw them draw nigh and turn up the lane. It would be mock heroism to say that it did not. She knew that Tom Murdock, the murderer of her husband, must be one of the prisoners, but she did not know why they were bringing him there—for the police had now made the turn. She thought the magistrate might have spared her that fresh excitement—that renewal of her hate. But the magistrate was one of those who had anticipated the law by his sense of justice and his practice. He was one who gave everyone of his Majesty's subjects fair play, and it was therefore his habit to have the accused face to face with the accuser when informations were taken and read.

Poor Winny was rather fluttered and disturbed when they entered, notwithstanding "the chief" had considerately prepared her for the visit. She did not lose her self-possession, however, so much as to forget the respect and courtesy due to gentlemen, besides being officers of the law. She asked them down into the parlour, and requested of them to be seated. They accepted her civility in silence, seeing enough in her manner to show them that she was greatly distressed, and required a little time to compose herself. She was, however, the first to speak.

"I suppose, gentlemen, you are come respecting

this sad affair. I told this gentleman here all I knew about it yesterday."

"Yes, but matters are still worse to-day, although there was no hope even then that they would be better. Of course it will relieve you so far at once to tell you that we are aware of the position in which you now stand towards the deceased."

"Yes, sir. It was with a wish that the world might know it I took the step I did. I had Father Farrell's approval of it, and my own parish-priest's as well; but subsequently—"

"My good girl, we did not come here to question the propriety or otherwise of either your actions or your motives. Nor do I for one hesitate to say that I believe both to have been unexceptionable. But it will be necessary that you should make an information upon oath as to what took place from the first moment the men came to the door, until the shot was fired by which Rory Lennon came by his death."

"I suppose, sir, you must have much better evidence than mine as to the firing of the shot. I can only swear to the fact of two men having tied me up and carried me away on a cart, and that there was a third man on horseback with a mask upon his face; that when we came to Boher bridge, the deceased Rory Lennon and his father came to our rescue; that there was a long and distracting struggle at the bridge, which lasted with very doubtful hopes of success for my deliverance until Jamesy Doyle, our servant-boy, came up with the police; that the man on horseback with the mask, whom I verily believe to have been Thomas Murdock, turned to fly; that the deceased Rory Lennon fastened in his horse's bridle to prevent him; that a deadly struggle ensued between them; and that the man on horseback fired at the deceased, who fell, I may say, dead on the road. The sight left my eyes, sir; and except that we brought the dying man home on the cart, I know no more about it of my own knowledge, sir."

"A very plain, straightforward, honest story as I ever heard," said the magistrate. "But it will be necessary for you, when upon your oath, to state whether you know, that is, whether you recognised the man on horseback at the time."

"I could not recognise his features, sir, on account of the mask he wore; but I did recognise his voice as that of Tom Murdock, and I knew his figure and general appearance."

"That will do now, Mrs. Lennon. I shall only trouble you to repeat slowly and distinctly what you have already said, so that I can write it down."

The magistrate then unlocked his leather writing-case, took out the necessary forms of informations, and was not long embodying what Winny had to say in proper shape.

He then went through the same form with old Ned, with Biddy Murtagh, and with Jamesy Doyle. The reader is already acquainted with what each of these persons could tell the magistrate; and although we have given a sketch of what Winny had said, it will not be necessary to tire the reader with a repetition of what he knows so well.

When the magistrate had all the informations

taken and arranged, he directed Sergeant Driscoll to bring in the prisoners, that he might read them over, and swear the several informants in their presence. Winny became very nervous and fidgety, and would have left the room, but the magistrate assured her that it was absolutely necessary that she should remain, at least while her own informations were being read. He would read them first, and she might then retire. He regretted very much that it was necessary, but he would not detain her more than a couple of minutes at most.

Tom Murdock and the other prisoner were then brought in; and Winny having identified the other man, her informations were read in a loud distinct voice by the magistrate, and she acknowledged herself bound &c. &c.

"You may now retire, Mrs. Lennon," said the magistrate; and she hastened to leave the room.

Tom Murdock stood near the door out of which she must pass, his hands crossed below his breast in consequence of the handcuffs. He knew that there was no chance of escape, no hope of an alteration or mitigation of his doom in this world. Everything was too plain against him. There were several witnesses to his deed of death, and the damning words by which it was accompanied, and he knew that the rope must be his end. Well, he had purchased his revenge, and he was willing to pay for it. He determined therefore to put on the bravado, and glut that revenge upon his still surviving victim.

"Rory of the Hills is dead, Miss Cavana," said he, as Winny would have passed him to the door, her eyes fastened on the ground, "but not buried yet," he added with a sardonic smile. "I wish I were free of these manacles, that I might follow his *remains* to Shanvilla chapel-yard."

"You would go wrong," she calmly replied. "He is indeed dead, but not buried yet. But he is my dead husband, and will lie with the Cavanas in the chapel-yard of Rathcash, and rise again with them; and I would rather be possessed of the inheritance of the six feet of grass upon his grave than be mistress of Rathcash, and Rathcashmore to boot. Where will you be buried, Tom Murdock? within the precincts of—the jail. To rise with—but no! I shall not condemn beyond the grave: may God forgive you! I cannot."

Even Tom Murdock's stony heart was moved. "Winny Cavana, do you think God can?" he said, turning towards her; but she had passed out of the door.

The magistrate then read the informations of the other witnesses, while Tom Murdock and the other prisoner stood apparently listening, though they heard not a word.

Jamesy Doyle's informations were word for word characteristic of himself. He insisted upon having the flash of lightning inserted therein, as an undoubted fact, "if ever he saw one knock a man down in his life."

The witnesses having been all "bound over" to prosecute at the next assizes, nothing now remained but to commit the prisoners to the county jail; and in less than a quarter of an hour the police escorted them down the lane, and turned to their right towards C. O. S.

The magistrate and "the chief" had then some conversation with old Ned and Winny, who had returned at their request to the parlour. It was of a general character, but still respecting the melancholy occurrence, or indeed occurrences, the magistrate said, for he had heard of the death of the man who had been killed by "the watch-dog." Ere they left they took Jamesy aside upon this subject, as the only person who knew anything of this part of the business, and the magistrate requested him to state distinctly what he knew of the transaction.

Jamesy was *distinct* enough, as the reader will believe, from the specimens he has already had of his style of communicating facts.

"Tell me, my good boy," said the magistrate, "did you *set* the dog at the deceased?" laying a strong emphasis on the word.

"Begorra, your honour, Bully-dhu didn't want any settin' at all. The minnit he seen the man in the kitchen, he stuck in his thrapple at wanst. I knew he'd hould him tal I came back, and I med off for the police."

"Are you aware, my young champion, that if you set the dog at the deceased, you would be guilty of manslaughter at least, if not murder?"

"Of murdher is id? Oh! tare an' ages, what's this for? Begorra, af that be law it isn't justice. Didn't they tie th' ould masther neck an' heels? Didn't they tie Miss Winny an' carry her off to murdher her, or maybe worse? Didn't they tie Biddy Murtagh? an' wouldn't they ha' tied me af they could get hoult of me? an' would you want Bully-dhu to sit on his boss, lookin' on at all that, your honour?"

"That may be all true, Jamesy, but I do not think the law would exonerate you, for all that, if you set the dog at the deceased man."

"Well, begorra, I pointed at the man, your honour; but I tell you, Bully-dhu wanted no settin' at him at all; af he did I'd have given it to him; and I think the law would onerate me for that same. See here now, your honour. Af th' ould masther had a double-barrel gun, an' shot the two men as dead as mutton that was goin' to tie him up, wouldn't the law be well plaised wid him? and if I had a pistil, an' shot every man iv 'em, wouldn't your honour make a chief iv me at least, instead of sending me to jail? and why wouldn't Bully-dhu, who had on'y a pair of double-barrel tusks, do his part an' help us? I'm feedin' an' taichin' that dog, your honour, since he was a whelp, an' he never disappointed me yet—there now!"

There was certainly logic in all this, which the magistrate, with all his experience of the law, found it difficult to contradict. A notion had come into his head at one time, that if Jamesy Doyle had set the dog at John Fahy, he might be guilty of his death, notwithstanding the said John Fahy had been committing a felony at the time. But there was no proof that he had set the dog at the man, beyond his own admission, and the question had not been raised. Jamesy was willing to avow his responsibility, as far as it went, in the most open and candid manner, and not only that, but to *justify* it, which he had indeed done in a most extraordinary, clever manner. Then what had been his conduct all through? Had it not been that of a courageous, faithful boy, who had risked his own life in obstructing the escape of the murderer? and was he not the most material witness they had—the only one who had never lost sight of the man who had shot Rory Lennon, until he himself had secured him for the police? "No, no," reflected the magistrate; "it would be absurd to hold Jamesy Doyle liable for anything, but the most unqualified approbation of his conduct from first to last."

"Well, Jamesy," said he, out of these thoughts, "we will take your own opinion in favour of yourself for the present. There is no doubt of your being forthcoming at the next assizes."

"Begorra, your honour, I'll stick to the ould masther and Miss Winny, an' I don't think they're likely to lave this."

"That will do, Jamesy. Come, Mr. ——, I think we have taken up almost enough of these poor people's time. We may be going."

They then left; and the reaction of being alone after so harassing a visit of two hours from these officials, although kindly conducted, wrought so upon Winny's mind and heart that she threw herself upon her bed, and through sheer misery and fatigue she sobbed herself to sleep.

A word or two about old Mick Murdock ere we close this chapter, as the reader, not having seen or heard of him for some days, will no doubt be curious to know what he had been doing, and how he comported himself during so trying and exciting a scene.

During the period which Tom had spent in the obscure little public-house upon the mountain road in the county Cavan, his own report that he had gone to the north had done him no service; for the addition which he had tacked to it, about "going to get married to a rich young lady," was not believed by a single person for whose deception it had been spread abroad. That sort of thing had been so often repeated without fulfilment that people reversed the cry of the wolf upon the subject.

There was nothing now for it with those to whom Tom was indebted but to go to his father, in hopes of some arrangement being made to even secure them in their money. Several bills of exchange—some overdue, and some not yet at maturity—with his name across them, were brought to old Mick for sums varying from ten to fifteen and twenty pounds. Old Mick quietly pronounced them one and all to be *forgeries*. Tom and he had had some very sharp words before he went away. He had called the poor old man a "—— old niggard" to his face, and he heard the words "cannot last very long," as Tom slapped the door behind him.

Old Mick would have only fretted at all this had his son returned in a reasonable time to his home, and, as usual, made promises of amendment, or had even written to him. It was the first time that ever a forged acceptance had been presented to him for payment, and Tom's prolonged absence without any preconcerted object to account for it weighed heavily upon the old man's heart as to his son's real character. Tom was all this time, as the reader is aware, planning a bold stroke to secure Winny Cavana's fortune to pay off these forgeries. But we have seen with what a miserable result.

It was impossible to hide the glaring fact of Tom Murdock's apprehension and committal to jail upon the dreadful charge of murder from his father. It rang from one end of the parish to the other. But instead of rushing to meet his son, clapping his hands, and exclaiming, "Oh! wiristhrue, wiristhrue! what's this for?" poor old Mick was completely prostrated by the news; and there he lay in his bed, unable to move hand or foot from the poignancy of his grief and disgrace.

Nancy Feehily, however, watched the dispensary doctor passing, and brought him up; and to his experience and Nancy Feehily's nurse-tending we must leave him for a time.

If Tom Murdock has broken his poor old father's heart, and that he never rises from that bed, it is only another item in his great account.

CHAPTER XXXV.

THE reader will recollect that the incidents recorded in the two last chapters took place towards the latter end of June. We will, therefore, have time, before the assizes come on, to let him know how far Winny's fancy map was perfected.

For herself, then, first. She had determined to become a member of a convent in the north of Ireland, giving up the world with all its vanities—she knew nothing of its pomps—and devoting her time, her talents, and whatever money she might finally possess, to religious and charitable purposes. She had not delayed long after the magistrate and "the chief" had left, and she had experienced a refreshing sleep, in taking her father into her confidence to the fullest extent of her intentions, not only as regarded herself, but with respect to those friends whom she had set down upon the map to be provided for.

"Father," she said, continuing a conversation, "there is no use in your moving such a thing to me. It is no matter at what time you project it for me; my mind is made up beyond even the consideration of the question. I never will marry. Do not, like a dear good father that you have ever been, move it to me any more."

"Indeed, Winny, I could not add a word more than I have already sed; an' if that fails to bring you round, shure I'm dumb, Winny asthore. God's will be done! I'm dumb."

"It is His will I am seeking, father. What matter if we are the last of the *C* Cavanas, as you say? Besides, my children would not be Cavanas; recollect that, father."

"I know that, Winny jewel; but they'd be of th' ould stock all the same. Their grandfather would be a Cavana, if he lived to see them."

"Be thankful for what you have, father dear.

There never was a large clan of a name but some one of them brought grief to it."

"Aye, Winny asthore; but there is always wan that makes up for it by their superior goodness. Look at me that never had but the wan, an' wasn't she, an' isn't she, a threasure to me all the days of my life? Look at that, Winny."

"And there is your next-door neighbour, father, never had but the one, and instead of a treasure, has he not been a curse? Look you at that, father."

Old Ned was silent for some moments, and Winny did not wish to interrupt his thoughts. She hoped he was coming quite round to her way of thinking with respect to her never "getting married;" and she was right.

"Well, Winny asthore," he said, after a pause, "shure you're doin' a good turn for your sowl hereafter at any rate; an' I'll be led an' sed by your own sinse of goodness in the matther. For myself, Winny, wheresomever you go I'll go, where I'll see you sometimes—as often as you can, Winny. Be my time long or short, I know that you will never see me worse, if you don't see me betther nor what I always was. But it isn't aisy to lave this place, Winny asthore, where I'm livin' since I was the hoith of your knee with your grandfather an' your grandmother—God rest their sowls! There isn't a pebble in the long walk in the garden, nor a pavin'-stone in the yard, that I couldn't place upon paper forenent you there this minnit, and tell you the colour of them every wan. There's scarcely a blade of grass in the pasthure-fields that I couldn't remember where it grows in my dhrames. There isn't a furze-blossom in the big ditch but what I'd know it out iv the bud it cum from. There isn't a thrush nor a blackbird about the place but what I know themselves an' their whistles as well as I know your own song from Biddy Murtagh's or Jamesy Doyle's. Not a robin-redbreast in the garden, Winny, that doesn't know me as well as I know you; an' I could tell you the difference between the very chaffinches—I could, Winny, I could."

"I know all that, father dear, and I know it will not be easy to break up all them happy thoughts in your mind. But then you know, father dear, I could not stop here looking across at the house where that man lived. God help me, father, I do not know what to do!"

Poor old Ned saw that she was distressed, and was sorry he had drawn such a picture of his former happiness at Rathcash. The recollection of these little matters had run upon his tongue, but it was not with any intention of using them as an argument to change Winny's plans.

"Winny," he said, "I didn't mane to fret you; shure I know what you say is all thrue. I could not stop here myself no more nor what you could, Winny, afther what has happened. Dear me, Winny jewel, how soon you seen through that fellow, an' how glad I am that you didn't give in to me! But now, Winny asthore, let us quit talking of him, and listen to what I have to say to you. 'Tis just this. My landlord, who you know is member for the county, tould me any time I had a mind to sell my inthcrest in Rathcash, he'd give me a hundred pounds more for it than any one else. I'll write to him to-morrow, plaise God, about it. You know Jerry Carty? Well, he is afther offerin' me seven hundred pounds into my fist for my good-will of the place. As good luck would have it I did not put any price upon it when my landlord spoke to me about sellin' it. I can tell him now that I have a mind to sell it, an' I won't hide the raison aidher. I can let him know what Carty is willin' to give me for it, an' he's sure to give me eight hundred pounds. You know, Winny, that your six hundred pounds is in the bank bearin' inthcrest for you, an' what you don't dhraw is added to it every year. But that's naidher here or there, Winny, for it will be all your own the very moment this place is sould, an', as I sed before, you may make ducks and dhrakes iv it. Shure I know, Winny, that you'll never see me want for a haporth while I last, be it long or short. But, Winny dear, let us live in the wan house; that's all I ax, mavourneen macree."

"That will be about fourteen hundred pounds in all, father."

"A thrifle more nor that, I think, Winny. Maybe you did not know how much or how little it was, when you laid it out the very way you tould me."

"No, not exactly, father; but I knew I must have been very much within the mark; I took care of that."

"Go over it again for me, Winny dear, af it wouldn't be too much throuble."

"Not in the least, father. You know I took Kate Mulvey first, and determined to settle three hundred pounds upon her for a fortune against 'she meets with some young man,' as the song says. And I believe, father, Phil M'Dermott, the whitesmith, will be about the man. He is very fond of Kate, but he would not marry any woman until he had saved enough of money to set up a house comfortably and decently upon. Three hundred pounds fortune with Kate will set them up in good style, and I shall see the best friend I ever had happy. Then, father, there are the Lennons, my poor dear husband's parents, whom I shall next consider. Pat Lennon, poor Rory's father, risked his life most manfully in my defence. Were it not for his resolute attack upon the two men with the cart, and the obstruction he gave them, they would have carried me through the pass long before the police and Jamesy Doyle came up; and the probability is that you would never have seen your poor Winny again. I purpose purchasing the good-will of that little farm and house from which the Murphys are about to emigrate, and settle a small gratuity upon them during their lives."

"Annuity, I suppose you mane, Winny; but it's no matther. How much will that take, Winny?"

"About two hundred pounds, father, including the—what is it you call it, father?"

"Annuity, Winny, annuity; I didn't think you were so—"

"Annuity," she repeated before he had got the other word out, and he was glad afterwards.

"Well, Winny, that's only five hundred out of somethin' over six."

"Then I'll give Biddy Murtagh a hundred pounds, and she must live as cook and housemaid with Kate; and I'll lodge twenty pounds in the savings-bank for Jamesy Doyle. Perhaps I owe him more than the whole of them put together."

"That will be the first duck, Winny."

"How is that, father?"

"Why, it's well beyant the six hundred, Winny, which was all you were goin' upon at first; but you may now begin with whatever we get by the sale of Rathcash."

"Well, father, I would only wish to suggest the distribution of that, for you know I have no call to it, and God grant that it may be a long day until I have."

"Faix, an' Winny, af that be so, you've left yourself bare enough. But don't be talkin' nonsense, child. What would I want with it? Won't you take care iv me, Winny asthore? an' won't you want the most iv it where you are goin'? an' didn't you tell me already that you'd like me to let you give it to the charities of that religious establishment? Shure, there's no use in my askin' you any more not to go into it."

"None indeed, father, for I am resolved upon it. But you shall live in the town with me, and I can take care of you the same as if I was in the house with you. There shall be nothing that you can want or wish for that you shall not have, and no day that it is possible that I will not see you."

"What more had I here, Winny, except the crops coming round from the seed to the harvest, an' the cattle, an' the grass, an' the birds in the bushes? Dear, O dear, yes! Hadn't I yourself, Winny asthore, forenent me at breakust, dinner, an' supper; an' warn't you for ever talkin' to me of an evenin', with your stitchin' or your knittin' across your lap; an', Winny jewel, wasn't your light song curling through the yard, an' the house, afore I was up in the mornin'? But now—now—Winny—O Winny asthore, mavourneen macree! but your poor old father will miss yourself, no matther how kind your plans may be for his comfort. Shure, the very knowledge that you were asleep in the house with me was a blessin'."

There was an outbreak of love and tenderness in all this, more perhaps in the manner than the words, which went to Winny's heart, but had not done so without passing through her head also. Her judgment as well as her feelings had been touched by it, and as she kissed her father's cheek a revolution was wrought in her thoughts.

"Father," she said, "God bless you! I will be back with you in a few minutes—do not fret;" and she left him, and shut herself up in her room.

But he did fret; and he was no sooner alone than the big tears burst uncontrollably forth into a pocket-handkerchief, which he continued to sop against his face.

Winny had thrown herself upon her knees at the bedside, and prayed to God to guide her. Her thoughts and prayers were too dignified and holy for tears. "But they had made a free course to the pinnacle of the mercy-seat, and she rose with her soul refreshed by the glory which had responded to her cry for guidance.

She returned to her father, a radiant smile of anticipated pleasure playing round her beautiful lips. There was no sign of grief, or even of emotion, on her cheeks.

"Father," she said, "I have been seeking guidance from the Almighty in this matter; and the old saying that 'charity begins at home'—that is moral charity in this instance—has been suggested to my heart. We shall not part, father, even temporarily. Where you live, I shall live. I have been told, father, just now, while upon my knees, that to do all the good I have projected need not oblige me to join as an actual member of any charitable or religious society. No, father, I can carry out all my plans without the necessity of living apart from you; we will therefore, father dear, still live together. But let us remove when this place is sold to B——, where the establishment I have spoken of is situated, and there, with my knitting or my stitching on my lap before you in the evenings, I can carry on all my plans in connection with the institution without being an actual member, which might involve the necessity of my living in the house. But, father dear, I hope you do not disapprove of any of them, or of the distribution of the money, so far as I have laid it out."

"Winny, Winny, I always knew you were my daughter, an' now I'm sure of it. But didn't I tell you you might make ducks an' dhrakes iv it? Winny, God will reward you for not lavin' me in a cowld lodgin'-room by myself, while you were sleepin' on a bed iv down in that big house you spoke of; an' shure when I'm gone, Winny asthore, you can join them without frettin'."

"No, father, that I could not. But do not speak that way, there is no fear of your going, thank God; and if my stopping with you can help to cheer and gratify you, I shall never be away from you, except perhaps for a few hours in the day-time; the way you used to be from me upon the farm."

"An' welcome, Winny dear, for shure won't I know that you are earnin' glory for your soul, Winny—won't I, mavrone macree?" And the old man threw his arms round his daughter's neck and gave her a long fond hug to his beating heart.

It was then quietly and finally arranged between them that as soon as Rathcash was sold, and the stock and furniture disposed of, they would remove to B——, in a northern county. They there intended to take a small house, either in the town or precincts—the latter old Ned preferred—where Winny could join the Sisters of Charity, at least in her acts, if not as a resident member. The money was to be disposed of as Winny had laid out, and legal deeds were to be prepared and perfected; and poor Winny, notwithstanding the sudden cloud which had darkened the blue heaven of her life, was to be as happy as the day was long.

But, alas! no ray of this world's hopes could ever penetrate the silent gloom that shrouded her young heart's memory.

CHAPTER XXXVI.

Time has rolled on, and brought us to the closing chapter of this sad tale.

Within a month from the scene between Winny and her father, described above, Rathcash had been purchased and paid for. There had been "a great auction entirely" of the stock, crops, and furniture. The whole population of the townlands of Rathcash, Rathcashmore, and Shanvilla, besides many others, had been wandering with impunity, not only through the farm and the garden, not only through the haggard and the offices, but through the house itself, turning the furniture upside down, kicking tubs and buckets out of their way, and looking in the big glass over the "chimley-piece,"—some of them wondering "what this would go for," or others "what that would bring." Poor Bully-dhu knew it was no use to bark where there were so many persons drawing to the house together, and was hunted from post to pillar by the crowd,—an indignity to which he submitted with an ominous silence. He seemed to have a presentiment that some great change was about to take place which no energy of his could avert, and he thrust his big, black, cold nose into Jamesy Doyle's hand; and finally drew himself into his wooden house with a long melancholy howl.

But this scene too had come to an end, and all had now more than a month passed by. The house was shut up, the door locked, and the windows bolted. No smoke curled from the brick chimneys through the poplars. No sleek dark-red cows stood swinging their tails and licking their noses, while a fragrant smell of luscious milk rose through the air. No cock crew, no duck quacked, no turkey gobbled, and no goose gabbled. No dog bayed the moon by night. Bully-dhu was at the flitting. The corn-stands and haggard were naked and cold, and the grass was beginning to grow before the door. The whole place seemed solitary and forlorn, awaiting a new tenant, or whatever plans the proprietor might lay out for its future occupation. Winny and her father had torn themselves from the spot hallowed to the old man by years of uninterrupted happiness, and to the young girl by the memory of a blissful childhood and the first sunshine of the bright hope which is nearest to a woman's heart, until that fatal night when vengeful crime broke in and snapt both spells asunder. Rathcash and Rathcashmore had been a by-word in the mouths of young and old for the nine days limited for the wonder of such things.

If the goodness of his only child had broken the heart of one old man from the reflection that her earthly happiness had been hopelessly blighted, and his fond plans and prospects for her crushed for ever, the villainy and wickedness of another had not been less certain in a similar result. Old Mick Murdock, —ere his son stood before an earthly tribunal to answer for his crimes,—had been summoned before the Court of Heaven.

Assizes, and trials, and convictions, and sentences,

and even executions, have been times upon times described in novels and other books, such as *The Detective*, *The Irish Police-Officer*, and many others of the kind. Some of them have been well done, and some of them have not. But where they have not, they have been pure inventions, not facts. Suffice it therefore to say, that the assizes came round, "the charge was prepared, the judge was arrayed—a most *ter*rible show."

Old Cavana and his daughter were, as a matter of course, summoned by the Crown for the prosecution, as were also Pat Lennon, Jamesy Doyle, Biddy Murtagh, and the policemen who had come to the rescue. Even poor Bully-dhu, though not summoned, was in attendance, as he could not, indeed would not, be left behind in a strange place—"his lone." Poor fellow! could he have spoken, he would have cheerfully testified to his own share in the transaction, and triumphantly have ascended the dock, to be tried for murder, as a set-off to Tom Murdock's case against his friend Rory, who had once saved his life.

Old Ned was the first witness, Winny the second, Jamesy Doyle the third. Then Biddy Murtagh and Pat Lennon, and finally, before the doctor's medical evidence was given, the policemen who came to the rescue, particularly he who had seen the shot fired and the man fall.

This closed the evidence for the Crown. There was no case, there could be no case, for the prisoner, beyond the futile cross-examination of the witnesses, by an able and tormenting counsellor, old Bob

B——y, whose experience in this instance was worse than useless.

The reader need hardly follow on to the result. Tom Murdock was convicted, and sentenced to death; and ere three weeks had elapsed he had paid the penalty of an ungovernable temper and a revengeful disposition upon the scaffold.

Poor Winny had pleaded hard with the counsel for the Crown, and even with the Attorney-General himself—who prosecuted in person—that Tom Murdock might be permitted to plead guilty to the abduction, and be sentenced to transportation for life. She had already so far succeeded with the counsel for the prisoner, that he too proposed the matter to the Crown, stating that the unfortunate shot had been fired in a scuffle in the heat of the moment, and was not premeditated, &c. But the Attorney-General, who had all the informations by heart, said that the animus had been manifest all through, from even prior to the hurling-match, which was alluded to by the prisoner himself as he fired the shot, and that he would most certainly arraign the prisoner for the murder.

Old Bob B——y said he thought it was a very harsh and vindictive proceeding; which imputation the Attorney-General scornfully repudiated, and thereupon a wordy scuffle ensued between his majesty's representative and the counsel for the prisoner, through which old Bob B——y bore himself with his usual intrepidity. The public were delighted and edified by old Bob's pluck; but it was remarked by the knowing ones how vehemently pathetic the Attorney-General's "statement" was, and how he wrung tears from the jury while he coiled the rope around the neck of the unfortunate culprit. And so he was found guilty; and Winny, with her heart full of plans of peace and charity, was obliged to forge the first link in a chain the succeeding ones of which dragged Tom Murdock to an ignominious grave.

But "time and the hour ran through the roughest day." These things ceased not only to be spoken of, but to be thought of. Old Ned and Winny, accompanied by faithful Bully-dhu, had returned to B——, where the old man read and loitered about, watching every figure which approached, hoping to see his angel girl pass on some mission of holy charity, dressed in her black hood and cape.

Accompanied by Bully-dhu, he picked up every occurrence in the street, and compiled them in his memory, to amuse Winny in the evenings, in return for her descriptions of this or that case of distress which she had relieved. Thus they told story about, not very unlike tragedy and farce! When Winny had ended some heart-stirring detail of sad distress, old Ned "broke in" with some laughable description of how some poor small dog, who had purloined a bone at the risk of his legs, if not of his life, had been attacked, and rolled over and over, almost under the wheels of a cart, and finally robbed of his booty, by some dog double his size, until Bully, fired with indignation at the cruelty and injustice, had rushed forward and punished the plundering, surly villain, and restored the bone.

Then came Winny's turn about a pallet of damp straw and a half-starved, emaciated figure, followed again by old Ned's, about a dark-faced man with a barrel-organ and a monkey, which got in at a window and ran away with an old lady's cap. Old Ned must have designedly picked up these incidents, as a set-off against the monotony of his daughter's mournful stories, for we do not accuse him of having invented them. The streets of the populous town in which they lived furnished ample materials, without any invention on his part.

A sufficient time had now elapsed, not only for the deeds to have been perfected, but for the provisions which they set forth to have been carried out. Pat Lennon had already removed to the comfortable cottage upon the snug little farm which had been purchased for him by Winny, and the "annuity" she had settled upon him was bearing interest in the savings-bank at C. O. S.

"He had the most beautifullest little small Kerry cow in all Irelant," and "a great milker intirely," and he had two fat pigs up to their eyes in clean dry straw. It would surprise you to hear them nestling and grunting in the sty.

Phil M'Dermott was one of the best-to-do men in that side of the country, and his wife (if you can guess who she was) was the nicest and the handsomest woman (now that Winny was gone) that you'd meet with in the congregation of the three chapels within four miles of where she lived. Jamesy Doyle had been transferred—head, body, and bones—to the establishment, where he excelled himself in everything which was good, and useful, and—*handy*. Many a figary was got from time to time after him in the forge, filed up bright and nice, and if he does not "sorely belie" his abilities and aptitude, he will one day become a "whitesmith" of no mean reputation.

Biddy Murtagh was to have gone as cook and thorough servant to *Mrs. M'Dermott;* but the hundred pounds which had been lodged to her credit in the bank soon smoothed the way between her and Denis Murrican,—a Shanvilla boy, you will guess, —who induced her to become cook, but not thorough servant, I hope, to himself; so Kate M'Dermott— how strange it seems not to write 'Kate Mulvey'! —was obliged to get somebody else.

Poor Winny! blighted in her own hopes of this world's happiness, had turned her thoughts to a surer and more abiding source. She had seen her plans for the happiness of those she loved carried out to a success almost beyond her hopes. Her poor old father, getting whiter and whiter as the years rolled on, attained a ripe and good old age, blessed in the fond society of the only being whom he loved on earth. Winny herself found too large a field for individual charity and good, to think of joining any society, however estimable, during her father's lifetime, and was emphatically *the* sister of charity in the singular number.

But poor old Ned has long since passed away from this scene of earthly cares, and sleeps in peace in his own chapel-yard, between *two tombs*. Long as the journey was, Winny had the courage and self-control to come with her father's bier, and see his coffin laid beside that of him who had been so rudely snatched away, and whom she had so devotedly loved. Poor Bully-dhu was at the funeral, and gazed into the fresh-made grave in silent, dying grief. When all was over, and the last green sod slapped down upon the mound, he could nowhere be found. He had suddenly eluded all observation. But ere a week had passed by, he was found dead upon his master's grave, after the whole neighbourhood had been terrified by a night of the most dismal howling which was ever heard.

Winny returned to the sphere of her usefulness and hope, where for many years she continued to exercise a course of unselfish charity, which made many a heart sing for joy.

But she too passed away, and was brought home to her last resting-place in Rathcash chapel-yard, where the three tombs are still to be seen. Were she now alive, she would yet be a comparatively young woman; not much past sixty-four or sixty-five years of age. But it pleased God, in His inscrutable ways, to remove her from the circle of all her bounty and her love. Had it not been so, this tale would not have yet been written.

www.ingramcontent.com/pod-product-compliance
Lightning Source LLC
Chambersburg PA
CBHW030305240426
43673CB00040B/1071